MW00558797

Organizational Project Portfolio Management

A PRACTITIONER'S GUIDE

Dr. Prasad S. Kodukula, PMP, PgMP

ISBN-13: 978-1-932159-42-4

Printed and bound in the U.S.A. Printed on acid-free paper.

10 9 8 7 6 5 4 3 2 1

Library of Congress Cataloging-in-Publication Data

Kodukula, Prasad.
    Organizational project portfolio management : a practitioner's guide / by
Prasad Kodukula.
        pages cm
    Includes index.
    ISBN 978-1-932159-42-4 (hardcover : alk. paper)   1. Project management.
I. Title.
    HD69.P75K656 2014
    658.4'04—dc23
                            2014011201

Direct all inquiries to J. Ross Publishing, Inc., 300 S. Pine Island Rd., Suite 305, Plantation, FL 33324.

Phone: (954) 727-9333
Fax: (561) 892-0700
Web: www.jrosspub.com

DEDICATION

To My Parents

TABLE OF CONTENTS

PREFACE

Organizations face project go/no-go decisions every day. Whether to invest in a new project or to continue or kill an ongoing one is a frequent dilemma for the executives as well as lower-level managers. Selecting the right projects that help the organization achieve both its near-term goals and long-term strategy is one of the most pressing challenges for the decision makers. Allocation of the right resources to the right projects at the right time is a constant struggle.

In many organizations project decisions are based more on subjective and political considerations and less on objective and rational criteria. Projects are typically selected as disparate entities without much consideration for their collective contribution. Project evaluation and selection process are not always consistent even within the same organizational unit, let alone across the larger enterprise. Projects are almost never killed, no matter their performance to date or their future potential to generate value or lack thereof. Project redundancy is prevalent, thanks to organizational silos where the "left hand doesn't know what the right hand is doing" and vice versa. Managers are generally more interested in projects that serve their fiefdoms rather than those that help build the enterprise. No coherent, systematic approach is employed in allocating resources—both monetary and human—to the right projects that serve the organizational strategy for long-term sustainable growth. If your organization is engaged in any of these practices, you are more than likely wasting resources and destroying shareholder value. The industry best practice calls for project portfolio management (PPM)—a relatively new business process in the project management arena—that offers an effective approach in executing organizational strategy and maximizing value for its owners and other stakeholders through systematic management of projects in the form of a formal portfolio. It forms a vehicle to collectively bring coherence to implementing new business initiatives. At the core, the PPM's focus is on efficient allocation of the right resources to the right priorities at the right time.

THE BOOK'S INTENT

I was motivated to write this book for several reasons, three of which stand out:

1. As project management has evolved over the last two decades, portfolio management has become the new frontier. Recognizing the need for certified professionals, the Project Management Institute (PMI®) launched a new credential called Portfolio Management Professional in early 2014. It has only been within the last ten years most of the books on portfolio management have been published, including the first edition (2006) of PMI's *The Standard for Portfolio Management*. Some of them focus on product portfolios, some on industry-specific portfolios, some on portfolio tools, and a few on general principles and processes. Others have dealt with themes related to organizational change management. But I have not found a book that provides practitioners a practical, process-based methodology for designing, building, and managing a portfolio along with a set of tools that can be applied across various industries. This is the strongest driving force behind this book.

2. Virtually every portfolio book that I have seen talks about how a portfolio can and should help you align projects with the enterprise strategy. Many projects, however, are not necessarily *directly* driven by the enterprise strategy. For example, projects in the lower organizational units of large enterprises are driven by their own strategic needs (albeit presumably aligned to the enterprise strategy) and operational demands, making it difficult to show direct alignment with the enterprise strategy. My book's intent is to present a methodology and a tool kit that can be applied to any portfolio irrespective of its location in the organizational hierarchy and type of projects it contains.

3. Any PPM process should offer the capability to create a portfolio with a desired mix of different types of projects. The objective is to provide a balance to reduce the risk of putting all your investment dollars in one type of project. Many books talk about balance, but none show the practitioner how to go about making it happen. My aim is to present a step-by-step process for creating a *balanced* portfolio that will allow you to create balance along any project characteristic (e.g.,

form of value generated by the project, size, risk, or development time) of your interest. Furthermore, I intend for this methodology to be easily applicable in organizations that are already employing "balanced scorecard" (BSC), a management framework that is becoming increasingly popular. The scorecard requires organizations to establish goals in different domains (financial, customer, business process, and employee) to create balance. The PPM methodology presented in this book will allow you to easily create a balanced portfolio that will reflect the same balance as in the BSC.

In essence, this book's intent is to offer a generic, practical methodology—along with a tool kit—to design, build, and manage a balanced portfolio at any level of the enterprise, irrespective of the industry. While anyone interested in learning PPM will find this book useful, the following groups may derive maximum benefit:

- **Portfolio Managers.** This group is the primary audience for this book. If you are a portfolio manager, you are on the hook for executing the PPM process. You may even be responsible for initiating and establishing the process itself in the first place. I believe this book will not only help you understand the portfolio management principles, but also walk you through the process and give you the tools you need to do your day-to-day job.
- **Senior Managers.** Senior managers can be at different levels of the organization starting with executives at the top. At the highest level, you have C-level executives (CEO, CFO, CTO, CIO, etc.), who are responsible for setting the strategic direction of the enterprise. At the lower levels, there are business unit managers, directors, department managers, etc., who are responsible for formulating the strategy and goals for their own organizational units. Although most of these managers may not be directly involved in the PPM process, they may be sponsors and supporters of PPM. This book helps them understand the framework through which their organizational goals are translated into desired results. They need to understand how the PPM process operates and why it operates in the way that it does.
- **Decision Makers.** This group may include senior managers from the previous group and other managers with decision-making authority.

If you are involved in initiating and implementing a PPM process for your organization, this is the right book for you. It gives you an overall methodology and the tools you will need. If you have the direct authority to make or indirectly influence project go/no-go decisions, you will find this book extremely useful. If you are given a budget and the authority to decide on how you spend that budget on projects or even operational activities, there are several tools in this book that will help you with their prioritization.

- **Project Sponsors.** As a project moves through the cycle of idea generation, business case analysis, implementation, and closure, the project sponsor is in the hot seat. It is her responsibility to shepherd the project through the portfolio process, get it approved and supported, and keep it going in the face of all the obstacles that will come up. Using this book, project sponsors can learn how to present their case and "sell" their projects to the portfolio.

- **PMO Staff.** The portfolio management process is typically housed in a project, program, or portfolio management office (PMO). One of the responsibilities of PMO directors and their teams includes execution and facilitation of the portfolio governance and other PPM processes. The methodology and tools I have presented in this book will be of great value to the PMO staff.

- **Program and Project Managers.** To the program and project managers, the portfolio is what stands between them and getting their program/project approved and supported. They need to understand the rules of the engagement just as the portfolio decision makers do. For them, learning how to best present their case to the portfolio stakeholders is important.

HOW IS THE BOOK ORGANIZED?

This book is divided into four sections followed by appendices. Section 1 (Chapters 1 through 5) introduces the theme of the book; defines the basic portfolio terminology; differentiates projects, programs, and portfolios; offers a "funnel & filters^{SM}" model for the portfolio process; and illustrates how principles of financial portfolio management are applicable to project portfolios. Section 2 (Chapters 6 through 10) has five chapters, the first of which introduces a PPM methodology with four phases, with the remaining four chapters focusing on each one of the phases. Section 3 (Chapters 11 through 16) is dedicated to PPM tools and techniques. Section 4 (Chapter 17) includes several mini case studies that illustrate how you can apply the methods and tools presented in the previous chapters. Let me now summarize each chapter.

Chapter 1, *Introduction,* introduces you to PPM and lays the foundation for the book. It offers a definition of a project portfolio that is simple, but comprehensive. It answers the questions of what PPM is and why it is needed. It offers a "project iceberg" metaphor where the project triple constraint (scope-time-cost) is just the tip of the iceberg. The chapter suggests that whereas many organizations tend to focus on the tip, you must plow deeper into the iceberg to discover the project characteristics that are critical to long-term organizational success.

Chapter 2, *Project Portfolio,* elaborates on the portfolio definition presented in the previous chapter and analyzes each element of the definition. For example, "value" is a buzzword that both academics and practitioners often throw around without defining what exactly they mean by it. This chapter defines it clearly in the context of the portfolio, and many subsequent chapters come back to this topic. It also outlines different types of portfolios and the nomenclature associated with them. Here, I introduce a new and important portfolio concept that I call the "portfolio triple constraint"—not unlike the project triple constraint that most project professionals are familiar with. To build and maintain an effective portfolio, you must keep the three components of its triple constraint in balance. A key responsibility of the portfolio team is to maintain this balance, which I discuss throughout the book.

Chapter 3, *Projects, Programs, and Portfolios,* differentiates between the three domains. There is a lot of confusion in the industry as to the differences between a project and a program, and a program and a portfolio. This chapter discusses the definitions and the distinguishing characteristics of the three domains with examples and scenarios.

Chapter 4, *Portfolio Model,* presents a conceptual model to illustrate how projects go through their life cycles within the context of the portfolio. I call this model "funnel & filters[SM]." Several people have referred to the portfolio as a funnel in the past, but I have clearly outlined how different parts of the funnel represent different facets of the PPM process. This chapter also differentiates the funnel & filters[SM] model from the well-known phase-gate model and shows why the former is needed to supplement but not replace the latter.

Chapter 5, *Project vs. Financial Portfolios,* compares and contrasts project portfolio management principles vis-à-vis financial portfolio management. Both portfolios contain components as either financial assets or projects and aim to align with a predefined strategy, create balance with the components, and generate value for the portfolio owners. Financial portfolio management is a well-established discipline and has been practiced for much longer than the project portfolio management. This chapter shows how, notwithstanding the limitations, project portfolios can utilize well proven financial portfolio principles and strategies. It also describes the "efficient frontier" of financial management and illustrates how it can be applied to portfolios containing projects that generate financial value.

Chapter 6, *Project Portfolio Management Methodology,* introduces a generic portfolio management methodology that can be employed at any organizational level in any industry. There are four phases in this methodology. In the first phase, you build the foundation for your portfolio by identifying the strategy and goals of the organization the portfolio is associated with. In the second phase, you design the portfolio in accordance with your organizational strategy, goals, risk tolerance, and other factors. In the third phase—a one-time event—you initiate a new portfolio by bringing the relevant projects in your organization under its purview. Once the new portfolio is built it moves into the fourth phase, which is "Monitor & Control Portfolio." This phase continues as long as the portfolio is alive and active. Each phase is characterized by specific key processes, which are identified in this chapter. The next four chapters discuss in detail each one of the four phases and the processes within that phase.

Chapter 7, *Build Foundation,* first draws the organizational big picture, generally referred to as the strategic framework, including the organization's mission, vision, strategy, values, goals, and objectives. It illustrates the importance of how every organizational unit should identify its own strategic framework that must align with that of the parent enterprise. The framework forms the foundation for the portfolio, so that the component projects can be aligned to the organizational strategy. The chapter also identifies the project/portfolio governance process, infrastructure for PPM, portfolio organizational structure, and the roles and responsibilities of key portfolio team members.

Chapter 8, *Design Portfolio,* delves into how to put together the design specifications for a portfolio. It is these specs that the portfolio team should follow to build a new portfolio and maintain it for the long haul. The effectiveness of the portfolio is dictated by the degree to which it adheres to the specs. The chapter delineates two types of portfolio balancing requirements: project categorization and portfolio triple constraint. It also describes the project selection criteria as well as the weightage factors for each criterion. It defines the success measures and performance indicators for the portfolio as a whole.

Chapter 9, *Construct Portfolio,* is about how to build a new initial portfolio if you are starting fresh with a new portfolio. In this chapter, I introduce a term called "portfolio calibration." It is the process of transforming the new portfolio to what I call a "steady state" portfolio. A portfolio is considered to be under steady state when it exhibits the design specifications. This chapter outlines the key steps involved in portfolio calibration.

Chapter 10, *Monitor & Control Portfolio,* focuses on the fourth phase of the PPM methodology. It discusses several processes critical to this phase: identify, categorize, and evaluate new projects; assess ongoing projects; prioritize new and ongoing projects; rebalance portfolio; select or terminate projects; and assess portfolio performance. It presents three levels of evaluation for every project: Level 1 is quick screening, where a project candidate is evaluated against key portfolio benchmarks. If the candidate passes muster, then it is subjected to Level 2, where the project is evaluated in more detail for its own merit based on the project selection criteria defined in the design phase. If the project passes Level 2, it then undergoes Level 3, where it is evaluated for its relative merit against the other competing projects in the portfolio. This chapter also reviews the commonly known sunk cost fallacy related to project termination decisions. More important, it discusses the lesser known sunk cost dilemma, how to overcome it, and when is the right time to kill a project.

Chapter 11, *Project Evaluation,* is dedicated to tools and techniques galore for evaluating projects for their investment worthiness. They are presented under two headings: financial and nonfinancial. The former set of tools include net present value, benefit cost ratio, return on investment, internal rate of return, etc. The latter set primarily focuses on scoring models.

Chapter 12, *Project Prioritization,* offers tools and techniques commonly used for ranking projects. It discusses how the efficient frontier principle can be applied to rank projects that produce financial value. For projects that generate a nonfinancial form of value, other ranking techniques such as forced ranking, paired comparison, and scoring models are presented. Data visualization tools discussed in this chapter include radar charts, bubble diagrams, scorecards, and dashboards. This chapter offers examples of a portfolio scorecard and a dashboard, among others.

Chapter 13, *Uncertainty and Risk,* first defines and differentiates uncertainty vs. risk. Several tools and techniques for understanding and quantifying uncertainty and risk are discussed in this chapter. Decision trees, sensitivity analysis, and Monte Carlo simulation are a few examples. This chapter elucidates different ways to understand and minimize portfolio risk. It also identifies major biases in decision making, which must be understood by the portfolio team.

Chapter 14, *Earned Value Management,* is a review of the basic project management tools and techniques. They include the work breakdown structure, Gantt chart, network diagram, bottom-up cost estimate, and the performance measurement baseline. This chapter demonstrates how earned value management can be applied to track and control not only the individual component project performance, but also the portfolio performance as a whole relative to cost and schedule targets.

Chapter 15, *Resource Planning,* first identifies the most ubiquitous challenge: managing the supply-demand (resources-projects) equation. It argues that the real challenge is not having enough resources but having too many projects. What this should mean to the portfolio is focusing on the few critical projects, while weeding out the trivial many. The chapter presents numerous resource allocation and planning tools that can help you efficiently manage the supply-demand equation.

Chapter 16, *PMO,* presents current practices of project/program/portfolio management offices. The topic of the PMO is included in the tools and techniques section, because it is considered a "tool" that facilitates the project, program, and portfolio management processes.

Chapter 17, *Case Studies/Exercises,* is dedicated to several mini case studies developed as a series of exercises. They are built as part of a fictitious company that is interested in employing a formal PPM process and tools to manage its project initiatives. Since the case studies are an important and integral part of the book, let me elaborate.

Case Studies

The objective of the case studies is to demonstrate how the methodology and some of the important tools presented in this book can be applied to design, build, and manage a portfolio. Since this is a "how to" book, I thought it would add value to show the practitioner how the methodology can be applied. The mini case studies unfold as a series of exercises along with exhibits that provide the background information to solve the problems and answer the questions posed in the exercises. The first few exercises focus on the portfolio foundation, design, construction, and control. The last exercise relates to building the key components of the business case for a new project culminating in a go/no-go decision. The solutions to the exercises are included in the appendix.

The exercises are built around a fictitious biotechnology company that aims to streamline its projects under a portfolio using a formal PPM process. I tried to keep the industry-specific jargon and details to a minimum and focus on the portfolio aspects. My hope is that you will not get intimidated with the technology details. I also tried to keep the financial aspects at a relatively high level, so you do not get too bogged down with the nitty-gritty. I made the size of the portfolio relatively small to avoid complexity and confusion, yet included a diverse mix of projects. The principles you would apply to a larger portfolio are still reflected despite the smaller size. My overall objective is to give you a flavor for how the methodology and tools can be applied to design, build, and manage a real-world portfolio.

Prasad Kodukula

ACKNOWLEDGEMENTS

First and foremost, I would like to thank Padma Kodukula for detailed reviews of multiple drafts of the manuscript. Her critical insights helped me fine-tune several key concepts presented in the book. Her input into the Case Study (Chapter 17) was immensely valuable. I would also like to thank Doug Campbell for his review comments and stimulating discussions on topics of great interest for both of us. Thanks to Kaushiki Bagchi for her substantive as well as editorial input. Special thanks to Raghu Saripalli for reviewing Chapters 5, 6, 11, and 13 and providing crucial comments on the financial and risk-related topics. Thanks are also due to Carl Pritchard for reviewing Chapter 14 on earned value management. I wish to acknowledge the review of the early drafts of Chapters 1 through 6 by Chandra Papudesu.

I learned about portfolio management not only through my own research and practice, but also through my interactions in many parts of the world with clients that hired me for help, students that participated in my classes, and delegates that attended my conference presentations. Thanks to all of them for a great learning experience.

Most important, I would like to thank my publisher, Drew Gierman, of J. Ross Publishing for being more than patient with me from the start to finish of this project. His encouragement and support especially towards the finish line are greatly appreciated. I also wish to thank Steve Buda and the J. Ross Publishing production team for their contributions and support. Finally, many thanks to my wife, Padma Gannavarpu, for her immense patience in bearing with me, as I spent most of the weekends during the last few years working on this book.

ABOUT THE AUTHOR

Dr. Prasad Kodukula, PMP, PgMP, is a multiple award-winning speaker, management coach, author, inventor, and entrepreneur with nearly 30 years of professional experience. He is the founder and CEO of Kodukula & Associates, Inc. (www.kodukula.com), a project management training, coaching, and consulting company based in Chicago, Illinois, USA. He has spoken to audiences in more than 50 countries on a variety of topics including project, program, and portfolio management; leadership; and creativity/innovation. Dr. Kodukula has trained or coached several thousand project/program/portfolio managers at more than 40 Fortune 100 companies, the World Bank, the United Nations, and the United States government. Examples of major companies where he taught include Abbott Labs, Boeing, Chrysler, Cisco, Corning, Dow Chemical, Ericsson, IBM, J.P. Morgan Chase, Motorola, Sprint, Stryker, Volkswagen, and United Technologies Corporation.

As cofounder and CEO of Neochloris, Inc., a Chicago-based green tech company, Dr. Kodukula is currently leading a team involved in developing a patent-pending technology that removes carbon dioxide from the atmosphere and converts it to biofuel. Previously, Dr. Kodukula held positions as research and development director at a bio-environmental technology start-up, senior engineer at a global petrochemical corporation, and senior project manager at a large engineering consulting firm. He also taught senior/graduate-level courses at the Illinois Institute of Technology, West Virginia University, and the University of Kansas.

The Project Management Institute (PMI) recognized Dr. Kodukula as "Best of the Best in Project Management" by honoring him with the 2010 PMI Distinguished Contribution Award for his "dedication to the profession and practice of project management and sustained performance and contribution to the advancement of project management." He was also recognized by the U.S. Environmental Protection Agency and the Kansas Department of Health and Environment for his outstanding contributions in environmental science and engineering. Constant Compliance, Inc., an environmental technology company that he cofounded and led as CEO for more than 10 years, was recognized by the State of Illinois as the most innovative small business in the environmental category.

Dr. Kodukula's educational background includes baccalaureate degrees in chemistry, biology, and education. He holds an M.S. in environmental science from Rutgers University, an M.S. in environmental engineering from Cornell University, and a Ph.D. from the Illinois Institute of Technology. He also has a Master's Certificate in project management from George Washington University. Dr. Kodukula is certified as a Project Management Professional (PMP®) and a Program Management Professional (PgMP®) by PMI. He holds two patents and has several others pending and is a coauthor or contributing author of seven books and more than 40 technical articles. His last book *Project Valuation Using Real Options: A Practitioner's Guide* was published by J. Ross Publishing in 2006.

Web
Added
Value™

This book has free material available for download from the
Web Added Value™ resource center at *www.jrosspub.com*

At J. Ross Publishing we are committed to providing today's professional with practical, hands-on tools that enhance the learning experience and give readers an opportunity to apply what they have learned. That is why we offer free ancillary materials available for download on this book and all participating Web Added Value™ publications. These online resources may include interactive versions of material that appears in the book or supplemental templates, worksheets, models, plans, case studies, proposals, spreadsheets and assessment tools, among other things. Whenever you see the WAV™ symbol in any of our publications, it means bonus materials accompany the book and are available from the Web Added Value Download Resource Center at www.jrosspub.com.

Downloads for *Organizational Project Portfolio Management: A Practitioner's Guide* include charts for managing resources, discounted cash flow and Monte Carlo simulation spreadsheets, and worksheets for portfolio and project case examples in the book.

SECTION 1

PROJECT PORTFOLIO BASICS

Section 1 introduces project portfolio management (PPM) and lays the foundation for the book. It answers the questions of what PPM is and why it is needed. It defines a portfolio, program, and a project and shows the differences between the three. A portfolio model, referred to as "Funnel & Filters^{SM}," is also introduced in this section. The model illustrates how the project life cycle fits into a portfolio and how project and portfolio management interact and interface with each other. This section also presents a discussion on similarities and differences between financial and project portfolios. More important, it highlights the financial portfolio management principles that can be effectively applied to PPM.

1

INTRODUCTION

As the speed of change in the business environment has accelerated over the years, organizations are continuously striving to stay competitive in the marketplace. They are shifting strategies, driving innovation, releasing new products and services, expanding into new global markets, reorganizing management structures, and so on. These actions are commonly managed through large strategic initiatives that are ultimately translated into projects. While many major projects are driven by strategic initiatives, others are a result of operational needs and demands. Furthermore, irrespective of whether or not your organization has generated profits, you will undertake projects to comply with ever-changing technology, health, safety, environmental, and other mandates. Thus, projects have become the lifeblood of every organization to respond to change, and project management has been adopted as a formal process to complete these projects "better, faster, and cheaper." Today, it is one of the hottest topics in business. As a management process, project management has reached—or even surpassed—the heights of total quality management and six sigma. Figure 1-1 shows the advent of project management (represented by a Gantt chart, PERT, critical chain, PRINCE, etc.) juxtaposed with the other major business and management theories and techniques of the past century.

The focus of project management has always been on managing individual projects to achieve scope, time, and cost targets. As organizations reach higher levels of maturity in managing projects as disparate entities, they shift their focus to managing them collectively as project portfolios using a formal project portfolio management (PPM) process. This transition seems to

3

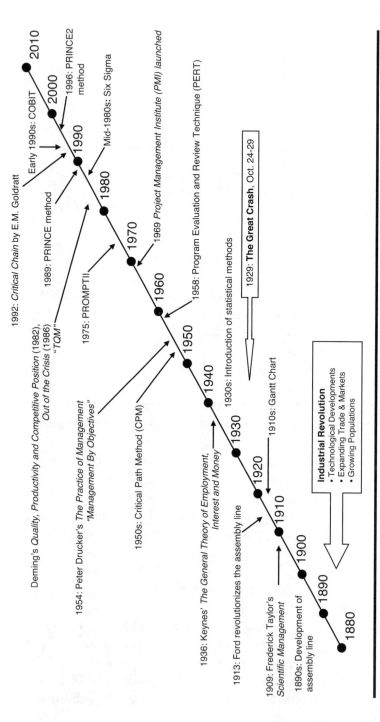

Figure 1-1 Project management and other management theories (Resch, 2011)

occur when the organization realizes that projects are investments, not expenditures. Investments require sustainable returns over the long haul. They must align with the strategy and goals of the organization providing the resources—both monetary and human. Most important, they must create value for the organization's owners as well as other key stakeholders (conjointly referred to as stakeholders hereafter). Project managers and sponsors may be more interested in their project cost targets, but executive managers are more focused on creating collective returns for the stakeholders from various project investments. They want to ensure that organizational resources are allocated to the best investments. Therefore, it has become paramount that projects are managed under a portfolio with a well-defined investment strategy that will help the organization create long-term sustainable value for the stakeholders. The purpose of this chapter is to define a project portfolio, introduce the portfolio management process, and set the stage for the book. In this chapter, you will also learn about my intent in writing the book and the audience I have in mind.

WHAT IS A PROJECT PORTFOLIO?

A project portfolio is a collection of strategically aligned, value-generating projects that help achieve organizational goals.

I will discuss this definition in detail in Chapter 2, but before going further, we need to establish a few basics. Any project portfolio by definition contains projects. But a "true" portfolio has projects that: 1) are aligned with the strategy of the organization sponsoring the portfolio, 2) help the organization achieve its goals, and 3) ultimately generate value for the stakeholders. This means that every project in the portfolio must, at a minimum, meet these requirements. The candidate projects for the portfolio must be evaluated for their alignment with the organization's strategy and goals and value creation potential, among other characteristics. This exercise is generally called "business case" analysis. Projects that meet the portfolio requirements showing a strong business case will stay in the portfolio and receive investment. As projects in the portfolio go through their respective life cycles, they are reevaluated periodically to ensure that they continue to meet the portfolio requirements. If they do not, their scope/time/cost targets may be revised or they are terminated.

WHAT IS PROJECT PORTFOLIO MANAGEMENT?

Project portfolio management—simply referred to as portfolio management—is a complex process that starts at the very top of the enterprise. It helps you convert the enterprise strategy into desired results. It is a key step in the overall strategy execution process (Figure 1-2). The external business environment is constantly changing. It may be a general shift in the economic conditions, or it may be changes driven by competition, customer needs, technology breakthroughs, new markets, regulatory controls, or a myriad of other causes. The changes may even be internal to the organization such as bloating bureaucracy and deterioration of employee morale. In response to the changes, the executive managers revise the enterprise strategy and formulate organizational goals. In the case of visionary leaders, transformational strategies and goals are introduced proactively. To achieve the desired results, new business initiatives are created. Programs and projects are the building blocks of these initiatives. They produce products and services that ultimately help achieve the organizational goals by creating value. Through a portfolio, the PPM process offers a vehicle to turn the strategy into value. PPM collectively brings coherence to implementing the business initiatives. It ensures that the right organizational resources are allocated to the right project priorities at the right time. PPM can be applied at any level of the enterprise. The principle is the same. Consider any organizational unit, for example, a division or a function. It must have its own strategy and goals. The PPM process will help you translate its strategy into value through projects at that organizational unit.

Whether you are a profit-driven, nonprofit, or government entity, your stakeholders expect the organizational resources to be invested in the right projects to deliver maximum value for them. They also expect you to invest in the right *mix* of projects balancing the benefits-cost-risk equation. PPM is tantamount to management of project investments to deliver value for your stakeholders. It translates to efficient allocation of organizational resources to the right project priorities. It involves evaluation, prioritization, and selection of projects integrated with investment decision checkpoints. The checkpoints include the initial invest/no-invest as well as the ongoing continue/cancel decisions, collectively called go/no-go decisions, spanning the life cycle of each project in the portfolio. The process behind the decision-making framework is the backbone of PPM.

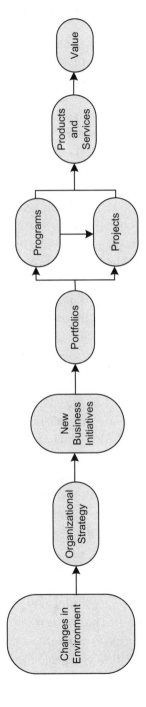

Figure 1-2 Role of PPM in strategy execution

WHY PORTFOLIO MANAGEMENT?

Successful organizations are those that are able to bring innovation to the market fast, alter their course swiftly to adapt to changes, leverage technology to gain competitive advantage, and manage risk effectively in today's uncertain world. This translates to first making the right strategic choices, investing in the right projects that align with those choices, and completing them successfully for the desired outcomes. All this at super speed! Portfolio management is about effectiveness (doing the right thing or selecting the right projects for investment), whereas project management is about efficiency (doing it right or implementing the projects faster, cheaper, and better). For PPM to be successful in your organization, you must first have a strong project management process in place. This is why, as mentioned at the outset, organizations typically initiate a PPM process as they reach higher project management maturity. The interconnectedness between the two processes will become clearer as we move through the book. Furthermore, if your projects are collectively managed under a program umbrella, an effective program management process will also be a requisite for a successful portfolio.

Project Iceberg

Organizations at the lower project management maturity spectrum manage individual projects focusing only on the well-known project triple constraint that includes scope of work, schedule, and cost. You may have completed a project meeting this constraint and concluded it was successful. But it is not truly successful if you delivered an inferior product or left the customer unhappy. On the other hand, let's say you not only met the constraint but also delivered a superior product and delighted the customer. This may not turn out to be a success for your organization, however, if no shareholder value was created in the long run. Then, what if you created enormous wealth for them, but in the process, damaged the environment, made fatal safety mistakes, destroyed employee morale, or violated laws or ethics? So the important question is whether the project ultimately produces value for the concerned stakeholders without destroying value for others.

PPM considers the project triple constraint just the tip of the iceberg (Figure 1-3). It helps you plow into the iceberg and assess a project from various facets, so you make the right investment that generates value for all the key

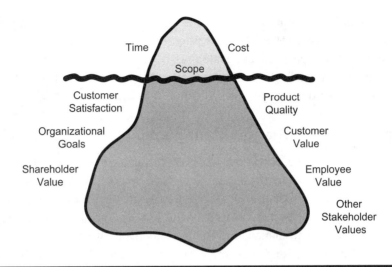

Figure 1-3 Project iceberg

stakeholders. Moreover, an enterprise-wide coherent PPM process provides you with an overarching strategy to manage the various icebergs in your organization. By assessing, monitoring, and managing the project icebergs collectively, PPM navigates your organization in the right direction for the distant future.

HOW CAN YOUR ORGANIZATION BENEFIT FROM PORTFOLIO MANAGEMENT?

As I alluded at the outset, today's organizations are evolving from project management maturity to portfolio management maturity. If your organization has already reached maturity in project management practice, you are more likely to complete your projects meeting the scope, schedule, and cost targets. But this does not necessarily mean that the project deliverables or outputs have indeed helped you generate value for your stakeholders and achieve your organizational goals. It is entirely possible that you selected and invested in a project not (or poorly) aligned with the organizational goals in the first place. Or, perhaps the original organizational goal the project was supposed to serve has changed before project completion. Apart from alignment, the value creation potential of the project may have been weak (or even nonexistent) to begin with or turned weak before the project was completed.

These scenarios are somewhat characterized by a "right solutions to wrong problems" syndrome resulting in a waste of organizational resources. Invest in enough of such projects, and watch your competitiveness evaporate in no time, potentially leading to extinction of your organization. The following paragraphs illustrate how your organization can benefit from PPM.

Organizational Change Management

Rapid changes in the economy, markets, technology, and regulations are forcing organizations to formulate new strategies or fine-tune the current ones more frequently than ever. As these strategies are translated into new initiatives supported by new programs and projects, portfolio management offers a framework to manage the change effectively. It helps you make the right investment decisions to generate value for stakeholders. It provides you with the right tools to rapidly alter the course of action in response to fast changes in the environment.

Clear Alignment

A well-designed and managed formal portfolio management process ensures that projects are aligned with the organizational strategy and goals at all times. New project ideas are evaluated for their alignment with the strategy and goals, and no projects are funded unless there is clear alignment. In addition, the degree of alignment is continuously monitored as the selected projects go through their individual life cycles. If an ongoing project no longer shows strong alignment, it may be terminated and the resources allocated to other higher priority projects.

Value Creation

Portfolio management helps you deliver value to your stakeholders by managing project investments through a structured and disciplined process. The justification for the projects is clearly identified by quantifying the expected benefits (both tangible and intangible) and costs. Only those projects that promise high value and rank high against the competing ones throughout their life cycles are funded. Portfolio management gives you a bigger bang for your investment buck in the long run because you are managing the investments in a systematic fashion.

Value Balancing

For a profit-driven company, the organizational goal may be to generate the maximum financial returns possible for the owners or shareholders. But if the projects selected for investment are based solely on financial value generation potential, interests of other key stakeholders may be compromised. PPM will help you create a balance among the projects to deliver not only financial value but other value forms as well.

Long-Term Risk Management

When projects are initiated and implemented without the portfolio framework, project sponsors and managers typically focus on the short-term risks related to the completion of the project and do not pay enough attention to the long-term risks and rewards. Furthermore, they are oblivious to the collective risk profile of the project investments. Under a portfolio structure, the risk-reward equation is examined for projects individually as well as collectively in the context of the overall business. By diversifying the investments and balancing the portfolio, you are able to create a proper mix of projects of different risk profiles and manage the risks more effectively.

Termination of Projects

Just because a project initially shows a strong business case does not necessarily mean it should continue to receive funding through its completion. Projects that no longer hold a strong business case as they go through their life cycles should be terminated. This helps you focus on those projects that will generate value and kill others, thereby maximizing the value of the portfolio as a whole. In most organizations, once a project receives authorization and enters into the implementation phase, it will most likely continue to receive funding until its completion. Terminating projects is a taboo in most organizations. It is a highly political and emotional issue for many decision makers and executives. Portfolio management helps make the project termination decisions more objective and less political or emotional.

Better and Faster Decision Making

Portfolio management brings more focus to the decision-making process making it faster and more effective. An integral part of PPM, portfolio and project governance provides a formal structure and process for making go/no-go project investment decisions. It places the responsibility of decision making in the hands of independent parties—rather than the project sponsors with possible self-interest—that can evaluate competing projects more objectively using the same measurements, metrics, and standards.

Reducing Redundancies

It is not uncommon in relatively large organizations to face a situation where the "left hand doesn't know what the right is doing." Organizational resources are sometimes wasted on different projects trying to produce the same output. The PPM process helps you eliminate or reduce redundancy yielding significant savings to the organization. When the portfolio management process is standardized across the whole enterprise, projects become more transparent and adequate checks and balances can help you detect redundancies early.

Better Communications

Many organizations have "silos" around each function that block effective communication, a critical ingredient of success for cross-functional projects. PPM is a mechanism that opens the channels of communication for people from various business and technical functions. Silos also undermine innovation that is critical to organizational success in today's hypercompetitive environment. PPM breaks the silo barriers creating opportunities for people to learn new insights from each other and become more innovative.

Efficient Resource Allocation

One of the biggest challenges for any organization is the efficient allocation of resources—both monetary and human. While every manager claims that she would like to see the biggest bang for her buck, only a few organizations have proper systems in place to prioritize her projects based on their return on investment. Allocation of the right people to the right projects at the right time is an even bigger challenge. You can rarely find a detailed inventory of the human resources vs. the project needs, that is, supply vs. demand. The situation becomes even worse when the project resources also have administrative and other operational responsibilities. One of the advantages of portfolio management is that it provides the structure and tools for efficient advance planning, needs prioritization, and resource allocation.

Consistent Performance and Growth over Time

One of the key portfolio management processes is the evaluation of projects for their financial value-generating merit. This involves forecasting the future cash flows of every project and its outputs over its life cycle. Cash flow analysis for the entire portfolio over future time increments enables you to estimate any investment gaps and corresponding projects to match the growth targets of the organization. The portfolio thus can offer consistent long-term growth and performance for the organization.

WHO NEEDS PORTFOLIO MANAGEMENT?

Every organization that wants to manage change through effective strategy formulation and execution needs portfolio management. If you aim to achieve your organizational strategy using new business initiatives supported by multiple projects that compete for the same resources, you can benefit from portfolio management. PPM is the main vehicle that helps you achieve organizational goals through projects. Irrespective of whether you are a profit-based enterprise, a nonprofit entity, or government, the portfolio provides the mechanism to achieve your goals. A profit-driven organization may establish a portfolio of projects that is aimed at profit growth, market share increase, process improvement, etc., whereas a nonprofit entity or government agency may initiate a portfolio of projects geared towards increasing customer satisfaction or reducing costs. The goals and metrics of success may be different, but the principles of portfolio management are the same. Fundamentally, the more project-centric your organization is, the stronger the need for portfolio management. It gives you more focus in making the right project investments and maximizes returns—financial or otherwise.

It is commonly believed that PPM is only for projects sponsored at the enterprise level or at a relatively high level in the enterprise such as a business unit. But in fact any organizational unit in the enterprise can take advantage of PPM. Wherever there are projects, and priorities need to be determined for allocating money and people, the PPM process can be applied. Any organizational unit with a budget, projects, resources, and the decision-making authority on how it wants to allocate its resources may serve as the "parent" of the portfolio that it supports. I like to call these units portfolio sponsoring organizations or PSOs. At the highest level, you may have an enterprise portfolio for which the enterprise itself is the PSO (Figure 1-4). The component projects of this portfolio are designed to achieve the enterprise goals. Moving down the hierarchy, you may have a portfolio for your own organizational unit, which may be a business unit, division, or a function. The component projects of your PSO are directly aligned to your own organizational unit's goals, which are presumably in alignment with those of the larger enterprise. Generally, at higher levels of the organization, the portfolio consists of large projects requiring relatively huge investments. They have more visibility simply because they are within the purview of executive management. The impact of the projects in the portfolio is considerably higher, because they are driven by the enterprise strategy and goals. The lower-level portfolios contain projects that are relatively small in size, with less direct impact on the enterprise's strategic goals. These projects may be tied more to the enterprise's tactical and operational goals, while being aligned to the strategy of their own PSO. There is no need to have a portfolio for every organizational unit unless there is a clear business case to support it. It depends on the unit's goals, overall investment available, number of projects to be executed, size of the resources to be shared, etc.

Is Project Portfolio Management for Discretionary Projects Only?

When you consider projects as investments, it may imply that they include only discretionary projects. But that raises the question of what is truly non-discretionary. Operations managers would argue that most of their projects, aimed at basic infrastructure and process improvements and commonly referred to as "keep the lights on" projects, are operational necessities and therefore nondiscretionary. This helps the project sponsors stay under the radar to avoid the rigorous analysis and justification that PPM requires of discretionary projects. A deeper analysis would reveal, however, that there is also a choice on these types of projects as to where you want to spend your resources. Therefore, a formal PPM process can be applied to what are generally considered nondiscretionary projects. The true nondiscretionary projects are those that are mandated by the government related to safety, health, environment, finance, IT, etc. Since PPM has the responsibility of efficient allocation of human resources, it requires that all projects, discretionary or

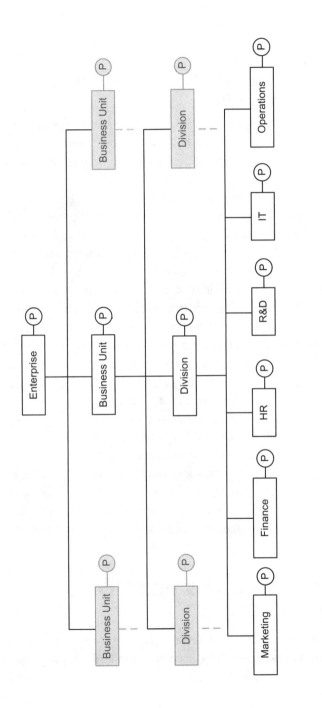

Figure 1-4 Portfolios at different organizational levels

otherwise, be linked to the portfolio. This is critical when the same resource pool is utilized for projects as well as routine operational support.

What Role Can Project Portfolio Management Play in Professional Service Firms?

One question that I am frequently asked in my teaching and consulting practice is how portfolio management can help professional service firms, such as those that provide IT, architectural, engineering, design, advertising or other types of services. The reason behind this question is that for a given client, the firm may be managing multiple projects, which collectively may be considered a portfolio. But this is not a "true" portfolio for the service firm because it is owned and managed by the client. The task of creating value lies with the client. The new project investment choices and the continue/cancel decisions on the ongoing projects are also under the control of the client and not the service provider, although the latter may have some input into it. True, the client owns and manages the portfolio, and the service firm is simply helping them implement the projects. But you can apply the portfolio management principles and tools to your business in selecting the industries and clients you want to work with and projects you want to implement for them in accordance with your organizational strategy, goals, portfolio of services you offer, and so on. A structured, formal portfolio management can help you select the right industries, customers, and projects to focus on your organizational goals and help you gain long-term competitive advantage. Furthermore, apart from the projects performed for the external clients, you always have internal business initiatives related to cost reduction, process improvement, infrastructure enhancement, employee training, and so on, which most likely require the same resources that are shared on external projects. Portfolio management can help you manage these priorities more effectively.

WHAT IS THE STATUS OF PORTFOLIO MANAGEMENT TODAY?

Whereas common terminology and methodology are emerging in project management, there are no universally accepted standards in portfolio management at this time. Even the definition of a project portfolio seems to be different in various organizations. Portfolio management is a relatively new concept, especially in the technology sector. The Project Management Institute published the first edition of its global standard for portfolio management in 2006. Recognizing the need for certified professionals in PPM, it launched the Portfolio Management Professional (PfMP^{SM}) credential in early 2014.

PPM has been practiced for a long time in the pharmaceutical industry, consumer products industry, and product development-driven organizations, albeit mostly in an ad hoc fashion. Its roots are in capital budgeting and product portfolio management. The former refers to planning of major capital investments involving physical assets, infrastructure, computer systems, etc. The idea is to assess the investment worthiness of these projects, since they involve major financial commitments. Product portfolio management, as the name implies, is managing a portfolio of products. It is concerned with the development and introduction of new products with a cohesive strategy to manage their benefit-cost-risk equation. It is considered a subset of PPM (Kendall and Rollins, 2003), wherein you apply the PPM principles to manage a product portfolio.

Many of the project assessment tools used in portfolio management today are similar to those used in capital budgeting and product portfolio management. Examples of such tools include financial models, scoring models, bubble diagrams, spider charts, etc. Their application, however, to project portfolios in a systematic fashion has been limited. Portfolio management software tools are becoming widely available now, but the cost seems to be relatively high. Recent trends include cloud-based tools with a choice of "pay as you go" or software-as-a-service. Mobile applications are starting to emerge. Project management offices (PMOs) have become common especially in the IT industry. Advanced PMOs have taken the responsibility for facilitating the PPM process.

2

PROJECT PORTFOLIO

A portfolio is a physical or virtual case (or bag, box, folder, etc.) that contains "things." It has different meanings to different people. An artist may think of it as a case containing one's drawings, paintings, photographs, and other such works. For a government official, it may mean a case with official documents or the position of a cabinet member or a minister of state (as in the portfolio for foreign affairs). In a financial context, it may be a collection of investments including stocks, bonds, and other such instruments. For a project management professional, of course, it refers to a collection of projects. Every organization—small, medium, or large—most likely is investing financial and human resources on various projects at any given time. If you make an inventory of the projects and place them in one group, it may be called a project portfolio. It may not be a "true" portfolio that is designed, built, and managed based on structured project portfolio management principles, processes, and best practices. It may be a *de facto* portfolio, which is simply a collection of projects that are selected for investment without much consideration for the characteristics of the component projects or the project mix. In this chapter, I would first like to elaborate on the portfolio definition I have already introduced in Chapter 1 and explain what a true project portfolio is. Then I will turn my attention to different types of portfolios that are most common in the industry.

WHAT IS A PROJECT PORTFOLIO?

As defined in Chapter 1:

> *A project portfolio is a collection of strategically aligned, value-generating projects that help achieve organizational goals.*

I elaborate briefly on each key element of the definition below and discuss the important characteristics of the projects that make up the portfolio. Subsequent chapters in the book will discuss in more detail the themes introduced here. For the sake of simplicity, a project portfolio is referred to as a portfolio in most of the following chapters.

Collection of Projects

Whereas our portfolio definition refers to a collection of projects, it can also be applied to a collection of sub-portfolios or programs. A sub-portfolio is essentially the same as a portfolio except that it is part of a larger portfolio. A program is also a collection of projects, where the projects may be "stand-alone" or sub-projects of a larger project, sometimes referred to as a mega project. (Programs are discussed further in Chapter 3.) A portfolio at the highest level of the enterprise consisting of large investments with oversight by executive management may contain programs. A portfolio with a relatively small investment pool managed by a smaller organizational unit (say, a department) may be made up of projects. These projects may be completely "stand-alone" or part of one or more programs. This can get confusing when the definition of a program is not clearly known. While it is theoretically possible to include both programs and projects in the same portfolio, the combination is not common because of the differences in their size and objectives, among other factors. Irrespective of the type of the components of the portfolio and their sizes and complexity, the general methodology and tools discussed in this book will apply. For the sake of convenience, the portfolio components are simply referred to as projects, instead of projects *and* programs, throughout the book.

Relationship between Projects

Every project in a portfolio must be able to create value by itself. It should not have to depend on any other project(s). If a combination of projects is needed to create value, they should be combined into one larger, value-creating project or even a program. The projects are selected for investment in the portfolio based on their value-creation potential, among other characteristics. Therefore, if an individual project does not produce value of one form or another, it cannot be evaluated for its merit and prioritized against the other value-creating projects. Projects in a portfolio are independent of each other except for the fact that they compete for the same pool of financial and human resources.

Alignment

Every portfolio must be linked to one single organizational unit. It must contain only those projects that align with the strategy of that unit. Typically it is the same organizational unit, also called a portfolio sponsoring organization (PSO), that sponsors the portfolio and holds the go/no-go decision-making authority. As mentioned in Chapter 1, portfolios may exist at different levels of the enterprise starting at the very top and moving down the organizational hierarchy to the functional or departmental level. Every PSO in the enterprise, irrespective of its location, must clearly articulate its strategy to provide the guiding force for the portfolio. When every PSO's strategy is aligned with that of the enterprise, every portfolio and its component projects will ultimately serve the enterprise's overall mission. Linking projects to their own PSO—rather than the enterprise—gives more focus to the portfolio. Since the PSO is presumably aligned with the enterprise, the portfolio serves the enterprise strategy, albeit indirectly.

Value

For many of you, value may sound like a management buzzword because it is often used as "management speak" without much consideration for what it really means. Everybody seems to have a different interpretation of the word. For most people, value simply means benefit. But it is only part of the complete equation. Value must consider the benefit in relation with the cost. It is essentially the return on the investment that you make. The cost part of this equation can be deceptive, if the "true" cost of the project is not taken into account. For example, if you do not consider the risk, the cost will be low and the value will look more attractive. Therefore, value should also include the cost associated with the risk. Thus, value translates to a benefit-cost-risk equation.

Value exists in different forms. Shareholder, financial, customer, employee, environmental, and societal value are a few examples. Investment decisions are obviously made based on a project's *potential* to create value rather than the *actual* value delivered. Value is not typically delivered until after the project's products and services are completed and delivered to the stakeholders. In fact, depending upon the product or service, it may take many years before substantial value is generated and the investment recovered. Therefore, the go/no-go decisions are always based on estimates of the future performance of project outputs. Whereas potential for value generation is a key project selection criterion, the true portfolio success depends on the *actual* value ultimately delivered by the project. While potential to create value is an important project characteristic, it is not sufficient to make it investment worthy. It must also show alignment with organizational strategy. Similarly, projects that exhibit alignment with little potential for value generation should not be pursued either. Each condition by itself is necessary but not sufficient for investment in a project.

Organizational Goals

The purpose of a portfolio is to help its sponsoring organization achieve its goals. The management team associated with the PSO identifies the goals every so often, typically annually, as part of the organization's strategic plan. It is the portfolio's responsibility to select only those projects that are necessary as well as sufficient to achieve those goals. Furthermore, for the portfolio to be effective, the component projects must be aligned with not only the current goals of the organization, but also its strategy. A project with great potential to generate revenue will likely contribute to one of the organizational financial goals, but it is not worthy of investment if it is not in the same business supported by its PSO's strategy. Alternatively, the portfolio will also be ineffective when the component projects are aligned with its PSO's strategy but not tied to its current goals. For instance, if your organizational strategy is to enter emerging markets and the current goal is to introduce products into Brazil, a project opportunity in India may not be the right fit in the portfolio at this time.

Right Mix of Projects

Although our portfolio definition does not specifically mention the combination or "mix" of the component projects, it is implicit that any portfolio must be balanced by selecting different types of projects in the right proportion.

The right project mix will help you manage the risk more effectively so as to create value and achieve organizational goals consistently over the long run. If your strategic plan already accounts for balance by formulating goals in different domains, as is done under the balanced scorecard framework, the portfolio can be designed to contain projects mirroring the same balance. Projects within a given domain can further be designed to exhibit their own desired mix.

Portfolio Life

A portfolio is not a temporary entity per se. It does not have a "finish" as a project does. It exists as long as its sponsor supports it and keeps it alive. At any given time it contains projects that are temporary with specified start and finish dates. Once a project has produced its deliverables and is completed, it exits the portfolio. However, since a portfolio is responsible for helping an organization achieve its goals and creating value for its stakeholders, a comparison must be made of the actual value delivered by the past projects against the promised value, and feedback loops established to improve the portfolio effectiveness. This may be facilitated by a project management office.

WHAT MAKES A PORTFOLIO EFFECTIVE?

An effective portfolio helps your organization achieve its strategy and goals consistently over the long haul. It serves as a vehicle for executing strategy and delivers what was promised (or even more) when it selected the projects for investment. Unfortunately, however, most of the time, you will not know whether you have made the right investments until long after the projects have been completed. A key indicator of the long-term effectiveness of a portfolio lies in whether it exhibits the design specifications of the portfolio. So an effective portfolio contains the right mix of aligned projects with great potential to generate value. It invests the right resources in the right projects to achieve the right goals striking a consistent balance among the three, while maintaining alignment with organizational strategy. Any change in one of the three will affect the other two which creates an imbalance. An effective portfolio makes proper adjustments to bring the balance back. Any imbalance would suggest that you have:

- Too many or not enough goals compared to the projects and resources,
- Too many or not enough projects compared to the goals and resources, or

- Too many or not enough resources compared to the goals and projects.

Thus the portfolio has a triple constraint, consisting of goals, projects, and resources. (Please see the following box for further illustration of the portfolio triple constraint.) When the triple constraint maintains consistent balance, the chances of portfolio success will be high.

PORTFOLIO TRIPLE CONSTRAINT

Before discussing the portfolio triple constraint, let us briefly visit the project triple constraint, which is known to virtually every project professional. There are slightly different versions, but the most popular one consists of project scope, time, and cost. Scope is considered to include not only the project requirements but also the quality associated with them. The cost component includes both labor and nonlabor cost, although sometimes the human resources contributing towards the labor cost are considered a separate constraint by itself. It is the project manager's responsibility to keep the triple constraint in "balance" for the entire project life cycle and to finish the project without exceeding the scope, time, and cost targets. As part of this "juggling act," you must first start with a project that has adequate time and budget to meet a clearly defined scope target. When any one of the three changes as the project goes through its life cycle, either one of the other two or both must change to keep the triple constraint in balance.

Just as with projects, we can consider portfolios as having a triple constraint. A portfolio's effectiveness to deliver value is controlled by three important elements, namely, organizational goals, projects, and resources (Figure 2-1). Resources are the investment the organization makes in terms of both money and people. To achieve a given set of organizational goals in any portfolio, you need appropriate projects and adequate resources to support those projects. The projects should be necessary as well as sufficient to achieve the goals. Unnecessary projects waste resources. If the projects are not sufficient, all your goals will not be achieved. To support the required projects, you need adequate resources. If you do not have enough resources, some projects may be delayed and you may not achieve your goals on time. When the goals change, the other two components of the triple constraint have to quickly shift in the right direction to keep the balance. This makes the portfolio very dynamic and portfolio management a tough balancing act. Imagine juggling three objects that keep chang-ing (balls, to knives, to scarves, and so on) continuously during the act. This is the challenge the portfolio team has in keeping the portfolio triple constraint in balance while ensuring that the portfolio is always aligned with the organizational strategy.

TYPES OF PORTFOLIOS

Classification of portfolios into groups can be complex because it can be done in so many different ways. The larger the size of the organization, the more ways you can classify them. If you are a relatively small organization executing only a few projects at a time, you may just have one portfolio that includes all those projects. You may call it the "enterprise" portfolio with no need for any more portfolios or further classification. On the other hand, if you are a behemoth corporation, with multiple business lines, management

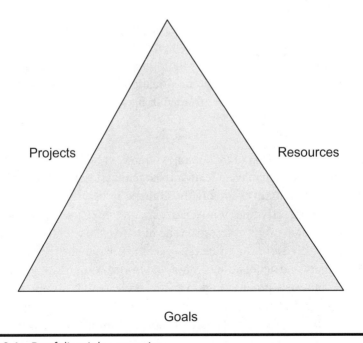

Figure 2-1 Portfolio triple constraint

layers, functional departments, product lines, technologies, markets, etc., you may have different types of portfolios across the organization. My intent here is not to elucidate every single possible way to classify the portfolios as an academic exercise, but to show a few key principles that a practitioner can apply in designing and establishing an effective portfolio structure. There are basically two approaches by which portfolios may be classified into groups based on one or more attributes:

- Organizational unit
- Project type or category

Organizational Unit

Any organizational unit that has the authority to spend resources for projects can create a formal portfolio. Therefore, a portfolio may exist at any level of the organization where that authority lies, as shown in Figure 1-4 in Chapter 1. The portfolio will be sponsored and supported by that organizational unit which is also known as the PSO. The PSO will be the single body with the decision-making authority for that portfolio on how it wants to spend its resources—both monetary and human. This body is represented by the executive or senior managers associated with that organizational unit. A portfolio hierarchy can be created reflecting the organizational hierarchy within the enterprise. Examples of portfolio classification based on the organizational units or PSOs are included in the following paragraphs.

Enterprise Portfolio

At the highest level of the organization, you may create an enterprise portfolio that is designed to manage a relatively large investment for major business initiatives. These initiatives are highly strategic in nature, meaning that they are designed to directly help you achieve the organizational goals identified in the strategic plan of the enterprise. The initiatives may cut across different business lines, divisions, and functions, if it is a large enterprise. Examples include mergers and acquisitions, major enterprise resource planning implementations, business process improvement projects, education and training projects, large infrastructure projects, and global expansion projects. If the organization is relatively small without separate business lines and divisions, new product development projects and major enhancements of existing products, among others, may be included in an enterprise portfolio.

Business Unit Portfolio

In a large enterprise with multiple business units, each unit may have its own investment pool that it manages as part of its own portfolio. Referred to as a business unit portfolio, it may be similar to an enterprise portfolio in many characteristics. Portfolios from different business units may constitute the larger enterprise portfolio, depending upon how the portfolios are structured in the organization. Looking at it differently, lower-level portfolios can be "sub-portfolios" of higher-level portfolios.

Divisional Portfolio

A divisional portfolio can be similar to an enterprise or business unit portfolio in terms of component projects, the difference being the location of the portfolio. Divisional and business unit portfolios are also highly strategic in nature and may cut across different functional departments within the given division or unit.

Functional Portfolio

Functional portfolios are managed at the functional level and are more focused on the immediate needs of the function. Examples of functional portfolios are IT portfolios, finance portfolios, and R&D portfolios. As the portfolios move down the organizational hierarchy to the functional level, they tend to become more operational and tactical and less strategic. This is not to say that the projects in a functional portfolio are not aligned to any organizational strategy because they still must be aligned to that function's strategy. Most often a functional PSO's strategy is focused on achieving its operational needs.

Project Type or Category

A portfolio may also be classified based on the type of projects it contains. Projects in any given type, commonly referred to as a category, will have certain common characteristics and would differ from other categories of projects in those characteristics. These characteristics are considered to be mutually exclusive between the categories. In most cases, the objective behind categorization (discussed in more detail in Chapter 8) is to build a portfolio that provides a balance between different categories of projects. Instead of risking all your investments in one category, it will allow for diversification.

Portfolio classification by project categorization is arbitrary and can be done in numerous ways. A few common categorization examples are given below:

1. The most commonly used categorization is based on how a project may help your business: change the business, grow the business, or run the business. The first category would consist of projects that will take your organization to the next level and may even transform the business landscape you are in. The projects may involve totally new technologies, new markets, game changing innovations, and radically different products and services compared to the current offerings. "Grow the business" category projects are those that help you grow steadily. They may include new applications of current technologies, current product and service enhancements, and incremental innovations. The third category of projects, also referred to as "keep the lights on" (KTLO), are operational necessities to keep the business running. These may include infrastructure enhancement, asset maintenance, process improvements, and the like.

2. Project categories may be based on a particular project characteristic such as the size (small/medium/large), development time (short-term/medium-term/long-term), cost (low/medium/high), and risk (low/moderate/high).

3. Another example of a project characteristic is the organizational goal or group of goals the project is expected to serve. As already mentioned earlier, if your organization is using balanced scorecard as a strategy management tool, you are required to develop goals in four major areas, namely, financial, customer, business process, and employee, for which you may create four portfolio categories:

   ◆ Financial Value Portfolio: Projects generate financial benefits and directly contribute to the share price of the company or wealth of the owners.

   ◆ Customer Value Portfolio: Projects generate customer-related benefits such as an increase in customer satisfaction and customer loyalty.

   ◆ Business Process Value Portfolio: Projects generate cost reductions through business process improvements.

◆ Employee Value Portfolio: Projects generate employee-related benefits such as an increase in employee morale and improving a current skill set or acquiring a new one.

4. You may also classify portfolios based on broad project domains:

◆ Capital Portfolio: A portfolio of capital projects involving construction of major new facilities, renovation of existing ones, and the purchase of large physical assets such as buildings and computer hardware.

◆ M&A Portfolio: A portfolio of projects dealing with mergers and acquisitions. Depending upon the size of the enterprise, these M&A portfolios can involve large investments.

◆ Product Portfolio: A portfolio of products or services offered by its PSO. It may include new product development or improvements to existing products.

◆ KTLO Portfolio: As mentioned before, it is an operations-driven portfolio consisting of projects that help you keep the lights on.

◆ Compliance Portfolio: A portfolio of projects that are mandatory because of regulations. For example, these can include health, safety, environmental, and Sarbanes-Oxley based projects.

The organization of each one of the above portfolios is arbitrary and can be structured in different ways:

1. Each category can be considered and managed as a distinct portfolio supported by a different PSO. In the third categorization example above, you may have four distinct and separate portfolios, each containing projects that generate a different form of value and supported by a different PSO.

2. The categories can be grouped into a larger portfolio supported by a single PSO wherein each category will act as a "sub-portfolio." Using the third categorization example again, you may have a larger portfolio supported by one single PSO with four sub-portfolios, one for each value form.

It should be evident from the preceding that a portfolio can be described using both location and project category because they are not mutually exclusive for categorization. For instance, you may have an enterprise capital portfolio, which refers to a portfolio at the enterprise level consisting of capital projects.

3

PROJECTS, PROGRAMS, AND PORTFOLIOS

The definition of a project—a temporary endeavor undertaken to create a unique product, service, or result—as espoused by the Project Management Institute (PMI, 2013a) has been well embraced by virtually the entire global project management community. However, there does not seem to be a consensus on the definitions of a program and a portfolio. PMI itself revised them through the three editions of their global standards for programs (*The Standard for Program Management*, PMI, 2013b) and portfolios (*The Standard for Portfolio Management*, PMI, 2013c) within the last six years. Table 3-1 presents the definitions for the three domains promoted by PMI in these global standards. Why is it important for your organization to clearly define a project, program, and a portfolio? Effective management of these domains requires different processes, methodologies, standards, tools, and techniques. It in turn means that you will need people with different skill sets to make projects, programs, and portfolios successful in your organization. Therefore, understanding clearly the definitions of and the differences between these domains will help you apply the right processes and resources to manage them more effectively. If overall project management is a key competence in your organization, you may also want to establish a clear career path in this discipline, identify different positions in that path, delineate the roles and responsibilities of each position, and develop the competencies required. In the absence of clearly defined structure and processes, the responsibilities of and relationships between the three domains may be overlapping, redundant,

Table 3-1   PMI definitions of a project, program, and a portfolio

Project	A temporary endeavor undertaken to create a unique product, service, or result.[1]
Program	A group of related projects, subprograms, and program activities that are managed in a coordinated way to obtain benefits not available from managing them individually.[2]
Portfolio	A component collection of programs, projects, or operations managed as a group to achieve strategic objectives. The portfolio components may not necessarily be interdependent or have related objectives. The portfolio components are quantifiable, that is, they can be measured, ranked, and prioritized.[3]

[1]PMI (2013a)
[2]PMI (2013b)
[3]PMI (2013c)

and blurred making this all extremely confusing. More important, it makes achievement of project, program, and portfolio management success in your organization more difficult.

Before we go too far into the book, I would like to define and differentiate projects, programs, and portfolios in this chapter. For many of the clients I have worked with, defining a program and distinguishing it from a project and a portfolio has been the most challenging. Therefore, my intention is to give you a better understanding of how a program differs from and is related to a portfolio and a project. I must state an important caveat here. There are numerous ways you can structure and assign roles and responsibilities to these domains. For the sake of simplicity—and clarity—I took the liberty to confine the discussion to typical scenarios and broad generalities. The differences and the relationships I have discussed in this chapter are most applicable when you have all three domains well established and integrated in your organization.

PROJECTS

Every project has a specific beginning and an end and is executed to produce a unique deliverable or a set of deliverables. Deliverables are also referred to as outputs and typically include products and services. One individual, referred to as the project manager, typically manages the project. She is given a budget, a time frame, and a specification of what the customer expects. A team is chosen by the project manager or given to her. It is not my intention here to discuss project management in any detail. That is left to the many dozens of books on the topic including PMI's *A Guide to Project Management Body of Knowledge*, commonly referred to as the *PMBOK® Guide* (PMI, 2013).

PROGRAMS

There is no one commonly accepted definition of a program, and as such, many different definitions prevail. Some definitions sound much like that of a project, and others are similar to a portfolio. However, it is commonly recognized that a program is a collection of related projects, managed together to gain a benefit that is not available from managing them individually. Managing them together gives you better control and more efficiency because of synergies. Many elements common to two or more of the component projects (e.g., resources, procurement, risks, stakeholders, etc.) can be coordinated together more efficiently at the program level. A program manager is assigned to be responsible for the coordination of the component projects and any related work outside the scope of the individual projects. Project managers are assigned to each one of the component projects and typically report to the program manager. While the definition is conceptually easy to understand, the confusion seems to occur as to how it applies in real-world scenarios where the "relationship" between the component projects is difficult to define. Let's examine two common scenarios that help us better understand this relationship.

1. Group of Related Projects with a Common Goal ("Mega Project")

A program in this scenario is similar to a project. It is enormous in size and complexity involving a large budget and numerous resources. It is temporary with a specific finish date and produces a major, unique deliverable such as a product or service, as in the case of a project. Therefore, the program in this scenario is commonly referred to as a "mega project." It consists of many related or interdependent projects working towards one common goal. Most often no single component project of the program is able to deliver value by itself. The value is generated after the program deliverable(s) has been produced. Examples include the development of a new passenger aircraft, the global launch of a major technology product, and the cleaning up of a massive contaminated waste site. In some cases the value may be delivered incrementally through completion of some of the projects in the program such as in the case of a global implementation of a major new enterprise resource planning system launched in increments.

The reason the above scenario represents a program is that it meets the two important conditions of the program definition: 1) it is a collection of related smaller projects, and 2) managing the effort as a program offers you better control and efficiency, which you may not have by managing the component projects individually. The key question here is at what point should the effort be considered large and complex enough where you will start to gain better control and efficiency by managing it as a program. This is a gray area, and each organization needs to develop its own standards or guidelines to provide clarity. In the absence of that clarity, differences between a project and a program become blurred and the terms end up being used interchangeably. More important, it becomes difficult to apply proper methodologies and tools consistently across the organization.

2. Group of Related Projects with Independent Goals

The second common program scenario includes a group of projects with independent or unrelated goals. They produce value independent of each other but are interrelated through a common theme such as a product line, technology, funding source, resources, client, or stakeholders. Depending upon the nature of the relationship, the component projects may be collectively managed either as a program or a portfolio. A portfolio structure may be the right fit if: 1) your own organization has the go/no-go decision-making authority over the projects; 2) the projects are competing for the same resources (financial, human); 3) they can be ranked based on their relative merit; and 4) lower ranking projects can be eliminated from further consideration for go/no-go investment decisions. Otherwise, the projects can be managed as a program, as long as the coordinated effort yields more benefit and better control compared to managing them individually. Here are a few examples:

- If you are a professional services firm implementing a group of projects for a particular client, you may organize it as a program. This is not a true portfolio in your organization because you have no authority in making the final go/no-go decisions. You may provide some of the necessary project information that is critical to the decisions. It is your client that has the ultimate authority.

- If you are an IT department in a large organization implementing projects for the business functions involving different applications and tools associated with a particular technology or service (e.g., Big Data), the projects may be organized as a program. This is similar to the above scenario, although an external client is not involved. It is the business functions in your organization that have the final decision-making authority, not your department.

- If you are going to launch a new product, which would be followed by future releases with improvements and enhancements over a period of time, each launch may be considered a project and the overall effort a program. Each launch is independent but related to the others through the common theme of the core product. It is not a portfolio, because the launches cannot be ranked based on their merit for rejecting the lower ranking ones. On the other hand, if there are multiple product opportunities associated with a particular technology platform that can be prioritized and selected or rejected based on their relative merit, a portfolio is more appropriate.

PORTFOLIOS AND THEIR RELATIONSHIP TO PROJECTS AND PROGRAMS

In Chapter 1, I presented the definition of a portfolio for the context of this book and then elaborated on it in Chapter 2. Now that we have defined all three domains, let's examine their hierarchical relationships and differences. There are numerous ways to structure the hierarchy and the relationships, but Figure 3-1 summarizes the most common ones. Projects are always at the bottom of the hierarchy and serve as the building blocks of both portfolios and programs. A portfolio is typically at the top of the hierarchy and consists of sub-portfolios, projects, or programs. It does not typically contain both programs and "stand-alone" projects. The reason is that programs and projects have different objectives and are of a different magnitude in terms of scope, cost, and complexity; and therefore, are better managed under separate portfolios of different sizes and characteristics accordingly. A portfolio may include projects from a single program or from different programs. Since it

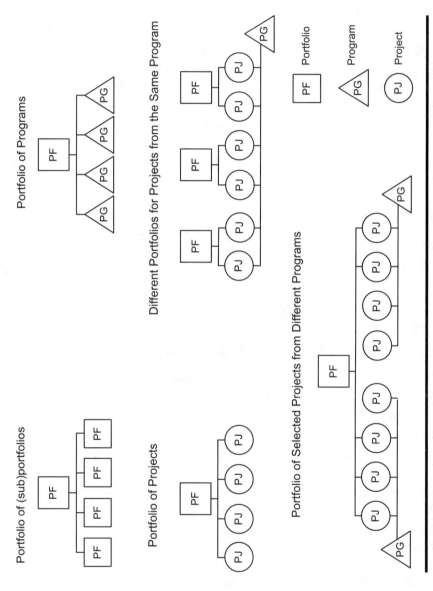

Figure 3-1   Examples of hierarchical relationships between projects, programs, and portfolios

can get confusing because of several possible relationships between the three domains, the key is to keep it simple and define the differences clearly.

Table 3-2 summarizes the key differences between projects, programs, and portfolios. (As mentioned in the introduction to this chapter, the differences are most applicable when the three domains are well established and integrated in your organizations.) In essence, projects focus on creating deliverables, programs on delivering benefits, and portfolios on allocating resources. Once the differences are articulated in your organizational context, establishing the required processes and tools for each domain becomes easier. Roles and responsibilities of managers of these domains and their staff can then be defined easily as well.

What is the Difference between a Project and a Program?

Of the two program scenarios described earlier, the mega project scenario seems to cause more confusion in differentiating programs from projects. While such a program appears to be a "normal" project, there are key differences. In the mega project scenario, as the name implies, a program is basically a large project that is broken up into several smaller projects. The rationale is simple: several small projects are much easier to manage than one large project, and there are synergies in managing them together. The teams are large, most often working in a virtual and global environment. The supply chain elements are more extensive and involve multiple vendors. The stakeholders are typically from various organizations in the enterprise with potentially conflicting interests. The impact of the program deliverables is far wider and deeper within the enterprise as well as externally in the marketplace. Most important, the component projects are interdependent. All this creates complexity, particularly in terms of integration. Just by the size and enormity of the programs, they tend to have large budgets or investment capital. Clearly there is more at stake. All this naturally creates risk. Programs have higher risk compared to projects. Project risks relate to the project triple constraint, namely, scope, schedule, and cost. Program risks are several-fold:

- Risks of individual component projects
- Risks of integration of different component projects
- Risks of producing the ultimate program deliverables, meeting the program's time and budget targets
- Long-term business risks of delivering value after the program outputs have been launched

Table 3-2 A comparison of projects, programs, and portfolios

	Project	Program	Portfolio
Components	Tasks or activities.	Projects that are related to each other.	Projects, programs, or sub-portfolios that generate value independent of each other.
Orientation	Tactical	Strategic	Strategic
Focus	Create deliverables.	Deliver benefits.	Allocate resources.
Objective	Meet project triple constraint (scope, time, cost).	Deliver benefits, manage stakeholders, integrate component projects.	Achieve organizational strategy and goals; balance portfolio triple constraint (goals, projects, and resources).
Success Criteria	Producing project deliverables meeting scope, time, and budget targets.	Delivery of desired benefits through program deliverables.	Generating promised return on investment; achieving organizational goals and strategy.
Scope	Defined scope and objectives; sometimes progressively elaborated through the project life cycle.	Larger scope, often progressively elaborated through the program life cycle because of uncertainty of future work.	Larger scope defined by the organizational strategy and goals.
Change	Change is managed as exception to "baseline;" involves managing and controlling its impact on project triple constraint.	Change is expected. Seen as an opportunity. Managed proactively to deliver promised benefits.	Change drives the portfolio. Investment priorities must change in accordance with changes in organizational strategy and goals.
Life Time	Temporary with a clearly defined finish. Relatively short term.	Temporary or ongoing. Relatively long term.	Ongoing with no definite finish.

Value Generation	Generates value over a period of time after the launch of deliverable(s).	Generates value incrementally through completion of individual project deliverables or all at once at the end of the program.	Generates value continuously as deliverables from component projects are launched.
Risks	Related to the project triple constraint. Short-term impacts.	Component project risks, project integration risks, benefits realization risks, and overall business risks. Long-term impacts.	Related to the portfolio triple constraint. Component project risks and high-level business risks. Long-term impacts.
Governance/Decision Making	Involves go/no-go based on project's performance to date as well as its individual and relative business case merit. Performed by senior or executive management; facilitated by PPM process.	Involves go/no-go based on program's ability to deliver desired benefits. Depends on performance to date as well as its individual and relative business case merit. Performed by executive management; facilitated by PPM process.	Involves decisions on investment choices and portfolio balance. Done by executive management.
Frequency of Performance Monitoring	Weekly	Monthly	Quarterly
Management	Project manager manages the project team; manages creation of project deliverables.	Program manager manages project managers, program staff, project interdependencies, and benefits creation process; provides leadership to the overall program team.	Portfolio manager manages portfolio team and staff; manages project investments; facilitates project/program governance process.

Both projects and programs need a formal governance structure. This structure most importantly includes, among others, the decision framework required to navigate the project or program course to a successful completion. This is particularly important for programs just because the investments are relatively large and more is at stake. The decision-making authority in both cases is represented by a high-level committee that steers the progress through what is generally known as a "phase-gate" process discussed in more detail in the next chapter. At the end of each phase (also called stage), the committee reviews the project or program status and decides whether it should move forward to the next phase. The final go/no-go decision is determined by the project or program's individual and relative business case merit at a higher level facilitated by a formal portfolio management process.

What is the Difference between a Portfolio and a Program?

A portfolio and a program can be misconstrued as the same because both are collections of projects. Differentiating the two becomes even more challenging because a program may involve different scenarios depending upon the relationship between its component projects, as discussed earlier. Let's consider the two major program scenarios and differentiate them from a portfolio.

1. Group of Related Projects with a Common Goal

This is the mega project scenario for the program, where the component projects have a common goal. The differences between this type of a program and a portfolio exist with respect to many characteristics.

- **Project interdependency.** In a program, interdependency among the component projects exists because of the common goal. One project's output is an input to one or more other projects ultimately leading to the final program output. In a portfolio, projects are not interdependent, although they may have a common relationship created by their competition for the same monetary and human resources. A program that is equivalent to a mega project typically generates value after all the component projects have been completed. The components may not generate value by themselves because of the nature of their interdependency. Projects in a portfolio, on the other hand, generate value independent of each other. What this means is that the portfolio components can be ranked so as to eliminate the low ranking ones in accordance with your investment priorities. But you cannot do the same with the program components when it is a mega project.

- **Governance.** Program governance mainly encompasses the go/no-go decision process for the program to continue from phase to phase based on its performance to date and its business case merit. A program steering committee is held responsible to review the program status. Typically it reports to an executive body, which ultimately decides on whether the program will continue to receive funding. In the case of a portfolio, the governance involves go/no-go decisions based on not only the individual but also the relative merit of its components through a prioritization process. The decision-making authority lies with a portfolio committee with executive power. Based on the analysis and recommendations from a portfolio management team, the executive committee makes the go/no-go decisions.

- **Risks.** Programs, as mentioned earlier, encompass risks related to the component projects, integration of the components, production of program deliverables, and ultimate delivery of value. Some of the portfolio risks are similar but others are different. First, a portfolio carries the risks of its component projects. Second, there are market risks associated with the commercial success of the products and services produced by the projects. And third, there are broader decision risks related to making the right project bets to deliver value consistently over the long term. These risks address the following questions: Are you selecting the right projects that will deliver expected value? Do you have the right mix of projects creating a balanced portfolio? Are you investing for the short term only? Are your investments going to help your organization achieve sustainable growth for the long haul? And so on.

- **Success criteria.** The program success is primarily determined by whether it has delivered the promised benefits. The portfolio success depends on the return it generates on the investments made and how it helps the organization meet its strategy and goals consistently in the long term.

2. Group of Projects with Independent Goals

A program comprising projects with independent goals appears similar to a portfolio, but there are differences in key areas.

- **Project interdependency.** Projects in this type of a program are independent of each other in producing value just as those in a portfolio. Each component project produces value by itself, but they are related to each other by a common theme such as a resource pool, technology platform, product, service, geographical region, client, etc. The difference is that the projects in a portfolio can be ranked based on their relative merit, so that the higher ranking projects can be selected for investment. Typically there is no such ranking associated with the program components, and all or most of them must be completed to meet the program requirements.

- **Governance.** Whereas the overall program decision authority in this scenario lies with the program steering committee, the component project go/no-go decisions are typically made by the respective project sponsors (or the project steering committees) based on their performance to date. (If your program consists of projects that you are performing for an external client, you obviously do not have any authority over the go/no-go decisions on those projects, because the governance lies with the client.) The portfolio governance primarily dictates the fate of its components (projects or programs) based on their individual and relative merit.

- **Risks.** The program risks are similar to those in the first scenario except that there are no major integration risks because of the "independency" of the component projects. Portfolio risks were already mentioned in a previous section.

- **Success criteria.** The program success is determined by the ultimate benefit the component projects generate. The portfolio success, as mentioned before, depends on the return it generates on the investments made and how it helps the organization meet its strategy and goals consistently in the long term.

4

PORTFOLIO MODEL: FUNNEL & FILTERS^{SM}

Conceptual models help us easily understand complex processes. They explain the relationships of different elements in a process in simpler terms without going into intricate details. They can easily be translated into powerful visual images to illustrate difficult concepts. In this chapter I offer a conceptual model that I named funnel & filters^{SM} in order to easily understand the basic elements of the portfolio management process. Chandra Papudesu and I introduced this model in a book on "real options" (Kodukula and Papudesu, 2006). Throughout this chapter I delve into details of this model. First, I illustrate how the model describes the movement of projects through the portfolio funnel. I also explain the difference between the funnel & filters^{SM} and the commonly used phase-gates models. Finally I describe the role of project portfolio management (PPM) in the overall value-creation process.

FUNNEL & FILTERS^{SM}

The funnel represents the portfolio containing the project candidates, projects, and the products and services created by the projects. Filters are the decision checkpoints for go/no-go decisions related to the fate of project candidates and projects (Figure 4-1). Each new project idea enters at the front end of the funnel as a candidate. Its aim is to travel through the funnel competing with other candidates and ongoing projects for resources, so it can create a new product or a service. Inside the funnel, it is scrutinized against

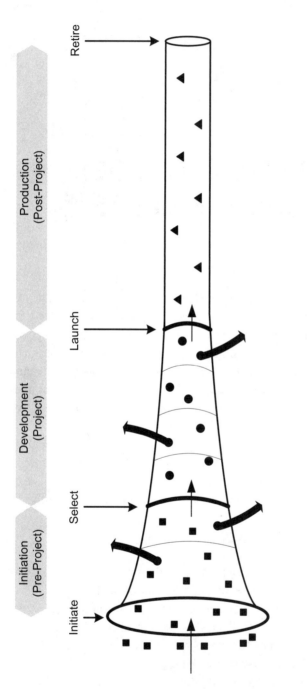

Figure 4-1 Funnel & Filters^{SM} (Kodukula, 2014)

the portfolio benchmarks at each filter. Go/no-go decisions are made based on its own business case merit as well as its relative merit compared to the competing projects.

As a new project idea is initiated at the front end of the funnel, upon receiving the final "go," it becomes a project, where it will start receiving resources to develop the product or service it is supposed to create. Once the project is completed, the product (or service) would go into "production" or "operations." Thus, a project candidate may transform into a project and then a product going through three broad phases as it travels through the portfolio funnel:

- Initiation (pre-project)
- Development (project)
- Production (post-project)

Let us say that you have submitted a project idea for developing a new software application to be considered for the portfolio in your organization. You want to develop, launch, and implement this application, because you believe it aligns with your organizational goals and will create value to the organization by increasing employee productivity thereby reducing costs. There are also several other attractive project ideas submitted for consideration for the same portfolio. All the competing ideas enter the front of the funnel and start the journey. Their journey inside the funnel is controlled by the initial invest/no-invest and the subsequent continue/cancel decisions to be made at the filters.

Initiation (Pre-project)

In the initiation phase, a new project idea is initiated and an evaluation is made as to whether it aligns with the organizational strategy and goals and has a strong business case. Furthermore, it is compared as part of a prioritization process, against the other new project ideas that are also in their respective initiation phases, as well as the ongoing projects that have passed this phase and are already underway. Thus, each idea is evaluated on its own merit as well as its relative merit against the other competing projects—new and ongoing—in the portfolio. The objective of the filter at the end of the pre-project phase is to filter out those candidates that are not worthy of investment. If the project idea receives a "no-go," it is rejected from the funnel.

If, on the other hand, it receives a "go," it is selected to enter the development phase. Let's say your new software development project idea has been evaluated and found to exhibit a high degree of strategic alignment and a strong business case. Also, as it is compared and prioritized against the other competing projects, it ranks high and is deemed worthy of investment. This means that after passing through the formal hurdles of funding approval, the project candidate becomes a formal project and moves forward to the development phase.

Development (Project)

The development phase involves execution of the project where the well-known generic project management phases apply: planning, implementation, and closeout. The generic phases can be replaced by industry specific ones discussed later in this chapter. At the end of the development phase, the product or the service developed by the project is launched. In our software project example, you will develop the software by navigating through these phases. Once the development is completed and the stage is set for launching, your project enters the production phase. The role of the filters in the development phase is discussed later.

Production (Post-project)

In the production phase, the deliverable or the output of the project goes into production or operations. The product or service developed in the development phase is marketed, sold, and supported in this phase. In the case of a product, it may also involve its physical production. This is the phase where the project benefits are realized. At the end of this phase, the product or service becomes obsolete and is no longer sold or supported by the organization and it "retires" from its life cycle. Using our example, during this phase your software application becomes part of normal operations in the organization. The end users keep using it while you are providing them the needed technical, operational, and maintenance support. The desired benefits of productivity enhancement and cost reduction are hopefully achieved. At some point your application may reach the end of its life, once it is removed from the system or integrated into a larger system, and you will no longer provide any support for the application. If you desire to make enhancements to your application and release future versions, they would be considered new project ideas and therefore, placed at the front of the funnel again to seek resources.

Filters

The filters represent the decision processes associated with portfolio management; hence the name "decision" filters. Both the initiation and development phases in the funnel have decision filters. The former phase filters are for initial project screening and go/no-go investment decisions associated with the new project candidate. This process may be facilitated by three levels of evaluation:

- **Level 1**: This is the initial screening of the project candidate based on preliminary information submitted by the project initiator. The objective is to weed out marginal projects quickly without having the initiators or the portfolio team spending a significant amount of time preparing or evaluating the business case, respectively.
- **Level 2**: Once a project request passes the initial screening, the project initiator presents a detailed project business plan (commonly referred to as a "proposal") for further consideration. A Level 2 evaluation involves evaluation of the project for its own merit. If it passes muster at this level, it will go to Level 3.
- **Level 3**: At this level, a project is evaluated for its *relative* merit against the competing projects in the portfolio funnel by means of a prioritization process. The competing projects will include the other project candidates that have passed a Level 2 evaluation, as well as the old ongoing ones. Based on the resources available and several other factors, the go/no-go investment decision is made at this point. The selected new projects move on to the development phase.

The filters in the development phase are meant to evaluate each ongoing project and help management decide whether to continue to invest in it, halt it temporarily, or terminate it altogether. These are Levels 2 and 3 evaluations, where the ongoing projects are evaluated based on their own merit and relative merit, respectively, just as project candidates are. The difference is that for project candidates, the evaluation is based on their initial business case, whereas for the ongoing projects, it is based on updated business cases as well as their performance to date. There are no filters in the portfolio funnel in the production phase. However, the portfolio is responsible for comparing the project's promised value documented in the business case with the actual value delivered, as discussed in the last section of this chapter.

The funnel & filters[SM] model is broad and can be applied to any portfolio scenario in any industry. It can describe projects that result in both products and services. The project and post-project phase cycle times may be relatively long in industries such as airplane manufacturing and pharmaceuticals and short in the technology sector. In telecommunications, while major infrastructure investments (e.g., network build up) exhibit long development and production times, rolling out consumer products and services may have shorter lifetimes. In the oil and gas sector, the model may require a fourth phase to represent the major environmental cleanup that needs to be done before the project is completely closed. Industries where the asset decommissioning may involve a significant effort will also require a fourth phase.

Application of the funnel & filters[SM] model is illustrated in the box below showing an example from the drug development industry. It represents a product portfolio where industry-specific phases are defined in lieu of the three generic phases mentioned earlier.

FUNNEL & FILTERS[SM]

Funnel & filters[SM] is a common process in drug development and is being increasingly adapted in other industries to manage their project portfolios. Developing a new drug is a long, arduous, and costly process. The entire research and development effort leading up to the approval of a drug by the Food and Drug Administration (FDA) in the U.S. can take approximately 15 years, which can cost the drug company in excess of one billion dollars. Due to increasing scrutiny by the regulators, these numbers are getting larger every year. Standardized and controlled by the FDA, the drug development process consists of three broad steps including discovery, experimental research, and clinical trials. The first step involves synthesis and discovery of new molecules. The second one consists of experiments, some involving animals, wherein the drug characteristics (bioavailability, toxicology, etc.) are investigated. At the end of these experiments, an Investigational New Drug document is submitted to the FDA kicking off the formal regulatory process preceding the third step. The most critical part of drug development is clinical trials, which are divided into four phases. Each phase involves a higher level of testing with human subjects in a clinical environment. At the end of Phase 3 trials, an application for New Drug Approval is submitted to the FDA. Once the drug is approved and introduced into the market, Phase 4 is initiated, which involves more clinical trials to gain further understanding of the safety and efficacy of the drug. This phase may continue on indefinitely for as long as the drug is used in the market.

Out of 10,000 molecules synthesized, approximately 1,000 enter experimental research. Of those, about 10 make it to Phase 1 clinical trials with one drug finally approved by the FDA. This represents a classic funnel & filters^{SM} process (Figure 4-2), where each drug molecule is competing with others in the funnel to win the race to become a newly approved drug in the market. The filters in the funnel are the decision checkpoints and the government approvals to move the candidate drugs to the next phase. The go/no-go decisions are based on the performance of the individual drug, its own business case, and its relative merit compared to the competing drugs in the portfolio. As the organizational strategy shifts or resources become limited, even a promising drug may have to be filtered out of the portfolio. You may terminate its further development altogether, license it to another company, co-develop it jointly, and so on.

Considering the long development times and enormous investments—not to mention the market demand—drug companies are trying to weed out the losers and bring the winning drugs to market as fast as possible. The funnel & filters^{SM} approach has proven to be effective in managing the overall drug development process as a portfolio. It can easily be adapted to manage portfolios in other industries.

FUNNEL & FILTERS^{SM} VS. PHASE-GATES

A phase-gates model, described in more detail in the box on page 52, is widely used as a project life cycle model. It represents the different phases of a project. Typically these phases are industry specific and replace the three generic project phases (planning, implementation, and closeout) with go/no-go decision checkpoints strategically placed between the phases. The decisions are based on the individual project's performance and merit. Funnel & filters^{SM} is a portfolio model where a project's fate is determined not only by its own

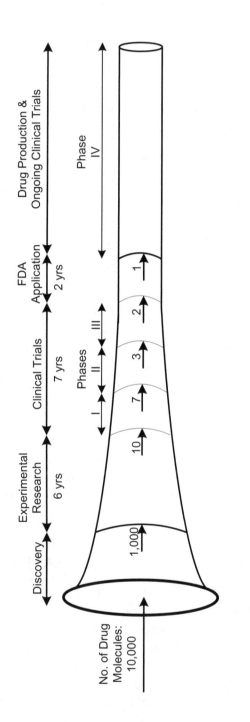

No. of Drug Molecules: 10,000

Not drawn to scale

Figure 4-2   Funnel & Filters℠: Drug development

merit but also by its relative merit against competing projects. Thus, a project that is part of a portfolio goes through its own phase-gates as it moves through the funnel & filters^SM. Conceivably, a project may show a strong business case and "pass" its phase-gate but may be a no-go at a funnel-filter, because it cannot compete with the other projects in the portfolio given the investment/resource constraints. When your organization has a formal PPM process in place, it is important to differentiate the two models (Table 4-1). Furthermore, you need to identify the governance structure and clearly delineate the roles and responsibilities of decision makers associated with it. Otherwise the role of the project sponsor/steering committee vs. the portfolio management team and the portfolio executive board can become blurred. Typically the project sponsor/steering committee is responsible for monitoring and assessing the project progress to date and for evaluating its expected future performance until its completion. The PPM team reviews the project's business case merit as part of the phase-gate process, compares it with the competing projects as part of the

Table 4-1 Phase-gates vs. Funnel & Filters^SM models

Phase-gates	Funnel & Filters^SM
• For one project.	• For multiple competing projects in a portfolio.
• Phases represent major parts of a project's life cycle. Gates between phases are decision checkpoints where go/no-go decisions are made.	• Each competing project travels through the funnel, as it goes through its own phase-gates. Filters are decision checkpoints, where go/no-go decisions are made.
• Go/no-go decisions are based on project's performance to date, its expected future performance until completion, and its own business case merit.	• Go/no-go decisions are based on a project's own business case merit as well as its relative merit compared to competing projects.
• A "go" decision gives a green signal for the project to move to the next filter in the funnel where its business case will be evaluated and compared against the competing projects.	• A "go" decision means that the project is (or continues to be) investment worthy and will be authorized to move forward to the next phase.
• At the end of each phase, a project sponsor/steering committee reports on project results and makes a recommendation to the portfolio management team. Input data is provided by the project management team.	• A portfolio management team evaluates the project status for its own and relative business case merit and makes a go/no-go recommendation to the portfolio executive board. The board decides on the final go/no-go for the project.

funnel & filters[SM] process, and makes a go/no-go recommendation to the port-folio board. The board has the ultimate authority to make the final decision. The timing of a project's gate reviews most likely will not coincide with the filter reviews. But the integration of the two processes must be made efficient through a clearly defined governance structure.

PHASE-GATES MODEL

A phase-gates model—originally introduced as stage-gates by Robert Cooper (Cooper, 2000)—was initially used for new product develop-ment. It describes a product's life cycle, as it goes from one phase to the next in the development process, for example, from design, to build, to test. Gates are strategically placed between the phases as checkpoints. The first phase is typically initiation where the business case for the new product is presented. The gate following this phase helps you decide whether the product should receive investment based on its business case. If the product is a "go" at this gate, it will move on to the next phase. At the subsequent gates following each remaining phase in the development process, go/no-go decisions are made. The decision may be a continuation of the development process as is, a minor or major change, a temporary suspension, or termination altogether. It is based on a review of the performance to date, expected future performance until the completion of the devel-opment process, and the business case merit. A steering committee consisting of the product sponsor and senior managers is typically re-sponsible for the go/no-go decisions. While the committee may meet more frequently to review the project progress, decisions are made at the gates. The phase-gate process has been used in new product development for many years. Recently it has become common in soft-ware development, technology, telecom, biotech, and other indus-tries. The phase-gate process is adopted as a project life cycle model wherein the generic phases include initiation, planning, implementa-tion, and closeout. The overall implementation phase may consist of phases that are specific to the industry. For instance, in software de-velopment, those phases may include requirements definition, design, development, testing, and launch of the final product.

VALUE CREATION PROCESS

Portfolio management is responsible for overseeing the various processes as-sociated with value creation. In the initiation phase, the portfolio assesses the value creation potential of the project candidate. In the development phase it continues to verify the value creation potential, as value is being developed by the project. In the production phase it validates the value delivered by the products and services. The relationship of the overall value creation process to the portfolio funnel is illustrated in Figure 4-3 and is discussed below.

Value Assessment

Every project candidate for the portfolio funnel is evaluated in terms of its value creation potential in the initiation phase as part of the business case. The initial value assessment involves an estimation of the type(s) and quantity of the benefit the project candidate is expected to deliver upon its completion. The estimated benefit is weighed against the estimated cost and risk involved. Based on the benefit-cost-risk equation, which represents the project's value, a go/no-go decision is made. Once the project is selected and formalized, it goes through the development phase. In this phase, the benefit-cost-risk equation must be revisited and revalidated on a regular basis as part of the ongoing value assessment process. Any one or more of the components of this equation can change during the development phase and make the project no longer attractive. The initial and the ongoing value assessment is based only on estimates, and you do not know whether your assessment is on the mark until the value is delivered in the production phase.

Value Development

Once a new project idea formally becomes a project, the value development process begins. This culminates in producing the project outputs. Costs expended in this process are in the form of monetary and human resources. The development process continues as long as the project receives a "go," as it moves through the filters in the portfolio funnel. The go/no-go decisions are based on the ongoing value assessments.

Value Delivery

Value is delivered in the production phase as the project outputs are launched. Most often it is delivered over an extended period of time. (It is possible, albeit not common, to deliver value incrementally during the project phase itself.) Value delivery is the flip side of value realization, and one cannot

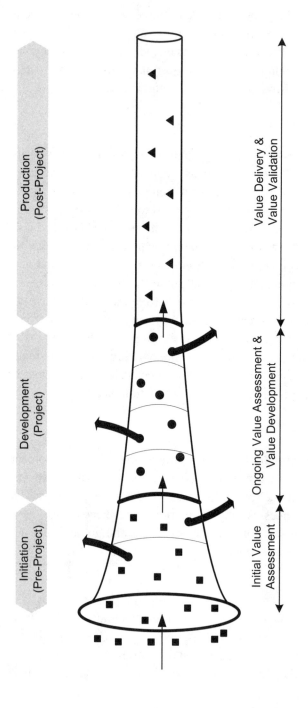

Figure 4-3   Funnel & Filters^SM: Value creation

exist without the other. As the organization delivers value, the targeted stake-holders realize value.

Value Validation

The true test of portfolio effectiveness lies in whether its component projects actually delivered the promised value. Value validation involves comparing the actual value delivered in the production phase with the value assessments from the previous phases. Lessons learned from the validation analysis can be applied in a "feedback" fashion, so that the value assessment process is constantly improved.

5

PROJECT vs. FINANCIAL PORTFOLIOS

There are portfolios of many different "things" (an artist's drawings, a government official's documents, an investor's financial instruments, etc.), but a project portfolio has more in common with a financial portfolio than any other. While managing project investments through a structured project portfolio management (PPM) process may be relatively new, management of financial investments has been practiced for decades using well-established principles and tools. There are many similarities as well as differences between these two types of portfolios. There are several lessons that we can delineate from the financial discipline that can be applied to project portfolios. It may be easy to discredit the lessons because of the differences, but the striking similarities can offer key insights into how we can design and manage project portfolios successfully. The differences must be clearly understood, so we know the limitations of the application. In this chapter I first present the key differences between the two types of portfolios. Then I discuss how basic financial portfolio principles can be applied to project portfolios. I must caution that most of the discussion in this chapter pertains to portfolios with projects that are expected to generate financial value but not of other forms. I lay the foundation in this chapter from which I derive a generic PPM methodology introduced in the next chapter.

PORTFOLIO COMPONENTS

Both financial and project portfolios contain assets that belong to different categories (normally referred to as classes in the financial arena) and subcategories. In fact, multiple levels of categories may exist. The financial assets are instruments such as the individual stocks and bonds, whereas a project portfolio consists of projects. A category is a group of assets with common properties. Examples of financial categories include stocks and bonds. Within each category of stocks, for example, there can be a subcategory of large, medium, and small "cap" stocks. Within the large cap stocks, there can be a further categorization to include stocks of different industrial sectors, and so on. As mentioned in Chapter 2 and discussed in more detail in Chapter 8, projects can be categorized and subcategorized in multiple levels based on different factors including size (small/medium/large), development time (short/medium/long), and risk (low/moderate/high). The financial assets are continuously divisible. For example, you can invest in a publicly traded company by buying its stock in multiples of its share price. On the other hand, project investments are virtually "all or nothing," although some may have the flexibility for a "staged" investment. Financial assets are traded in public markets and can be bought and sold virtually instantaneously, which means that investments can be made and returns realized at any time. The "buy/sell" asset decisions can, in fact, be completely automated through computer based algorithms. Project investments are not tradable in public markets. Most often the return on a project investment is not realized immediately but rather over a period of time after the project is completed. Project go/no-go decisions cannot easily be made instantaneously. The decision process requires people, discussion, and debate, and it takes time. Terminating ongoing projects involves loss of "sunk cost" (an investment that has already been made) with or without any salvage value.

STRATEGY

Most of the financial investments are managed by institutions run by professionals with financial management experience. Every institution has an overall organizational strategy that serves as the guiding light for their portfolios. Even an individual investor that likes to manage her own financial portfolio must have a clear strategy to provide direction for the portfolio. Similarly, organizations have a strategic framework including strategy and organizational goals that their project portfolios are expected to help achieve.

PORTFOLIO OBJECTIVE

The objective of investing in assets of either portfolio is to create value and maximize the return for the owners consistent with your investment strategy. This must be done in the context of risk for sustainable long-term performance. For a financial portfolio, the value of interest is obviously of monetary form. For a project portfolio of a profit-based company, it is primarily financial value. Project investments are also made to generate nonfinancial value, but ultimately they are expected to indirectly enhance the financial returns in some fashion. In both cases, the portfolio manager needs to continuously monitor its performance and make necessary changes relative to its makeup to maintain long-term portfolio success. This means terminating investments in assets that are not performing according to expectations and investing in new attractive assets.

PORTFOLIO VALUE

The value of a financial portfolio is equivalent to the value of the assets it contains at any given time. It is simply determined by summing up the market value of the individual assets in the portfolio after accounting for the transaction costs. The value of a project portfolio is far more difficult to enumerate for two important reasons: 1) The value generated by a project may not be of financial form and not objectively quantifiable, and, 2) Irrespective of its form, most often the value is realized over a long period of time rather than instantaneously, after the project has been completed. So the value of a project portfolio at any given time is only an estimate of its value generation *potential* long into the future.

PORTFOLIO RISK

Another critical difference between financial and project portfolios relates to the nature of the risk associated with the portfolio components and how it can be characterized. Financial portfolio risk is primarily market driven, while market risk is only a part of a project portfolio's overall risk. The former carries the risk associated with each individual asset (e.g., stock of a company) in the portfolio as well as the relationship risk characterized by the extent the asset categories (e.g., stocks of companies in a particular industry) in the portfolio move up and down together. For a portfolio of projects expected to generate financial value, the ultimate success of the component projects is driven by the market risk. But nonmarket risks such as technology feasibility, resource skill set, resource availability, production capability, and management effectiveness, among others, may also exist. Project portfolio risks have been studied and modeled to a far lesser degree than the market risks of financial assets and portfolios. Projects in a portfolio may reinforce each other synergistically by enhancing the return side of the equation. For example, a large market share in an operating system is likely to enhance revenues of other software products in the same organization. On the other hand, there may be "cannibalization," where a new product may diminish revenues from an existing product in the same portfolio. Very little information is available in the literature on how these phenomena can be accounted for in selecting assets in a project portfolio. Risk is a key driver in selecting the asset components of either type of portfolio, and its tolerance is largely dictated by the strategy and culture of the organization owning or sponsoring the portfolio.

APPLYING FINANCIAL PORTFOLIO PRINCIPLES TO PROJECT PORTFOLIOS

Notwithstanding the differences, some of the well-established principles of financial portfolio management can be applied to project portfolios. These principles relate to four themes, namely, alignment, value creation, portfolio balancing, and long-term performance. The first three of these can be traced back to the portfolio management theory developed in the early 1950's by Harry Markowitz. Known as the Modern Portfolio Theory (MPT), it laid the foundation for today's financial portfolio management. The three key principles of MPT are:

- The portfolio should be constructed in accordance with the overall investment strategy and goals.
- The portfolio has two sources of risks:
  - ♦ Individual risk related to a given asset of the portfolio itself, for example, an individual stock
  - ♦ Relationship risk of how a given asset is related to the others.
- These risks are minimized by diversification through avoiding overdependence on one asset or one asset category. Investing in multiple assets and asset categories and evaluating and adjusting the portfolio

makeup on a periodic basis using a well-structured approach is generally referred to as portfolio balancing.

- For a given level of investment risk, an optimal portfolio generates the highest value. Therefore, there is a spectrum of optimum portfolios creating the highest values for different levels of risks. Economists call this spectrum the "efficient frontier."

The four key themes applicable to project portfolios are discussed below, and a PPM methodology based on these principles is presented in the next chapter.

Alignment

A financial portfolio is constructed based on the overall investment strategy and goals of the investor. Different investors have different needs and therefore, different strategies and goals. An investor may be interested in building a portfolio that will help him reduce the overall tax burden, increase investment at a steady rate over the long term, provide reliable and consistent income regularly, or achieve some other objective. He might like to avoid specific assets (e.g., a stock of a particular company), or asset categories (e.g., tobacco company stocks), while favoring others (e.g. green technology stocks). According to MPT, you must build the financial portfolio in accordance with the strategy and goals of the investor. Similarly, for a project portfolio, you must select and invest in those projects that align directly with the strategy and goals of the organization sponsoring the portfolio. It may be the enterprise at the highest level of the organization, or a business unit, or a department at a lower rung that sponsors the portfolio. Whatever the case may be, alignment must be a key criterion in selecting the projects for the portfolio.

Value Creation

Another key criterion in selecting a project must be its potential to generate value, as in the case of a financial portfolio. While objective estimation of the financial value is possible because of quantitative tools, intangibles are not so easily quantifiable. If a project portfolio exclusively consists of projects that are designed to generate financial value only, the efficient frontier principle of financial portfolios can be applied to identify the right mix of projects that would generate the highest value. But an adjustment must be made for the expected value of each project for the risk it poses. If all the projects in a portfolio are "normalized" for their respective risks, a direct relationship can be developed between the total value to be generated and the cost of all the projects in the portfolio. Accordingly, for a given investment cost of a portfolio, among numerous possible portfolios (that is, combinations of projects), there exists one that would yield the highest possible value for the risk level acceptable to the organization. Therefore, if the total available investment for a portfolio is known, the particular mix of candidate projects that would give you the maximum value can be determined from the efficient frontier. (Please see the accompanying box for further discussion on the efficient frontier.)

EFFICIENT FRONTIER

If a project portfolio consists solely of projects that generate financial value exclusively, the efficient frontier principle can be applied to identify the right combination of projects that would give you the maximum financial return for any given level of investment. This principle is a key element of the MPT introduced in the early 1950's by Harry Markowitz. He and others that further developed the theory won a Nobel Prize in economics in 1990 for their groundbreaking work. The efficient frontier principle does not apply to portfolios that generate nonfinancial forms of value.

Let's say you have ten projects in your portfolio that are being evaluated for their merit, and you want to determine what mix of projects will give you the highest financial return. Here are the basic steps to identify the efficient frontier:

1. Compute how many possible portfolios are theoretically possible (2^{10}, that is 1,024), and identify the individual projects in each one of those portfolios.
2. Plot the investment cost of the portfolio (the sum of costs of all the projects in the portfolio) vs. the net present value (NPV) of the portfolio (the sum of NPVs of the projects in that portfolio). (The discount rate used in calculating the project NPVs must be adjusted for the individual project risks, as discussed in Chapter 12.)

Figure 5-1 illustrates the results in the form of a schematic without real data. Each bubble represents a portfolio. There should be a total of 1,024 bubbles for all the possible portfolios (not all portfolios are shown in the figure for the sake of simplicity). The efficient frontier curve consists of the portfolios that are expected to yield maximum value for a given level of portfolio investment. This analysis can be helpful in many ways:

- Knowing how much investment is available, you can select the portfolio with the right mix of new projects located at the frontier. For example, for an investment of $X in Figure 5-1, the portfolio at the efficient frontier (circled in the figure) yields the highest NPV compared to any other portfolio requiring the same amount of total investment. Accordingly, you would choose to invest in those projects that make up that particular portfolio.

- You can identify an investment level beyond which the increase in the total portfolio return is minuscule. In Figure 5-1, beyond a total investment of approximately $Y, for every unit of additional investment, the incremental increase in the portfolio value is small and diminishing. The portfolios yielding the highest value are on the lower part of the frontier where the slope of the curve is steeper. Thus you can identify those projects that will give you the biggest "bang for the buck."

- Similar analysis of an existing portfolio can reveal useful insights. You can identify those projects in the portfolio that may be offering no/low value or only incrementally higher value compared to the rest of the projects. Optimization of the portfolio by terminating such projects may result in significant investment cost savings for the same value or insignificantly lower value. You can determine what projects can be terminated to lower the investment cost by identifying the right project mix that is closer to the steeper portion of the frontier as illustrated in Figure 5-2. Alternatively, you may maximize the portfolio value by altering the project mix of the portfolio while keeping the investment at the same level (Figure 5-2).

The number of theoretically possible portfolios with every possible combination of projects increases exponentially with the number of projects to be considered. This makes it increasingly difficult to do the calculations manually, but a computer program can help you create the numerous scenarios and generate the efficient frontier curve more easily. You may also develop the efficient frontier manually using a simplified approach, as illustrated with an example in Chapter 12. It must be reiterated that this analysis cannot be applied to projects that generate nonfinancial value.

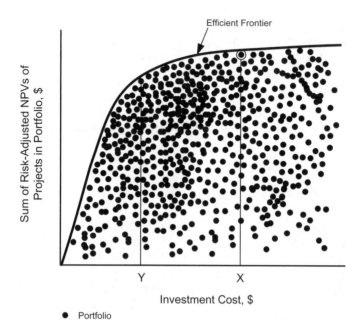

Figure 5-1   Efficient frontier

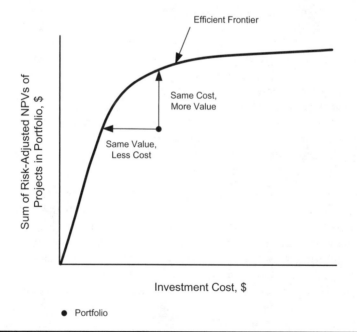

Figure 5-2   Efficient frontier: portfolio optimization

Portfolio Balancing

As mentioned before, to minimize individual and relationship risks, MPT suggests that you create a diversified portfolio containing assets belonging to various categories and subcategories to produce the desired balance. The balance must be a function of the portfolio strategy and goals as well as the portfolio owner's risk tolerance. Similarly, a project portfolio can be diversified with respect to project categories and subcategories. For instance, projects may be divided into revenue generating and cost reduction projects, and the former can be further divided into categories based on the development cost. Investments can be made in accordance with predefined proportions within these categories and subcategories.

Long-Term Performance

A financial portfolio is considered successful when it maximizes value over the long-term horizon, although the portfolio returns may ebb and flow due to economic cycles. For a project portfolio, the same principle must apply. However, valuation (quantifying the value) of a project portfolio and tracking it over time is a tricky process, especially if the portfolio contains projects that generate nonfinancial value.

The value of a financial portfolio at a given time is easily calculated by summing up the individual values of each component asset at that time. In a project portfolio consisting of financial value-generating projects, the value of each component project is represented by its estimated *future* cash flows. The value of the portfolio as a whole at any time is the summation of the estimated values of the component projects at that time. It is important to estimate the portfolio value, not only at the present time, but also in time increments into the future to ensure that appropriate project investments are made to generate value consistently over the long term without any major "dips." The portfolio value in the future can change depending upon the value of the projects entering and leaving the portfolio. It should be tracked regularly, so that advance planning can be made to introduce the right projects into the portfolio to maintain consistent value generation. All this can become complex, because projects, unlike financial assets, typically have a long lag time before they start generating value and most often generate value over an extended period of time. Portfolio valuation for long-term performance requires sophisticated processes, metrics, and analysis and certainly warrants higher levels of portfolio management maturity.

The focus of the foregoing discussion is comparison of the financial value-generating project portfolios with financial portfolios. But the principles behind the latter portfolios are applicable even to those project portfolios that generate nonfinancial value. Alignment with organizational strategy and goals, maximizing value creation, balancing through diversification, and long-term performance are the foundational principles of any type of project portfolio.

SECTION 2

PROJECT PORTFOLIO MANAGEMENT METHODOLOGY

Section 2 focuses on a practical methodology for designing, building, and managing a balanced portfolio. The first chapter in this section introduces four key phases of portfolio methodology: Build Foundation, Design Portfolio, Construct Portfolio, and Monitor and Control Portfolio. The first two phases include portfolio planning processes, whereas the latter are about building and maintaining the portfolio. Building the portfolio foundation involves understanding the strategic framework and goals of the organization that is sponsoring and supporting the portfolio and establishing the infrastructure required to implement the overall project portfolio management (PPM) process. Portfolio design is a critical phase that involves putting together the design properties or specifications for the portfolio. The effectiveness of a portfolio is a direct function of how closely it adheres to these specifications. Portfolio construction deals with building the new portfolio and calibrating it to reflect the specifications. The last PPM phase is about monitoring and controlling the portfolio to ensure that it continues to exhibit the design specifications. Processes specific to each one of the four phases are discussed in different chapters.

6

PROJECT PORTFOLIO
MANAGEMENT
METHODOLOGY

Using the foundation I have laid out so far, let us now delve into a structured, process-based methodology to design, build, and manage a new project portfolio or improve an existing one. The methodology presented in this chapter is generic and is universally applicable to project portfolios of any kind and at any organizational level. The chapter starts with the basics of the financial portfolio management process founded upon the principles presented in Chapter 5. Taking the lessons learned from financial portfolio management, I then present a project portfolio management (PPM) methodology. As I alluded to in Chapter 5, there is a school of thought that believes there are many differences between financial and PPM and feels strongly that the former is not an effective guide for project portfolios. For those skeptics, I offer the following:

1. The differences should not be the cause for unequivocal rejection of financial portfolio principles to be applied to project portfolios. We can learn a great deal from the similarities between the two types of portfolios but must be aware of the limitations. However, we should not overextend the application to a point where it loses the validity. I hope that the previous chapter has shed adequate light on the topic to help you understand the limitations.

2. Ask if a given project management methodology makes sense and can stand on itself independent of the financial portfolio principles. If the answer is yes, it does not matter whether financial portfolio principles apply. In fact, you may consider them to validate the project portfolio methodology. I believe the methodology introduced in this chapter stands on its own and passes this test.

The methodology presented herein involves four phases, one of which is construction of the initial or new portfolio. This phase is only a one-time event. Once the initial portfolio is built, it becomes a three-phase methodology in the long run. Each phase is characterized by several individual processes, which are briefly mentioned in this chapter. The subsequent four chapters are dedicated to a detailed discussion of each of the four phases.

CREATING AND MANAGING A FINANCIAL PORTFOLIO

Let's say you win a lottery for a few million dollars. First you pay Uncle Sam his portion of the proceeds. You splurge on the quick luxuries you always wished to enjoy. Then you prudently decide to invest the remaining jackpot—hopefully you have some left! You want to make it grow, so you and your family can have a decent living for the rest of your lives—perhaps without having to work like most people. Except for personal checking, you have never had any investment or retirement accounts. You hardly have any experience in personal investing, so you hire a financial advisor for help. After a few meetings with you, the advisor will most likely apply the following four steps to help you manage your investment:

1. Build the foundation for your portfolio by capturing your long-term financial strategy, needs, and goals; income/expense requirements; personal risk characteristics; and so on.
2. Develop the design specifications for the portfolio in terms of the asset categories (cash, treasuries, bonds, stocks, etc.) and subcategories and their "mix" (percent investment allocation for each category/subcategory) aligning with the foundational requirements from the first step.

3. Construct the new portfolio by selecting and buying specific assets in each category/subcategory that fit your portfolio design specifications from the second step.

4. Monitor the performance of the portfolio regularly and control it by making changes (sell some assets and buy others) in accordance with your financial strategy, goals, and portfolio design specifications.

You will basically stick to this approach, unless your portfolio foundation shifts. If your long-term financial goals change, perhaps because of your age, family needs, general economic conditions, or a myriad of other things, you may:

- Revise the portfolio foundation (Step 1).
- Change the design of the portfolio (Step 2).
- Revise the makeup of the portfolio and continue monitoring and controlling the portfolio (Step 4). (Step 3 is the construction of the new portfolio, which is a one-time event, therefore, it is not repeated.)

Obviously financial portfolio planning and investing are much more complex than the above four steps, but these simple fundamentals of personal finance set the tone for financial portfolio management.

PROJECT PORTFOLIO MANAGEMENT METHODOLOGY

Reflecting the financial portfolio process presented above, I have identified a methodology to manage a project portfolio that consists of four major phases (Figure 6-1):

- Build Foundation
- Design Portfolio
- Construct Portfolio
- Monitor & Control Portfolio

Each phase is characterized by specific processes that are listed in Figure 6-1. The first two phases deal with the planning side of portfolio management,

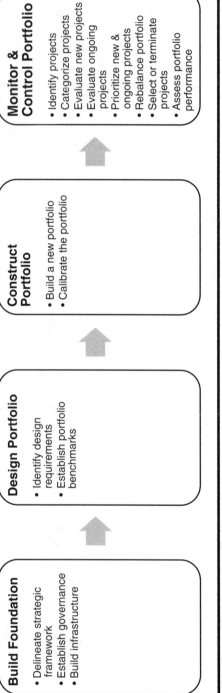

Figure 6-1   PPM Phases & Processes (Kodukula, 2014)

whereas the other two are about implementation. Each phase is described briefly below.

Build Foundation

The first phase of the methodology involves building the organizational foundation that needs to be in place before a portfolio is designed and constructed. It is a prerequisite to the initiation of any PPM process in your organization. Without the foundation, the PPM process will be weak and ineffective. The organization must clearly articulate its strategic framework including its mission, vision, strategy, and goals which provides the foundation on which the portfolio can be built. A governance process must be established to facilitate decision making, risk management, and accountability, among others. You also need to have the necessary infrastructure, such as the information management systems and physical facilities in place for the PPM process to work efficiently. Accordingly, the key processes involved in this phase are:

- Delineate strategic framework
- Establish governance
- Build portfolio infrastructure

The foundational requirements are not expected to change often. They are revised only when there is change in the strategy and goals of the organization sponsoring the portfolio.

Design Portfolio

The second phase of the methodology deals with the design of the portfolio. It precedes the initial portfolio construction and must be completed before the very first project is placed in the portfolio. It involves developing the portfolio design specifications (also referred to as properties or characteristics) that constitute the portfolio design template or the blueprint. The design specifies screening criteria for project candidates to become serious contenders for the portfolio, investment benchmarks the projects must meet to receive investment, project termination criteria, the desired balance between different project categories, risk contingencies, and so on.

The individual projects in the portfolio and their relative mix should meet the requirements specified in this phase. The evaluation, prioritization, and selection of projects in the portfolio construction and monitor/control phases must follow the specifications developed in this phase. The two important processes of this phase are:

- Identify design requirements
- Establish portfolio benchmarks

The design specifications for this phase, to a large extent, depend upon the foundational aspects of the portfolio from the first phase and should be revised whenever the foundation shifts.

Construct Portfolio

The third phase of the PPM methodology involves construction of a new portfolio that fits the portfolio design specifications. Once you have built the foundation (phase 1) and developed the portfolio design (phase 2), you are ready to build the new portfolio. Presumably projects are already being funded by your portfolio sponsoring organization (PSO) and are at various phases of their life cycles. Therefore, portfolio construction starts with the creation of the new portfolio by pooling the ongoing projects in the PSO. The new portfolio will not likely meet the design specifications developed in the previous phase. Your task now is to transform the new portfolio to an ongoing "steady state" portfolio that meets the portfolio design requirements. The transformation is done through a process that I call "calibration." A steady state portfolio consistently exhibits the characteristics required by the portfolio's design template, despite the dynamic throughput of projects in the portfolio. The projects in a steady state portfolio align with organizational strategy and goals, have a strong business case, meet the investment benchmarks, rank relatively higher in their merit, and exhibit the right mix to achieve the desired balance. Calibration of the new portfolio involves termination of projects that do not meet the portfolio design specifications, and completion of remaining projects and addition of new projects, so that the new portfolio will evolve into a steady state portfolio. Obviously this process takes time. The key portfolio construction processes are:

- Build a new portfolio
- Calibrate the portfolio

Construction of the new portfolio, which eventually transforms to a steady state portfolio, is a one-time process. Once the steady state is attained, you enter the next phase of the PPM process, where the objective is to maintain that steady state. From this point on, the Construct Portfolio phase is no longer part of the PPM process. PPM will now be characterized by three phases:

1. Build Foundation
2. Design Portfolio
3. Monitor & Control Portfolio

These three phases are ongoing and iterative (Figure 6-2). When there is a significant change in the business environment, a PSO's strategy and goals are revised which shifts the portfolio foundation. It warrants revisions to the portfolio design specifications. The revised design will become the blueprint for the processes associated with the next phase of the PPM methodology.

Monitor & Control Portfolio

This phase of the PPM methodology involves day-to-day, ongoing, and iterative activities aimed to keep the portfolio in steady state. It includes many

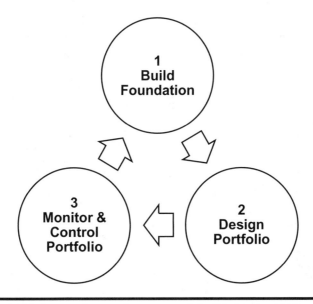

Figure 6-2   PPM phases of a steady state portfolio (Kodukula, 2014)

key processes as shown in Figure 6-3. New projects are identified, evaluated, and selected for the portfolio. Performance of ongoing projects as well as their business cases are reviewed and revalidated. The new and ongoing projects together are prioritized and the portfolio rebalanced. Final go/no-go decisions are made. Portfolio performance is continually evaluated and the PPM process improved based on the lessons learned. Project "churning" makes the portfolio highly dynamic, which in turn makes portfolio control complex and challenging.

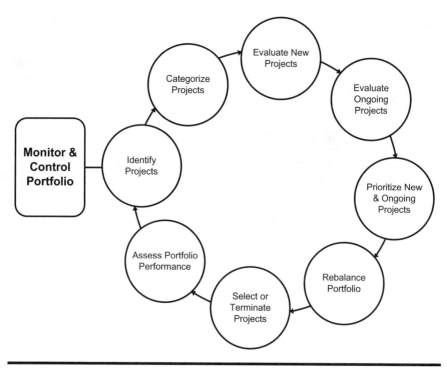

Figure 6-3   Iterative processes of "Monitor & Control Portfolio" (Kodukula, 2014)

7

BUILD FOUNDATION

Let's say that you have been given the charter to initiate a formal project portfolio management (PPM) process in your organization. Whatever methodology you want to implement, certain prerequisites must be in place before you build the new formal portfolio. For example, the organizational "strategic framework" must be articulated, so that the right projects that align with the framework can be selected. The goals of the portfolio sponsoring organization (PSO) must be clearly defined and made visible to the portfolio team. This will facilitate the alignment of projects with the goals. The PPM methodology, governance process, infrastructure, etc. must also be put in place. Collectively these prerequisites build the foundation for the portfolio. Without a proper foundation, a portfolio can be easily manipulated, weakened, and destroyed by forces such as internal politics, strong power bases, and poor support structures. I have met hundreds of portfolio managers and staff over the years that are extremely knowledgeable and effective with the implementation side of PPM. But they are particularly frustrated by the foundational factors that they have very little control over. In this chapter I discuss in detail the processes associated with laying the portfolio foundation.

A key objective of a portfolio is to make sure that only those projects that align with the organizational strategy and goals and have a high potential to create value are selected for investment. This implies that the organizational strategy and goals must first be clearly articulated. Second, a governance process must be defined to facilitate an effective decision-making process. Third, the infrastructure that defines the portfolio team structure, portfolio information management system, required physical structures, etc., must be in place. Along these lines, three key processes are important in building the portfolio foundation:

- Delineate strategic framework
- Establish governance
- Build infrastructure

DELINEATE STRATEGIC FRAMEWORK

An organization's mission, vision, values, and strategy—commonly referred to as the strategic framework—are at the core of the foundation of the portfolio. Definition and the "hierarchy" of the terms associated with the strategic framework (Figure 7-1) vary depending on the organization. Every organization must have a reason to exist, which is often represented by its mission. Based on the mission, the vision for the future of the organization is defined. The essence of the vision is what the organization wants to be in the long term. The mission and vision show the direction for the formulation of

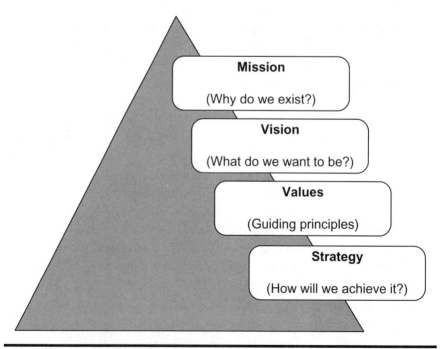

Figure 7-1   Major components of strategic framework

strategy. Strategy is a high-level framework of how you will accomplish an organization's vision and mission. It describes how you will get from an "as is" baseline state to a "to be" finish line state. Organizations also elucidate "guiding principles," which are the behaviors that guide the realization of their mission and vision. Often referred to as "values," they are not to be confused with value, that is, defined as benefits. The strategic framework developed at the helm of the organization cascades down to the lower-level organizational units. The lower units develop their own strategic frameworks that must be in alignment with that of the parent enterprise. The strategy of the enterprise is developed by the executive team, and at the lower organizational units, it is the responsibility of the management teams of the respective units.

Strategy Development

Formulation of enterprise strategy is a highly creative exercise that involves intense effort by the executive/management teams. Various tools and techniques have been developed over the years for strategy formulation and hundreds of books and thousands of articles have been written on the topic. Of the many strategy development tools and techniques available in the literature, the most common ones are competitive analysis (Porter, 1998); strengths, weaknesses, threats, and opportunities (SWOT) analysis; blue oceans (Kim and Mauborgne, 2005); and balanced scorecard (Kaplan and Norton, 1996). Strategy formulation is a complex process and will require many more tools than the aforementioned. Description of this process or the tools needed is outside the scope of this book. Of the several approaches available, the balanced scorecard framework offers a more clearly defined foundation for portfolio management. Therefore, it is described in more detail in the following box.

BALANCED SCORECARD

The balanced scorecard (BSC) framework, developed by Robert Kaplan and David Norton (1996), challenges the traditional view that a profit-based organization's sole purpose is to create financial value or wealth for its owners or shareholders. It is built on the premise that the goal of maximizing shareholder value causes management to focus on short-term profitability at the expense of long-term competitiveness. Therefore, it offers a framework that requires formulation of organizational strategy and goals in financial as well as other domains. Specifically, it presents four domains, also referred to as perspectives:

- Financial
- Customer
- Internal business process
- Employee learning and growth

Each domain corresponds to a different form of value including nonfinancials. Whereas Kaplan and Norton identified the above four domains as critical to the success of any organization, you may add more (or consolidate them into three) as you deem fit for your organization. BSC provides a comprehensive framework that translates an organization's mission and vision into a coherent set of goals and objectives in the four domains. Thus, it creates a balance at the strategic level with respect to the organizational goals, hence the name balanced scorecard. The scorecard also includes a quantitative approach to measure, monitor, and manage organizational performance using outcome measures and performance indicators corresponding to the goals or objectives.

Financial measures related to shareholder value include operating income, return on capital, economic value added, etc. Examples of customer-related measures are customer satisfaction, customer profitability, customer retention, new customer acquisition, and market share. Internal business processes may be unique to each industry or business, but generic measures in this domain include time to market, throughput, procurement, order fulfillment, project management, etc. Employee learning and growth perspective measures may include employee satisfaction, employee retention, and employee skill set.

If the organizational performance is measured and managed only by financial metrics, a project portfolio would invest in only those projects that expect financially attractive returns accordingly. Projects that show promise in enhancing customer satisfaction, process improvements, employee learning and growth, and other areas may be rejected, as they do not align with organizational value priorities and cannot compete with those that demonstrate financial merit. On the other hand, if your organization adopts the BSC approach with focus on multiple domains, the portfolio must select projects in all those domains based on the relative priorities for each domain. This lends to a balanced portfolio, a portfolio where a balance is created in terms of the form of value to be generated by a given project. If your organization is already using a BSC approach, PPM would be an excellent fit. The reason is that: 1) the BSC articulates the strategic framework with goals and objectives clearly defined forming the foundation for the portfolio; 2) different value forms are already identified as critical to the organization's success, which can be used as project categories in the portfolio to reflect the same balance as required by the scorecard; and 3) the quantitative framework offered by the BSC is an excellent means to evaluate the portfolio performance. Even if your organization does not use the BSC, categorizing the projects in your portfolio based on the value form is still an effective approach to creating a balanced portfolio.

Strategic Goals and Objectives

Enterprise strategy is translated into a plan commonly referred to as a strategic plan, which outlines the long-term goals—also called strategic goals—that help the enterprise achieve its shareholder expectations. It also contains high-level plans showing how those goals will be achieved. Strategic goals are high-level, long-term, and qualitative. They do not change considerably over short periods of time. Significant changes are typically made when external business conditions shift dramatically or because of change in leadership at the helm of the organization. In order to objectively monitor the organizational performance towards achieving the goals, each goal should be translated into corresponding objectives that are specific, measurable, agreed to (by the concerned stakeholders), realistic, and time bound (SMART).

Strategic Alignment

In a large enterprise comprised of several business units, each unit must define its own mission, vision, strategy, values, goals, and objectives, which must directly align with those of the enterprise. Furthermore, moving down the organizational hierarchy, each organizational unit must define its own strategic framework linked to that of its "parent" unit and ultimately to that of the enterprise (Figure 7-2). For example, an individual function (for instance, IT) must develop its own strategic framework in accordance with that of its parent unit, ultimately aligning with that of the enterprise up through

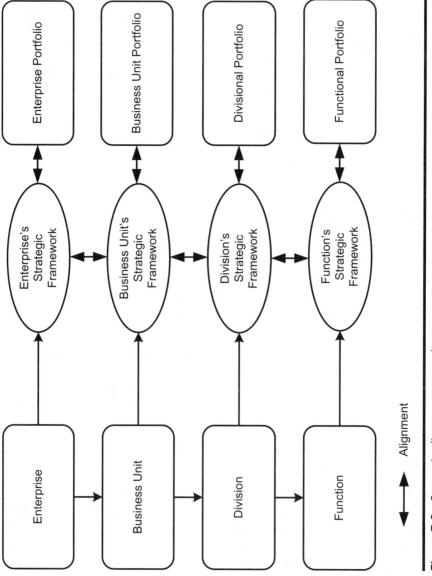

Figure 7-2   Strategic alignment across the enterprise

the organizational hierarchy. Starting at the highest level of the enterprise, strategic framework must be developed at every level of the organization by a cascading process making sure there is alignment throughout the entire enterprise. Most effective organizations are strategically aligned and strive to achieve their goals and objectives with laser-like focus. Their management teams clearly define the organizational strategy, goals, and objectives and communicate them effectively throughout the organization. If the strategic framework of the PSO is well defined and visible, you have the proper foundation to select the right projects for the portfolio. Ultimately a portfolio can produce effective results only when both the enterprise and the PSO have an effective strategy and goals providing the right direction for the portfolio. Otherwise, no matter how well the PPM process is implemented, organizational success is unlikely. PPM is about strategy execution but not formulation. It is a vehicle to get you to the destination you have chosen, but if the destination is wrong to begin with, the portfolio cannot deliver effective results.

ESTABLISH GOVERNANCE

Governance of any entity is the structure that:

- Identifies the relationships between and responsibilities of its major stakeholders.
- Provides framework to mitigate and manage conflicts of interests among the stakeholders.
- Defines the accountability of key players involved in managing the entity.
- Establishes policies, processes, and practices to be implemented to achieve the entity's objectives.
- Ensures the entity is managed in a responsible, professional, and transparent manner aiming for its long-term success.

Corporate governance has received increasing attention since 2001 especially in view of the high profile scandals involving large public companies such as Enron Corporation and WorldCom. The Sarbanes-Oxley Act was passed in 2002 in the U.S. (and similar acts in other major countries) to promote accountability and transparency in public companies. The overall theme of governance has become critical not only at the corporate level but throughout the enterprise including the portfolios and projects. The major activities related to portfolio governance are:

- Install portfolio management team organizational structure.
- Create the decision-making framework (e.g., funnel & filters[SM] and phase-gate processes).
- Define overall PPM methodology and standards to be followed by the entire organization.
- Define risk management processes and procedures.

Let's address the portfolio management team organizational structure in more detail here, while the other areas are covered in other parts of the book.

Organizational Structure

The portfolio management team organizational structure includes the portfolio stakeholders that are responsible for various executive, management, and operational functions. Several critical functions are associated with portfolio management, which require people with different roles/responsibilities and skills/competencies. Depending upon your organization, you may use a different organizational structure for managing your portfolio. As an example, typical elements of an organizational structure (Figure 7-3) are discussed below, not necessarily in any hierarchical form.

Portfolio Sponsoring Organization (PSO)

A PSO is the organizational unit that sponsors and supports the portfolio. It may be the enterprise itself or any of the units (business unit, division, department/function, etc.) at a lower level. It is responsible for initiating the portfolio and providing the financial and human resources to manage the portfolio. One of the most critical roles for the PSO is to make the organizational strategy and goals clearly visible for the portfolio team. The PSO is represented by the portfolio executive board (PEB).

Portfolio Executive Board

The PEB consists of executive or senior managers with the decision-making authority over the investment funds and human resources. The board

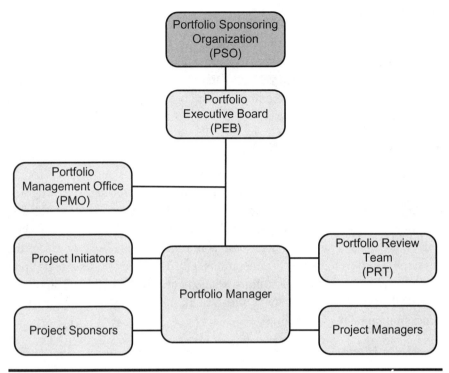

Figure 7-3 Common elements of a portfolio management team organizational structure

is responsible for making initial go/no-go decisions on new project opportunities as well as continue/cancel decisions related to ongoing projects. As a whole, the board represents the PSO and undertakes its responsibilities.

Project Initiators

Project initiators submit proposals for new projects to be considered for investment by the portfolio. As part of the proposal process, their responsibility is to perform project evaluation, often referred to as business case analysis, and provide the required information using the appropriate format. These initiators may already have the funds available to sponsor the project, if approved by the PEB. In some cases they may be seeking investment funds from elsewhere in the organization.

Project Sponsors

Project sponsors provide the investment funds for the projects in the portfolio and work closely with respective project managers in ensuring that the projects are performing according to the specifications and are completed successfully. They are key members of the project governance process and typically project initiators also.

Portfolio Review Team (PRT)

The PRT plays a critical role in the PPM process. It is responsible for reviewing the new project proposals, evaluating the performance of ongoing projects from the portfolio perspective, prioritizing them, and formulating go/no-go recommendations to the PEB. This team is cross-functional, typically consisting of subject matter experts in finance, marketing, engineering, research and development, IT, operations, etc. They may be an integral part or extension of the core portfolio management team. Depending upon the size of the portfolio, they may be full-time in this position or part-time with other functional responsibilities.

Portfolio Manager

Portfolio managers are the focal contact for the PEB, PRT, project managers, and the project sponsors. They have the primary responsibility of implementing the PPM processes. Specifically, the responsibilities are to:

- Collect and organize the project proposal information from the project initiators and the performance data of ongoing projects from the project managers and submit them to the PRT in the right format.
- Assist the review team with the tools and techniques they need.
- Collect and formalize portfolio performance information.
- Gather lessons learned and facilitate their use to improve the PPM process.

Portfolio Management Office (PMO)

The PMO can serve many functions including administrative support, building the portfolio infrastructure, establishing the information systems, facilitating the overall PPM process, and so on. In many organizations these functions are housed in what is generally called the project management office. Chapter 16 is dedicated to PMOs.

BUILD INFRASTRUCTURE

The objective of building the portfolio infrastructure is to facilitate the initial implementation of the PPM as a formal standardized process as well as its ongoing operation and maintenance, once it is in place. The key elements of the infrastructure include the required physical facilities to house the PMO and the management information system to gather, analyze, and report PPM information.

8

DESIGN PORTFOLIO

"Design Portfolio" is the second phase of the project portfolio management (PPM) methodology. Designing the portfolio is tantamount to developing a blueprint for the portfolio. The design requirements, also called specifications, established in this phase will dictate how the portfolio will be constructed and managed in the later phases of the PPM process. Therefore, the design must be in place before the very first project is placed in the portfolio. The design specifies the properties you want the portfolio and its component projects to exhibit. The specifications particularly relate to the individual project characteristics and their relative mix. They also include the investment benchmarks and the metrics to be applied. Without the specs, the next two phases will have no direction for evaluation, ranking, and selection of projects. In this chapter, I focus on the design principles and processes that support portfolio construction, monitoring and control. The two key design processes of phase 2 (Design Portfolio) are:

- Identify design requirements
- Establish portfolio benchmarks

Many design requirements and benchmarks depend on a number of external as well as internal factors. External factors include the overall economy, general industry conditions, competition, customer needs, regulatory atmosphere, etc. The internal conditions include, among others, the organization's growth phase, strategic framework, and resource capacity. Since both the external and internal conditions are prone to change, the portfolio design should be reviewed and revised appropriately at least annually.

IDENTIFY DESIGN REQUIREMENTS

Design requirements for the portfolio fall into two areas, namely, portfolio balance and project evaluation criteria. Within the former, two types of balance are critical to the portfolio:

- **Category Balance**: Balance between different project categories for portfolio diversification to manage risk effectively.
- **Triple Constraint Balance**: Balance between the organizational goals, projects, and the resources to ensure that there are enough (but not unnecessary) projects and resources to achieve the organizational goals and to optimize resource utilization.

Accordingly, identification of the design requirements involves the following steps:

1. Establish project categories and subcategories into which projects will be placed for ranking and selection to create category balancing.
2. Provide guidelines to ensure the balance of the portfolio triple constraint.
3. Identify criteria to be considered in evaluating new and ongoing projects.

The design requirements are developed and revised, as necessary, by the portfolio manager and the subject matter experts with input from and approval by the portfolio executive board (PEB).

1. Category Balance

It is just common business sense that in order to gain and maintain long-term competitive advantage in the marketplace, any organization must invest in diverse projects. Diversification creates a balanced portfolio that will help manage risks effectively for the long term. A balanced portfolio consists of projects of different categories, which are mutually exclusive. Each category represents a particular project characteristic. Examples include the form of value (financial vs. nonfinancial) the project generates, investment size, development time, markets, geography, product line, technology, risk level, etc. You may even create subcategories within a category. For instance, a portfolio may be categorized based on the value form (financial vs nonfinancial) at the first level, and subcategorized based on the investment size at the next. If your organization is adapting a balanced scorecard (BSC) framework for strategic management, it is fitting to use the four BSC domains (the value forms) for the first category level. There are no hard and fast rules as to how many category levels are optimal. The more category levels there are, the more complex the portfolio becomes making the project evaluation process increasingly difficult. On the other hand, having only one level may not give you the opportunity to balance enough project characteristics. Two levels are probably adequate. Portfolio balance is achieved by splitting the available resources among the categories in predefined proportions.

2. Triple Constraint Balance

One of the key design requirements for the portfolio must be that the triple constraint (goals, projects, resources) be in balance at any time. Balancing involves changing two of the components of the constraint until they match the third one, while keeping the latter unchanged. It is a continuous, iterative process and one of the most challenging tasks of PPM. The main objective of this juggling act is to ensure that there are sufficient and necessary projects as well as resources available to help achieve the current goals of the portfolio sponsoring organization (PSO).

A frequent question raised by many PPM practitioners is whether the resources component of the triple constraint should be monetary, human, or both. From a practical standpoint, this question translates to: Once the projects are evaluated and ranked, should you select only those that can be supported by the available investment money, human resources, or both. If it is to be based on both, it will add another layer of complexity to the balancing act. You may first match the projects with the available investment funds and then seek the required human resources to complete the projects. An easier approach is to establish in the design phase whether monetary or human resources, relatively speaking, are more important to the portfolio. This will determine the criterion of monetary or human resources to match against the projects in balancing the triple constraint. For example, in the case of a capital portfolio requiring heavy investment in terms of materials, equipment, and construction contractors, you may choose available money as the primary criterion in selecting the projects from a ranked list. On the other hand, you may consider the available human resources for selecting projects in a research and development portfolio that demands large amounts of human resources. In the portfolio design phase, you must specify whether money or people should represent the resource component of the portfolio triple constraint.

3. Project Evaluation Criteria

Identifying the right project characteristics or attributes as criteria for evaluating the investment worthiness of projects is critical to project ranking and selection. The characteristics should represent the true merit of the project and be measurable in some fashion, so that ranking can be more objective and rational. The criteria can be numerous, but an excessive number of criteria can make the evaluation process more cumbersome. On the other hand, insufficient criteria may not represent the true merit of the project. A proper balance must be struck for practical reasons. You may start with a long list of preliminary criteria relevant to your portfolio. Upon assessing the importance of these criteria, you may select the "vital few" and reject the "trivial many." To keep it simple, you may choose no more than five or six that will essentially capture the project's merit. At minimum, you should include the following three that are vital:

- Alignment
- Potential to generate value
- Risk characteristics

These criteria can be applied to any project category and any type of portfolio, thereby creating consistency across your entire organization. The criteria must be the same for every project within a category but may be the same or different between categories. Metrics will need to be defined for these criteria as discussed later for Levels 1-3 evaluations.

Alignment

This refers to how well a proposed project is aligned to the PSO's strategy and goals. As discussed in Chapter 7, strategy is a high-level framework of how you will accomplish an organization's vision and mission while adhering to its core values, and goals are major milestones to be achieved so that the strategy is realized. A key factor in determining a project's merit must be how it can help the PSO achieve its goals while at the same time demonstrating its fit with the PSO's strategy. As discussed previously, to make the project evaluation process more robust, you need to assess the alignment with the organization's strategy and goals separately. Alignment with the strategy ensures that the project will help the organization reach its long-term mission and vision while adhering to the organizational core values. Goal alignment ensures that sufficient and necessary projects are funded to achieve the organizational goals. It is not enough to show just one or the other. First let's take an example of a scenario where goal alignment exists but the strategic fit is poor. Say you are a car maker with a vision to be number one in Asia in revenue with a goal to increase revenues by 20% over the next three years. A candidate project proposing to develop the most innovative candy machine with high sales potential may meet the revenue generation goal, but it will not align with your company's mission and vision. Furthermore, if your company's core value is safety, a project candidate with high revenue generation potential that involves unsafe development methods does not align with your strategy. Alternatively, a project may demonstrate strategic fit but does not help the PSO achieve any of its goals. For example, a new product development project may fit with your general strategy that aims for product innovation, but your current goals may be limited only to product enhancements rather than new products. Therefore, assessing project alignment must include two criteria:

- Strategic alignment
- Goal alignment

Potential to Generate Value

Every proposed or ongoing project should exhibit the potential to generate value. The value may be:

- Financial
- Nonfinancial

If a project offers both value forms in some fashion, you may select the dominant form for ranking against other similar projects and take credit for the other value form in some fashion.

Risk Characteristics

Risks, by definition, can be either negative or positive, referred to respectively as:

- Threats
- Opportunities

Both types of risks can be experienced during the development (project) and production (post-project) phases. The risks during the former phase are related to the project triple constraint. The risks from the production phase, sometimes referred to as business risks, are primarily market driven, especially when the project deliverable is expected to produce financial value. Project evaluation should include criteria to address risks in both phases.

ESTABLISH PORTFOLIO BENCHMARKS

Benchmarks are standards and guidelines that the portfolio team needs to follow in constructing and managing the portfolio. They must be established in the design phase. Depending upon your organizational preferences and risk tolerance and the portfolio type, the actual values may differ, but the key benchmarks include:

- Project category allocations
- Project evaluation criteria
- Criteria weightage factors
- Discount rates
- Contingencies
- Tolerance limits
- Project termination criteria

The PEB should be responsible for developing the project category allocations. The chief financial officer or senior finance managers should specify the discount rates with input from the portfolio team. The portfolio team is responsible for developing the other benchmarks with input from and approval by the PEB. The benchmarks must be revisited periodically (preferably annually) and revised as necessary. Furthermore, the portfolio team should also specify the tools and techniques for measurements related to the benchmarks. (Section 3 of this book is dedicated to various tools and techniques associated with the PPM process.)

Project Category Allocations

Category allocation refers to the relative proportions by which the available resources (monetary and human) are split among the different project categories in a portfolio. The desired project mix, which translates to portfolio balance, must be specified as part of the portfolio design. The portfolio team needs to ensure that this balance is maintained in the portfolio monitor/control phase. The actual balance may not "exactly" match the design balance all the time due to the dynamic nature of the portfolio, but you must make every attempt to be as close to the design balance as possible. Tracking and maintaining the desired balance is easier when the category allocations are based on money rather than people. The reason is that many organizations do not have the right infrastructure for capturing the actual amount of time people spend on projects. The allocations are to be determined by the PEB with input from the portfolio manager. Figure 8-1 is a stack chart showing an example allocation. It also shows how the design vs. "actual" allocations can be tracked and compared over a period of time.

Project Evaluation Criteria

Once you have identified the project characteristics that would serve as criteria for Levels 1-3 evaluation (discussed in Chapter 4), you need to specify the metrics and the tools and techniques to measure them. In addition, you must also develop benchmarks and guidelines to evaluate the merit of the projects against the criteria. The project characteristics that serve as the criteria suggested in the previous section are:

- Alignment
  - Strategic alignment
  - Goal alignment
- Potential to generate value
  - Financial value generation potential
  - Nonfinancial value generation potential
- Risk characteristics
  - Threats
  - Opportunities

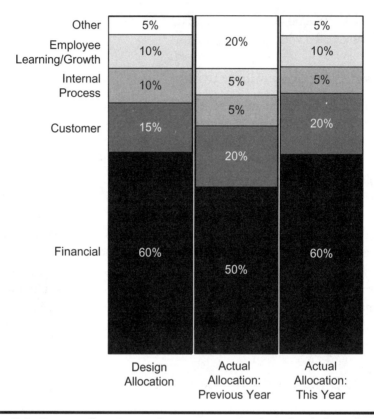

Figure 8-1 Percent allocations and project categories based on balanced score-card domains

Of these characteristics, only financial value is tangible and can be estimated in a quantitative fashion. Commonly used financial metrics include net present value (NPV), return on investment (ROI), benefit-to-cost ratio (BCR), and payback period. The intangibles are typically measured using semiquantitative tools such as scoring models. The metrics and their benchmarks are useful in three critical ways: 1) to screen the new project candidates (Level 1 evaluation) prior to performing a detailed evaluation, 2) to evaluate a project for its own merit (Level 2 evaluation), and 3) to evaluate a project for its relative merit (Level 3 evaluation). Further discussion on screening criteria for Level 1 evaluations is presented below. The same metrics for alignment, value generation, and risk that are used in Level 1 can also be applied to a Level 2 and 3 evaluation.

Project Screening Criteria (Level 1 Evaluation)

Project screening criteria are meant to weed out weak project candidates in their early stages. This initial screening eliminates the need for the project initiators to perform a detailed business case analysis and to put together an elaborate project business plan (discussed in Chapter 10) to be considered for investment in the portfolio, if it does not meet certain basic requirements. Furthermore, the time and effort by the portfolio team to conduct a detailed review is also minimized. A simple one or two page "project request form" (discussed in Chapter 10) by the project initiators may facilitate the screening process. Project screening criteria are the benchmarks that a proposed project must meet before a detailed project business case analysis is requested from the project initiator to facilitate subsequent detailed evaluation. If a proposed project does not meet the screening criteria, it will be rejected without further consideration; if it does, it will then go to the next phase that involves detailed business case analysis. This screening is the same as the Level 1 evaluation mentioned in Chapter 4. Examples of screening criteria include:

- **Project Size**. Projects requiring an investment that is below a certain threshold need not be considered by the portfolio. These are relatively small projects that would require significant PPM process efforts compared to their budget needs. The rigorous analysis required by the portfolio may be superfluous considering the project size. (Alternatively, you may create separate categories for different project sizes and have different levels of documentation and evaluation requirements. As the project size increases, more information will have to be submitted about the project's business case, and the evaluation will need to be more rigorous.)
- **Project Alignment**. The candidate project must show a minimum level of alignment with its PSO's strategy and goals. You may use a simple scoring model (discussed in Chapter 11) to measure the degree of alignment for a given project and identify a minimum acceptable score. Projects with scores less than the minimum acceptable score may not be considered for investment.
- **Project Value Generation Potential**. A proposed project may not be considered for the portfolio unless it meets certain investment benchmarks for financial metrics, such as BCR, ROI, payback period, etc. The financial metrics will apply only to those projects that generate

revenue. For nonfinancial value-generating projects, you may develop minimum acceptable scores as benchmarks using scoring models.

- **Project Risk**. A project may look attractive based on the benefit cost equation, but not if the risk is considered. Risk must be an integral part of any project evaluation. To screen out projects with a high threat level in their early stages, you can identify a risk threshold or an unacceptable risk level as a benchmark. These thresholds can be based on a scoring model. If a project exhibits risk that is greater than the threshold, the proposed project will be rejected. (It may be reconsidered at a later time, if mitigation actions are included in the project to bring the risk to an acceptable level, that is, lower than the threshold.)

Criteria Weightage Factors

The project characteristics used as selection criteria may not contribute equally towards a project's merit. Therefore, you need to assign weightage factors in accordance with their relative importance. The total percentage of weights of all the criteria must add up to 100. Project criteria and weightage factors must be the same for every project within a category. If the same criteria are used for different categories, the same weightage factors cannot be used for the categories. (If both are the same, there would be no differentiation between categories, hence no need for different categories.) You must use the same criteria and weightage factors in evaluating projects for the initial go/no-go as well as subsequent continue/cancel decisions. It is not unlike applying the same rules of the game from start to finish. It is the responsibility of the subject matter experts and the portfolio team to identify the weightage factors. These factors must be revisited and revalidated at least annually.

Discount Rates

A discount rate applies only to projects that generate financial value. As discussed in detail in Chapter 12, the discount rate used in financial calculations plays a key role in assessing a project's merit. This key rate is used in calculating the NPV of the project. The higher the project's risk is, the higher the discount rate should be. When the NPV is calculated using an "adjusted" discount rate, the resulting NPV is called risk-adjusted NPV. It is paramount that these rates are specified in the design phase. You may describe the level of risk in either an ordinal (e.g., low, medium, or high) or cardinal scale (e.g., a scale ranging from 1 to 10) and specify an appropriate discount rate corresponding to each risk level. The discount rates to be used depend on a number of internal and external factors and must be revised periodically as economic conditions change.

Contingencies

Contingencies, also referred to as reserves, are meant to cover cost increases caused by materialization of project threats. In a broad sense, there are two types of threats, namely, known and unknown. Known threats are those that have been identified by the project manager/team as part of the project risk management process. Unknown threats are those that are not identified. Contingencies established to address known and unknown threats are called project and management contingencies, respectively. The former is part of the individual project budget, and the project manager has the authority to utilize it, as known project threats materialize. Management contingency is held at the portfolio level for all the component projects together. This is tantamount to "self" insurance, and management approval is needed to expend this contingency when unknown threats materialize. At the portfolio level, you must track the available management contingency as well as the aggregate of all the project contingencies.

A simple and common method to calculate individual project contingency considers the project risk level as determined by a formal risk assessment process. A certain percentage of the total project budget is used as the contingency depending upon the project's risk level. For example, the following guidelines are common:

- Low-risk projects: 5%
- Moderate-risk projects: 15%
- High-risk projects: 25%

More sophisticated methods are available that involve detailed risk assessments, probability analysis, and simulations. There is no systematic method to calculate management contingency for a given project. It is commonly estimated as a certain percentage of the total portfolio investment based on historical information. The portfolio design must provide guidelines to calculate project and management contingencies.

Tolerance Limits

As part of the portfolio design, you must identify the tolerance limits for variance of performance for the portfolio and the component projects. For instance, at the portfolio level, as discussed in more detail in Chapter 14, you can develop and track a portfolio cost performance indicator based on the aggregate cost performance of the component projects. Similarly, you can also have cost as well as schedule performance indicators for each component project. These indicators must have tolerance limits that should be defined in the portfolio design phase. Typical limits are +/– 5% or +/– 10%. If a project or a portfolio exceeds these limits, you must investigate the reason for the variance and take appropriate action.

Project Termination Criteria

A project in the portfolio should exit the portfolio either because it is completed or terminated. The criteria for project completion should be negotiated between the project manager/team and the project sponsor. These will typically include completion of all the deliverables meeting the sponsor requirements. However, the criteria for termination must be predefined by the portfolio in its design phase. Without clearly defined criteria, termination decisions on poorly performing projects will likely be more political and less rational. Continuation of unworthy projects is a waste of organizational resources.

Changing business needs drive organizational goals, which in turn should drive what stays in the portfolio. This partly translates to keeping the portfolio triple constraint in balance or matching the projects with goals. If a project no longer aligns with the organizational goals or strategy, it must be considered for termination. Termination should also be considered if the project does not meet the portfolio benchmarks via a weak business case. For instance, if the expected ROI falls below its benchmark or the BCR is not acceptable any longer, the project should be recommended for termination. Even if a project shows strong alignment and business case, it may need to be suspended or even terminated if it cannot compete with the other projects in the portfolio, given the limited investment/resources available.

The termination criteria must be clearly spelled out in the design phase. Every ongoing project in the portfolio must be tested against the termination criteria. If it meets the criteria, the portfolio team must evaluate it further to decide whether that project should continue to receive funding/resources or be scaled-down, terminated, or halted temporarily for possible future consideration. A list of critical factors should be identified that the portfolio team must evaluate before recommending the project for termination. General reasons why a project should be terminated include:

- It no longer fits with the organization's strategy and goals.
- It no longer has a valid business case.
- It is no longer attractive because of higher completion costs compared to the benefits.
- The risk is totally unacceptable to the organization (unless mitigation is possible).
- It does not rank high enough compared to the other projects in the portfolio.
- The technology is no longer relevant.
- The competition has beaten you to the punch.
- Regulations have changed.
- Markets or economic conditions have changed for the worse.

9

CONSTRUCT PORTFOLIO

Whereas the last two chapters were about the planning side of portfolio management, this chapter focuses on implementation. The objective of the Construct Portfolio phase is twofold: 1) to place all the projects of the portfolio sponsoring organization's (PSO) interest in a new portfolio, and, 2) to initiate calibration of the new portfolio by purging those projects that do not meet portfolio specifications. Once the portfolio foundation is laid out and the design specs developed from the previous two project portfolio management (PPM) phases, you may place all the projects under the purview of the PSO in the new portfolio. Now the calibration process begins. Calibration refers to the process of transforming the new portfolio to a steady state one. A portfolio is considered to be in steady state when it meets the specifications developed in the design phase. Calibration is a time-consuming process that is initiated in the Construct Portfolio phase. It will continue into the next phase, namely, the Monitor & Control Portfolio phase, until the steady state is reached. Table 9-1 compares the characteristics of a new portfolio with those of a steady state one. Portfolio construction is a one-time process. It no longer exists once the portfolio moves into the Monitor & Control Portfolio phase. The Construct Portfolio phase consists of two processes:

- Build a new portfolio
- Calibrate the portfolio

Table 9-1 Portfolio transformation from new portfolio to steady state portfolio

Portfolio Characteristic	New Portfolio in Phase: Construct Portfolio	Steady State Portfolio in Phase: Monitor and Control Portfolio
Portfolio design requirements are met	Most likely no	Yes
Projects are aligned	Most likely no	Yes
Projects meet portfolio benchmarks	Most likely no	Yes
No projects have unacceptable risks	Most likely no	Yes
Portfolio is in balance with respect to project categories	Most likely no	Yes
Portfolio is in balance with respect to triple constraint	Most likely no	Yes

BUILD A NEW PORTFOLIO

The objective of this process step is to bring the projects of interest into the new portfolio and make the required information available to facilitate the calibration process in the next step. When you are introducing a new PPM process, it is unlikely that you will start a portfolio with all new projects. You will probably start it with projects that are already under way. You may also have a few new project requests for funding. A good practice is to build the new portfolio with both the ongoing projects and the new project proposals. The portfolio executive board (PEB) should give direction to the portfolio team as to what projects should go under the purview of the new portfolio. The key activities in building the new portfolio are:

- Identify and inventory the ongoing projects as well as the new ones that are waiting to be approved for funding. These are the projects within the PSO that are supposed to be under the purview of the new portfolio.
- Collect business case information for each project. This information may not exist depending upon the old project management practices in your organization. Even if it does, it may not be complete and formally and properly documented. It may be loosely available in disparate places.
- Gather past performance and current status information for each project, especially as it relates to cost and schedule.

- Gather data regarding an estimate to complete (ETC), that is, a budget required to complete the remainder of each project.
- Obtain a breakdown on how the ETC will be spent each quarter over the remainder of each project.
- Collect human resource estimates for each project that describe the resource needs over the next few quarters.
- Place the projects into the appropriate categories and subcategories identified in the design phase.
- Compile all the project information in the desired format for the portfolio team to facilitate project evaluations.

Once the projects are formally in the portfolio, their fate will be determined by the PPM process. The initial makeup of the new portfolio is unlikely to reflect the design specifications. The reason is that the ongoing projects were selected before the portfolio design specifications were developed. So you may find projects that may not align with the goals of the PSO, meet the investment benchmarks or risk thresholds, or hold a strong business case, etc. The projects, as a group, most likely do not reflect the design proportions of the project categories. They may not be sufficient or necessary to serve the current organizational goals.

Building the new portfolio is not an easy process for a number of reasons: 1) the required business case information on projects may not have been developed; 2) estimates on resource and budget needs may not be available; 3) proper documentation may be lacking; 4) most project teams will resist generating required information retroactively; and 5) project sponsors and teams may not embrace the new PPM process with open arms. The portfolio team may end up not having much choice other than to work with whatever little information is available. The key to the success of this process lies in constant communication from the senior management and the PEB regarding the importance of the new PPM process in the organization and their commitment to make it work.

CALIBRATE THE PORTFOLIO

The calibration process involves the purging of ongoing projects that are not worthy of investment and selection of the right new projects that deserve investment. As mentioned earlier, this is a process by which you strive to meet the portfolio design specifications and gradually move towards the steady state. It involves the following steps:

- Perform project evaluations (Levels 1 and 2) based on all the available information, and compare each ongoing and new project against the portfolio benchmarks of its category developed in the design phase. You may place those projects that do not meet the criteria on a list that you will later recommend for suspension or termination. Keep in mind project dependencies in making the evaluations and go/no-go recommendations.
- Analyze each ongoing project against the termination criteria developed in the design phase, and place those that match them on the list of projects for suspension or termination.
- Look for redundancies in the remaining projects, and make a list of any consolidations you would like to recommend. This list will have "revised" projects reflecting your recommendations.
- Evaluate and compare the to-be-consolidated and other remaining projects for their relative merit (Level 3 evaluation) and rank them within each category.
- Calculate the relative proportions of the budget required for the remainder of the year by the projects in each category.
- Identify the difference—there will most likely be a difference—between the current percent category allocations and percent design allocations. (This difference will gradually need to be closed in the next phase to achieve the design portfolio balance.)
- Map the projects to the current organizational goals and identify those goals that are not served, therefore not met, by any of the projects.
- Make recommendations to the PEB as to which projects should be consolidated, suspended, or terminated. Also, inform them about the difference related to the percent category allocation and the goals that will not be achieved due to project deficiencies.

Portfolio calibration as delineated above is certainly not a sequential process. It is iterative wherein the portfolio team, the PEB, and the individual project teams and their sponsors will actively participate in facilitating information gathering, project evaluations, and final go/no-go decisions. Termination of ongoing projects as part of the new PPM process will not be easy for political and emotional reasons. There will be resistance from the project sponsors and teams. Some organizations prefer not to terminate projects abruptly to avoid any political fallout. Instead, they choose to suspend them temporarily. They may even provide a meager amount of resources to keep them barely alive. The hope is that it will be easier to gradually terminate them. But if a project is unworthy of investment, it must be terminated to conserve resources, so that those resources can be spent on higher priority projects. Effective communication and a strong commitment by upper management to promote the new PPM process in the organization will be paramount.

By the end of this phase, you will have constructed the new portfolio with projects that meet most of the design requirements. The exception is that the portfolio does not exhibit the balance related to project categories and the portfolio triple constraint. After entering the Monitor & Control phase, over a period of time, the new portfolio will gradually reach steady state as you perform portfolio balancing.

10

MONITOR & CONTROL
PORTFOLIO

The objective of the Monitor & Control Portfolio phase of the project portfolio management (PPM) process is to maintain a steady state portfolio that
consistently delivers value and helps the portfolio sponsoring organization
(PSO) meet its goals. The first step in this phase is to continue the calibration process by balancing the new portfolio from the previous phase. The
portfolio balance will be achieved over a period of time by placing the right
proportions of new projects in the right categories in the portfolio, as the ongoing projects are completed or suspended/terminated. The triple constraint
balance will also be achieved by closing the project and resource gaps. It is
through this calibration process over a period of time that the new portfolio
will gradually attain the steady state. Then you must continue to maintain
this state by rebalancing the portfolio at regular intervals over its lifetime
(Figure 10-1).

The monitor/control phase consists of continuous review and analysis of
the business cases of new projects, business cases and status of ongoing projects, and the performance of the portfolio as a whole. The review and analysis
are performed in cycles at regular frequency, typically in quarters. At the end
of each cycle, the portfolio team makes go/no-go recommendations to the
portfolio executive board (PEB), which makes the final decisions. The key
decisions, among others, pertain to the selection of new projects and suspension or termination of ongoing projects. As these decisions are implemented,
the portfolio churns. The next cycle begins per the portfolio schedule. Thus,

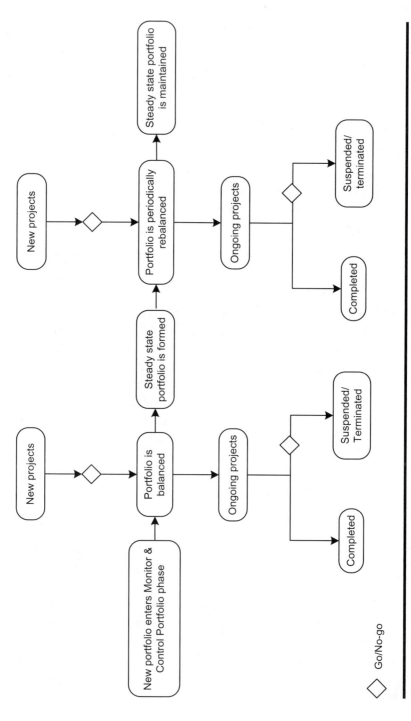

Figure 10-1   Steady state through balancing and rebalancing of portfolio

the portfolio monitor/control phase involves a series of cycles of review and analysis, where each cycle is characterized by the following key processes (Figure 6-3 in Chapter 6):

- Identify projects
- Categorize projects
- Evaluate new projects
- Evaluate ongoing projects
- Prioritize new and ongoing projects
- Rebalance portfolio
- Select or terminate projects
- Assess portfolio performance

Key activities involved in these processes are presented in the form of a flow diagram in Figure 10-2 and discussed in detail below.

IDENTIFY PROJECTS

The objective of the project identification process is to inventory the projects and document their business cases. For the ongoing projects, their current and expected future performance data is also documented. The key documentation includes:

- Project inventory of the portfolio (PIP)
- Project request form (PRF)
- Project business plan (PBP)
- Project performance report (PPR)

A project management office (PMO) can facilitate the maintenance of these documents through an information management system. Numerous templates for these documents are available in the literature. Some are bare bones and some are highly elaborate. You need to tailor these templates to your own specific portfolio's needs.

Project Inventory of the Portfolio

A PIP is simply an inventory of the new and ongoing projects denoting their status as they go through their respective life cycles. It is a living document

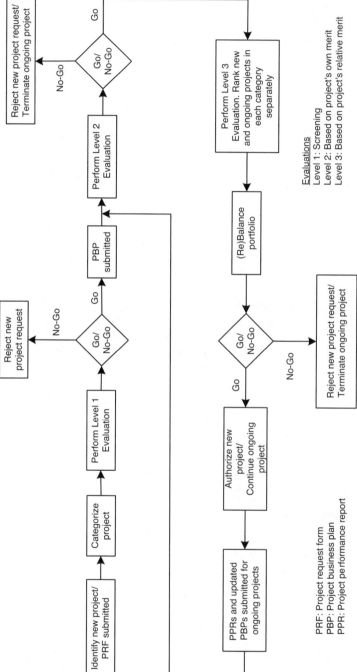

Figure 10-2   Process flow for project evaluation and go/no-go decisions

that should be revised regularly as the project status changes. Table 10-1 is a list of items to be included in the PIP. The inventory not only helps you collectively track the status of the projects in the portfolio, but can also provide metrics to evaluate the portfolio for future improvements. It is the responsibility of the portfolio team to update the inventory at regular intervals.

Project Request Form

A PRF is a form that is submitted by the project initiator requesting funding from the portfolio for a new project. It may contain the information listed in Table 10-2. A PRF does not require a detailed analysis. It is a high-level document that may not need any supporting documentation. Based on the information in the PRF, the portfolio review team (PRT) evaluates the project candidate against the screening criteria developed in the portfolio design phase. If it does not meet the criteria, the project request is rejected.

Project Business Plan

If a project candidate meets the screening criteria, its initiator may perform a detailed business case analysis and document it in a formal report called the PBP. Frequently referred to as a project proposal, it serves the purpose of

Table 10-1 Components of a project inventory of a portfolio

- Project request forms submitted for Level 1 evaluation
- New project requests that failed Level 1 evaluation
- New project requests that passed Level 1 evaluation
- Project business plans submitted for Level 2 and 3 evaluation
- New project requests that failed Level 2 evaluation
- New project requests that passed Level 2 evaluation
- New projects that failed Level 3 evaluation
- Ongoing projects that received Level 3 evaluation
- Ongoing projects that passed Level 3 evaluation
- Ongoing projects that were suspended because they failed Level 3 evaluation
- Ongoing projects that were terminated
- Projects on plan
- Projects off plan
- Completed projects

Table 10-2   Components of a project request form

• Background
• Business objectives
• Justification (How the project fits into the organizational strategy and serves the organizational goals)
• Project description
• Development time
• Key milestones
• Development cost
• Value to be generated (financial, customer, business process, employee, etc.)
• Expected financial benefits
• Expected nonfinancial benefits
• Expected cost savings
• Major threats
• Major opportunities

"selling" the project to the portfolio management team. It is akin to the business plan of a start-up company. An entrepreneur most likely will not be able to receive seed capital for his start-up without a business plan. Prospective investors will not even want to talk to entrepreneurs, unless they show a business plan to begin with. Similarly, a PBP is an essential component of the project investment decision process. It must, at minimum, include the components shown in Table 10-3. For ongoing projects, PBPs should be verified with periodic updates by incorporating the most recent project performance and business case information.

Project Performance Report

A PPR presents the current and expected future performance data for an ongoing project. The basic information to be included in the PPR is provided in Table 10-4. The project manager and the team are responsible for generating the report. The PPR is typically generated towards the end of each project phase as part of the phase-gate process. The PRT evaluates ongoing projects based on the information provided in the latest PPRs and updated PBPs. A PPR is not the same as a project progress report. Progress reports are generated more frequently, weekly or biweekly, to inform the stakeholders regarding the status of the projects. PPRs contain a project's current and expected future performance data that facilitate go/no-go decisions.

Table 10-3 Components of a project business plan

- Executive Summary
- Business need
- Alternative solutions
- Recommended solution
- Project's business objectives
- Project description
- Strategic fit with the organization
- Alignment with organizational goals
- Cost model
- Financial benefits: cash flows, NPV, IRR, ROI, payback period, etc.
- Other forms of benefit
- Sensitivity analysis: best/worst case scenarios
- Key deliverables
- Implementation plan and milestones
- Key stakeholders
- Risks
- Future opportunities
- Recommendation

Table 10-4 Project performance report

- Project status: Red/Amber/Green
- Milestones planned vs. completed
- Future projected milestones
- Baseline finish date/expected finish date
- Project percent completion
- Schedule variance
- Cost variance
- Reasons for variance (if any) from baseline
- Original baseline budget
- Estimate to complete
- Estimate at completion
- Contingencies used and remaining
- Resource needs
- Major outstanding issues
- Risks
- Constraints

CATEGORIZE PROJECTS

After the new projects have been identified and the ongoing project documentation is updated—and before the evaluation process begins—there is an important step that involves project categorization. The categorization (including subcategorization) can be based on any of the project characteristics discussed in Chapter 8. For example, the balanced scorecard (BSC) domains representing various forms of value to be generated by the project can be employed for categorization. One of the challenges you may face with the BSC domains is how to account for multiple values a project may offer. For instance, a "customer value" project that is expected to enhance customer satisfaction will likely also generate financial benefits. To keep the categorization and subsequent evaluation and prioritization processes simple, you may assign every project to one primary category. You may establish a mechanism for the project to receive extra "points" in the evaluation process to account for any additional value offered through another category.

EVALUATE NEW PROJECTS

Every project candidate must go through three levels of evaluation (introduced in Chapter 4) prior to a go/no-go recommendation. The first two levels are performed in this process step and the third one in the "Prioritize New and Ongoing Projects" process discussed later.

- **Level 1 (Screening)**: This is the initial screening of the candidate based on a review of the information provided in the PRF. The project is tested against the screening criteria. If it passes the screening, it will go to a Level 2 evaluation. If not, the project initiators may consider resubmitting at a later time with appropriate revisions or abandon the idea altogether.
- **Level 2 (Evaluation for its own merit)**: This involves a detailed evaluation of the candidate (based on the information provided in the PBP) against the category-specific project selection criteria and the investment benchmarks developed in the portfolio design phase. If the candidate holds merit, it is selected for a Level 3 evaluation. Otherwise, it is sent back to its initiator.
- **Level 3 (Evaluation for its relative merit)**: This process involves ranking of the project candidate along with the competing projects,

which include both new and ongoing projects that have passed a Level 2 evaluation.

The evaluations are performed by the PRT consisting of subject matter experts. The portfolio manager and the PMO can facilitate this process. The frequency at which the three levels of evaluations are performed depends on a number of factors. Level 1 evaluations should be done more frequently than Level 2 or 3 evaluations. They may take place as soon as or within a short period (say, one or two weeks) after a PRF has been submitted. This will facilitate a faster overall go/no-go decision process. Level 2 and Level 3 evaluations may be done less frequently. Table 10-5 summarizes the characteristics of the three types of evaluations.

EVALUATE ONGOING PROJECTS

The objective of this process is to perform a Level 2 evaluation on each ongoing project. The evaluation takes place in two steps. First, the project is evaluated on its performance to date and expected future performance. The project sponsor and the steering committee are responsible for the evaluation, which is typically performed at the end of each project phase as part of the phase-gate process. The evaluation results are documented in a PPR. The project sponsor is also responsible for updating the PBP based on the latest available information. In the second step, the PRT reviews the PPR and PBP and evaluates the project against the project selection criteria and the investment benchmarks for each project category. These are the same criteria/benchmarks used in selecting the project when it was requested for funding as a new project in the first place. The project will also be evaluated against the termination criteria developed in the portfolio design phase. Just because a project showed superior business case at the time of its initiation, that does not necessarily mean it still continues to show merit and should continue to be funded. Based on this overall evaluation, the portfolio team decides on whether the project should be terminated or whether it should move on to the next step in the evaluation process. At the end of this process step, you will have a list of the ongoing projects recommended for termination and a list of the remaining projects that go forward for a Level 3 evaluation where the project will be ranked along with the competing projects.

Reviews under Level 2 evaluation are not the same as project progress reviews. The latter are performed more frequently, weekly or biweekly, to

Table 10-5 Characteristics of Levels 1 through 3 evaluation

	Project Status	Evaluation		
		Level 1	Level 2	Level 3
Objective	New	To screen the project from further consideration	To evaluate whether it is investment worthy based on its own merit	To evaluate whether it is investment worthy based on its relative merit against competing projects
	Ongoing	Not applicable	To evaluate whether the project continues to be investment worthy based on its own merit	To evaluate whether it continues to be investment worthy based on its relative merit against competing projects
Documentation	New	Project request form	Project business plan	Project business plan
	Ongoing	Not applicable	Project business plan, project performance report	Project business plan, project performance report
Criteria	New	Screening criteria	Project selection criteria depending on the project category	Relative merit against competing projects
	Ongoing	Not applicable	Project selection criteria depending on the project category, termination criteria	Relative merit against competing projects
Frequency	New	Only once at the time of initial project request	Only once after the PBP is submitted	Quarterly or biannual
	Ongoing	Not applicable	As often as necessary. Typically at the end of each phase of the project or after a key milestone	Quarterly or biannual
Next Step	New	Pass here: Go to Level 2 evaluation; Fail here: Termination	Pass here: Go to Level 3 evaluation; Fail here: Termination	Pass here: Go to portfolio balancing; Fail here: Termination
	Ongoing	Not applicable	Pass here: Go to Level 3 evaluation; Fail here: Termination	Pass here: Go to portfolio balancing; Fail here: Suspension

review project progress. They involve the project manager and the team and the project sponsor. The focus is more on the progress to date and the project needs in the near future. The project business case is not a topic of concern, and no continue/cancel decisions are made in these reviews.

PRIORITIZE NEW AND ONGOING PROJECTS

In this process step, new and ongoing projects that have passed a Level 2 evaluation are compared against each other and ranked. Level 3 is comprised of evaluating projects for their relative merit. The subject matter experts of the PRT are responsible for this evaluation. The ranking is done separately within each project category. Several tools are available for project ranking, as discussed in detail in Chapter 12. Project ranking is not needed for every portfolio. At higher levels of the enterprise, if the projects are deemed worthy of investment (that is, they pass a Level 2 evaluation), they are typically funded without being ranked. They are usually large in scope and limited in number. The executive management will allocate the required resources. When resources are scant and there are many projects—low supply and high demand—projects need to be ranked. Higher ranking projects are selected in accordance with the resources available. Although project ranking is common in portfolio management circles, skeptics have challenged various aspects of it:

1. Some projects produce quantifiable tangible value, while others generate intangible value that cannot be quantified. Therefore, they cannot be combined for ranking purposes.
2. Even if the intangible value is measured using semiquantitative methods, the measurements are subjective, therefore, ranking does not represent "true" project priorities.
3. Ranking of projects becomes increasingly difficult and loses its validity as the number of projects on the list grows.
4. Ranking of projects based on either quantitative or qualitative project characteristics may not produce an optimum (that is, best) portfolio. Furthermore, using only one project characteristic for ranking ignores the value of other key characteristics.
5. Risk and uncertainty are generally higher with new projects compared to the ongoing ones because they decrease as a project goes

through its life cycle. Because of the differences in these characteristics and the difficulty in quantifying them, ranking of new and old
projects together may not be justified.

While these arguments may hold some merit, there are several ways to overcome the challenges of project ranking:

1. Rank the projects that generate tangible and intangible value sepa-
    rately. First categorize the projects based on the form of value they
    generate using the BSC domains as discussed previously, and then
    rank them separately within each category. (Categorization of proj-
    ects will also facilitate portfolio balancing.)
2. Subjectivity cannot be eliminated altogether but can be minimized.
    Find ways to quantify seemingly subjective evaluation criteria. If
    you are a measurements skeptic, Douglas Hubbard's book *How to
    Measure Anything—Finding the Value of "Intangibles" in Business*
    is a must-read. Subjectivity is not necessarily bad, especially when it
    involves experts with industry knowledge and experience.
3. When faced with an excessive number of projects, use the Q-Sort
    technique (described in Chapter 12) to separate projects into groups
    based on their merit; for example, excellent, average, and poor. You
    can further divide each group into smaller subgroups as well. You
    may use forced ranking techniques separately for each group. The
    idea behind this approach is that on any list of projects, top contend-
    ers as well as total misfits are always clearly visible. There are only
    a few projects in the middle of the pack, where true differentiation
    may be difficult. Top contenders can receive funding without having
    to go through formal ranking. Similarly, the misfits can be rejected
    without being subjected to ranking. Ranking the middle few will not
    be so overwhelming and can be done easily using the appropriate
    techniques discussed further in Chapter 12.
4. True, simple ranking methods may not produce an optimum portfo-
    lio, and a single project characteristic may not completely represent
    the true merit of a project. Therefore, whenever financial resources
    and subject matter expertise are available, sophisticated methods in-
    volving linear programming, utility theory, analytic hierarchy pro-
    cess, etc., are highly encouraged.

5. Several tools and techniques are available to help us understand and quantify risk and uncertainty (more on this in Chapter 13) to make the ranking process more objective. Additionally, a well-structured phase-gate process with strategically placed decision checkpoints will help us manage the uncertainty and mitigate the risk more effectively.

At the end of this process step you will have a ranked list of projects for every project category (or subcategory) of the portfolio. Once the projects are ranked, the objective is to rebalance the portfolio in order to meet the design requirements for an optimized portfolio.

REBALANCE THE PORTFOLIO

As mentioned previously, after the calibrated portfolio enters the monitor/ control phase, you must bring it to the initial steady state by going through the portfolio balancing process. Once this point has been reached, the portfolio must be *re*balanced at periodic intervals to maintain the steady state for as long as the portfolio is alive and active. A portfolio will never continue to be at a "true" steady state condition where all the portfolio design requirements are exactly met. Therefore, you assume that it is a "pseudo" steady state and strive to rebalance the portfolio to keep it as close to the steady state condition as possible. (Please see the following box for details on the steady state condition.) There are two types of portfolio balance that must be maintained to sustain the steady state: project category balance and portfolio triple constraint balance.

STEADY STATE AND "PSEUDO" STEADY STATE PORTFOLIO

Steady state is a commonly used term in chemical process engineering. It is a condition wherein a system is continuously maintained at fixed conditions to produce a target output at a desired rate. The properties of a system in steady state do not change with time. For example, let's say you are manufacturing a chemical in a reactor. The reactor continuously receives inputs, that is, the ingredients required to make the chemical, at a predefined rate. The chemical is produced at a desired rate, while keeping the reactor conditions constant. As long as the process is ongoing with constant rates of input(s) and output(s) with no changes to the properties of the reactor, it is considered to be in steady state. In a practical world, however, it is not possible to continuously keep the system exactly under constant conditions. Variations do take place, but we try to keep them to a minimum in order to maintain the steady state as closely as possible. Although the system may never achieve "true" steady state, we assume it has. In engineering, this condition is referred to as "pseudo" or "quasi" steady state.

A project portfolio, from a long-term perspective, should be considered to be in steady state when it generates the expected financial output (or other forms of value) consistently over the long run. However, for an operational purpose, it is considered to be in steady state when it consistently meets the portfolio design specifications. The presumption is that the portfolio will generate value consistently over the long run, as long as the desired design specifications are met continuously. The inputs to the portfolio are the new projects selected for funding, and the desired output is successfully completed projects that will generate value in the long term. Through a careful balancing act, you need to maintain the design specifications by selecting the right projects and rejecting the unworthy ones.

It is impossible to have a true steady state, where the portfolio balance exactly mirrors the design specifications. It is impractical to constantly keep the percent investment allocations for each project category at the exact design levels. It is also not possible to continuously keep the portfolio triple constraint in balance, when project vs. resource priorities often shift. Therefore, we strive to achieve pseudo state by keeping the portfolio balance as close as possible to the design specifications. This is done through a systematic reprioritization of projects and resources and rebalancing of the portfolio in cycles at regular intervals.

Category Balance

In a steady state portfolio, when an ongoing project from a particular category is completed or terminated, the percent investment allocation for that category will decrease with a corresponding increase in the other categories, assuming all the other projects in the portfolio will continue and no new projects are added. This will shift the portfolio balance and will result in a deviation from the design specifications. Similarly, the balance will tilt in the other direction when you add a new project to a particular category, assuming the same conditions of the previous scenario. But real world portfolios are extremely dynamic. They go through frequent churning because of completion, suspension, or termination of ongoing projects. Therefore, you need to keep the required project mix by rebalancing the portfolio continuously by adding the right projects to the right categories at the right time. This is probably one of the most daunting tasks in the PPM process. The key steps of category balancing are to:

- Compute the value of the total investment required for the remainder of the fiscal year to complete all the projects in each category. (It is a function of the time-based profile of the project estimate to complete [ETC]. Make sure to include project contingencies.)
- Calculate the relative percent investment allocation required for each project category for the remainder of the fiscal year.
- Compare the required allocations with the design specifications for each category and identify over-allocated categories with "surplus" projects and under-allocated categories with project deficiencies.
- In case of over-allocated categories, draw a line on the ranked project list to separate the projects that will and will not be recommended for funding. The position of the line will be dictated by the total available portfolio investment and the category's target percent allocation.

The allocation process is relatively easy if you are dealing with investment in terms of money compared to people. For example, in the case of a capital project portfolio that requires more financial resources compared to human resources, the process of dividing the available investment funds in accordance with the desired allocation proportions is easier. With a research and development portfolio where human resources are more significant, dividing people's time across the projects may be relatively more difficult. This requires a systematic planning effort. Chapter 15 presents several resource allocation and planning tools that will be useful in this regard. In "hybrid" situations where some component projects of a portfolio require mostly financial resources and others mostly human resources, you will need to have an estimate of the total value of the combined resources. This may be accomplished by assigning a certain financial value to each full time equivalent resource associated with the portfolio.

The surplus projects may be recommended for temporary suspension or termination. When you do not have the right projects in the portfolio to address all the organizational goals, you need to make appropriate recommendations to the PEB, so that those gaps can be filled through initiation of new projects. Thus, at the end of the portfolio balancing process, you will have a list of ranked projects within each category of the portfolio and a set of recommendations on project suspensions/terminations and deficiencies.

Triple Constraint Balance

Portfolio triple constraint balancing is a vigorously dynamic process, since its components are in constant change. The rate of change is usually the highest with the resources (especially people), followed by the projects, and then the organizational goals. In balancing the triple constraint, you first start with the most stable component which is the organizational goals, and verify if there are sufficient projects in the portfolio to achieve them. You do this by mapping the goals vs. ranked projects from the previous step and identifying the goals that are not currently served. This information has to be communicated to the PEB, so they can spread the message around the organization to initiate projects to fill the deficiencies.

Presumably your percent category allocations are consistent with the organizational goals. Otherwise, when you add new projects to the portfolio to make up for the deficiencies, it may create a conflict with the percent allocation balance by shifting it away from the design specification. (For example, say you added more financial value-generating projects to fill a deficiency. It will increase the percent allocation for such projects if your categorization is based on the value form. If BSC is employed to build your strategic framework, it requires that you identify goals for each of its domains and specific percent investment allocations for each domain. You may use the same domains and percent allocations for project categorization to minimize the aforementioned conflict.)

For the surviving projects in the portfolio, you also need to ensure that there are enough human resources. You must develop and implement an effective resource allocation plan that will make sure all the projects in the portfolio will receive the right resources at the right time. This plan must include the detailed needs in the near term and preliminary estimates for the long term. If there are not enough resources to support the surviving projects, you may need to scale down and revise the organizational goals accordingly. Thus, the balancing act continues—from goals, to projects, to resources and then back to goals and so on. Balancing the triple constraint is a highly iterative process.

At the end of each cycle of the overall balancing process, you will have a list of the PSO's goals that are not served by the current projects in the portfolio or excessive goals that cannot be achieved because of resource constraints, recommendations for suspending surplus projects and initiating new projects to fill in the deficiencies, and an updated resource allocation plan for the surviving projects.

SELECT OR TERMINATE PROJECTS

As a result of going through the processes discussed above, you will have a list of recommendations for the PEB:

- New projects that do not pass muster under Levels 1, 2, or 3 evaluation and therefore receive a "no-go" recommendation
- New projects that have received a "go" recommendation because they passed all three levels of evaluation
- Ongoing projects that need to be terminated because they did not pass the Level 2 evaluation
- Ongoing projects that need to be suspended because they passed Level 2 but failed the Level 3 evaluation (Management may want to terminate them. It is their decision.)
- A list of organizational goals that are not being served by the portfolio, so appropriate projects can be added to balance the portfolio with respect to its triple constraint
- A list of project categories and the differences between their current category allocations vs. design allocations
- An updated human resource plan showing detailed near-term and preliminary long-term resource needs

The portfolio team makes the recommendations but it is up to the PEB to make the final decisions. Deciding project selections and terminations is not an exact science. The PPM process provides structure and tools to make the decision-making process more objective and rational. The process may seem complex and daunting, but once it is streamlined in the organization, it is bound to become easier. As mentioned before, even when a portfolio contains an excessively large number of projects, the go/no-go decisions will most likely revolve around a few marginal projects in the "middle-of-the-pack." There will be clear leaders on the top and laggards at the bottom, where the decisions are no-brainers. There needs to be debate and discussion especially concerning the marginal projects in the middle. There must be strong communication between the portfolio team/PEB and the sponsors of these projects to facilitate final go/no-go decisions.

In the case of new projects that were considered investment worthy but could not compete with the other projects in the portfolio, the project sponsors should be given the opportunity to resubmit them for consideration at a later time. Similarly, ongoing projects may be suspended for later consideration. A "re-scoped" project or new market conditions may make it more attractive and investment worthy in the future, but there is no guarantee that it will be selected. A temporary halt typically puts the project at a disadvantage. Bringing it back to life requires additional resources, which may make the project even less competitive. Furthermore, the lost time may make the project nonviable. It may have lost its team (project manager included), sponsor enthusiasm and support, and momentum. In some organizations, a project suspension is not a particularly desirable option. They prefer to keep the project alive with minimal funding.

Project Termination

Termination of projects, even when they are failing, is not easy. As much as you try to make the overall PPM process objective and rational, there are always political and emotional considerations that can make project terminations excruciatingly difficult. Even experienced senior managers and decision makers frequently make the argument that a seemingly failing project should continue, especially because a significant investment has already been made. The idea behind this is the thought of wasting all the investment that has already been made on the project. This is known as sunk cost fallacy, which is described in more detail in the box that follows. Rational decision making suggests that the sunk cost, which is the cost already incurred, should not be considered in making project investment decisions. Instead, the decision should be based on the project's merit going forward. A rational decision at every decision cycle may suggest continuing the project, but it may culminate in a financial loss, because the project cost has far exceeded the expected benefit. Thus, by avoiding the sunk cost fallacy you may fall into the trap of a different phenomenon called the "sunk cost dilemma." The dilemma, also reviewed in more detail in the box that follows, discusses when it is the right time to terminate a project. The portfolio teams and upper management should clearly understand the ramifications of sunk cost in investment decisions.

SUNK COST

The sunk cost of a project is the cost that has already been incurred and cannot be recovered. It includes both human resources and monetary costs, and it is equal to what is commonly referred to as the "actual cost" in project management lexicon. Sunk cost contrasts with the ETC, which is the expected budget required to complete the project. At the beginning of a project before any effort or money is expended, there is no sunk cost, and the ETC is the total budget needed for the entire project. As the project progresses, the sunk cost increases. It may be the same as the budgeted cost of work performed to date showing zero cost variance. Or, it can be lower or higher indicating positive cost efficiency or cost overrun, respectively. With the passage of time, the ETC is expected to decrease but can in fact increase due to poor initial cost estimates, scope changes, technology changes, and a host of other reasons. Depending on the cost overruns to date and the increase in the ETC, the project's net present value (NPV) may remain about the same as anticipated, decrease gradually, or go into the negative territory. (NPV is the difference between the expected benefit and the ETC in "today's" monetary units. It applies only to those projects that generate revenue. It is discussed in more detail in Chapter 11.)

Sunk Cost Fallacy

Termination of failing projects is not easy for many managers, especially because of the sunk cost. Despite mounting sunk cost, some may want to continue the project, reasoning that it may only decrease the project value but not completely destroy it. Some may want to continue in spite of the fact that the project is failing. Their reason: "You can't walk away from all the millions we've already invested in the project." For others, shutting down an incomplete project with enormous investment sunk into it may look like a failure on their part. And, there can be many political and emotional reasons also. Therefore, they try to continue to pour more money into the project, hoping it will turn around and help recover the costs. This phenomenon is colloquially known as "throwing good money after bad."

According to the economic theory, sunk cost should not play any role in financial decisions. You should only consider the merit of the project at the time of the decision, accounting for the investment it requires to complete the project. It would be irrational to consider sunk cost in investment decisions. However, behavioral economics suggests that people's decisions in the real world are greatly influenced by sunk cost. This phenomenon has come to be known as the sunk cost fallacy. Misconceptions of sunk costs can lead to bad decisions involving continuation of investments in projects that are doomed to fail.

Sunk Cost Dilemma

Avoiding the sunk cost fallacy and making rational decisions based strictly on the project's merits may lead to another phenomenon known as the sunk cost dilemma. When you are deciding to make the go/no-go decisions as a project goes through its life cycle, the rational decision may turn out to be "continue" every time. But you may end up finishing the project at a loss because the total cost expended exceeded the expected benefit. For any project, the NPV increases as the project progresses and nears completion, because ETC approaches zero while the benefit still remains relatively high. Similarly, the benefit/ETC ratio increases exponentially. The reason is that the benefit presumably remains the same as the initial estimate, while the ETC becomes smaller. Therefore, when sunk cost is not part of the benefit-cost equation, ongoing projects look increasingly attractive as they move through the development phase and have less chance of rejection. However, in the end, a project may turn out to be a failure because of excessive sunk cost (due to cost overruns) exceeding the promised benefit. So the dilemma for the decision maker repeatedly is, "When is the right time to terminate the project?" It is not unlike the question of when to walk away from the gambling table as the losses continue.

How to Overcome the Sunk Cost Dilemma

The sunk cost dilemma, a common phenomenon on projects, is between choosing to continue a project with uncertain benefit vs. terminating it for a certain loss in the form of sunk costs. The dilemma will repeat itself at every decision point until the project is either completed or terminated. Here are a few strategies to overcome the dilemma:

- Be realistic in estimating your project costs and benefits. Don't be too overoptimistic.
- Use proper risk management methods to understand and analyze the uncertainty associated with the benefit/cost equation.
- Employ a well-structured phase-gate process that facilitates effective go/no-go decisions. Establish more decision checkpoints especially in the early phases.
- Be prepared to kill projects early when they do not meet milestones or show consistent cost overruns.
- Avoid all or nothing situations (where benefits are realized only after all the project cost is sunk) on heavy investment projects. Structure them into phases where each phase can deliver incremental benefits.
- Create low-cost exits by making smaller initial commitments, including escape clauses in contracts. Predefine "points of safe return" on project investments beyond which the project will be canceled.
- Use real options methodologies (discussed in Chapter 11) to defer decisions until a later time when uncertainty is diminished on the benefit.

ASSESS PORTFOLIO PERFORMANCE

The objective of portfolio assessment is two-fold. First, ensure that the portfolio is effective in achieving its objectives. Second, capture and apply the lessons learned to continuously improve the PPM process. The true test of PPM process effectiveness lies in the actual realization of the value outcomes. The outcomes can only be measured by monitoring the aggregate value delivered by every component project over the lifetime of the products and the services it has produced. This will be far into the distant future after ongoing projects have been completed. The portfolio should establish systems that facilitate the collection of required data on project value outcome measurements to prove the portfolio effectiveness.

You may compare the actual value generated vs. its anticipated value for various projects in a portfolio using basic statistical tools. In this comparison you may include different project categories to show differences between categories. You may make further comparisons along the timeline (say quarterly or yearly) to observe the correlation between the actual and estimated values. Data on various financial metrics (e.g., payback period, return on investment) should also be examined. With today's sophisticated data analysis, you may dissect the data in so many different ways to validate the PPM process and gain better insights. The fundamental challenges with this exercise, however, are:

1. Financial value can be measured and tracked through quantitative measures, but other value forms are difficult to quantify.
2. Even with financial value, it is a resource-intensive effort to forecast time-phased cash flows along the time horizon.
3. Typically there is a disconnection between the portfolio management team involved in the project initiation and development phases and the operations team responsible for the production phase.
4. Time lag between the project development phase where value is created and production phase where value is delivered can be long. It makes the comparison of planned vs. actual data difficult and less meaningful because of changes in so many variables over time.

These challenges are not particularly insurmountable and can be overcome through proper planning and implementation of effective information management systems. While the responsibility to define the systems to collect and analyze the required data lies with the portfolio team, the portfolio management office is responsible for establishing those systems and collecting the data over time to make it available for the portfolio team. Although true portfolio success can be assessed only "after the fact" far into the distant future, several performance indicators can be monitored to gauge the portfolio health while the projects are going through the development phase in the portfolio funnel. The indicators in essence show whether or not the portfolio is meeting the design specifications. Examples of key indicators are:

*   The total value of a portfolio at any given time is represented by the total NPV to be generated by the projects going through the develop-

ment phase in the portfolio (NPV can be replaced by an equivalent measure for projects generating nonfinancial value.).

- The percent portfolio return as characterized by the expected benefit from the projects in the portfolio vs. the total investment required to complete the projects.
- The total amount of investment required to complete the projects in the portfolio.
- The percent of the total funded projects in the portfolio that are completed each year.
- The percent of the total projects in the portfolio that have been initially funded, but are terminated before their completion.
- The percent of the total funded projects in the portfolio that are completed under target time and budget.
- The correlation between the design percent investment allocations vs. actual percent allocations across different project categories (this is an indicator related to the category balance).
- The fit between the organizational goals, projects, and resources (this is an indicator related to the triple constraint balance).

As mentioned earlier, PPM is about strategy execution. Just because the strategy has been executed effectively does not necessarily mean organization will be successful in the long run. If the strategy formulation is flawed and strategy and goals are wrong to begin with, PPM cannot guarantee long-term organizational success.

SECTION 3

PROJECT PORTFOLIO MANAGEMENT TOOLS AND TECHNIQUES

Section 3 consists of six chapters on numerous project portfolio management (PPM) tools and techniques. It starts with evaluation of projects for both financial and nonfinancial benefits. Financial metrics discussed include net present value, return on investment, benefit-cost ratio and others. Scoring models that are most useful in evaluating a project's attractiveness, especially related to nonfinancial criteria, are presented. Project ranking techniques and data visualization tools are also discussed. Uncertainty and risk are defined, and several tools and techniques are offered to analyze them. Strategies for managing portfolio risks are also included. One chapter in this section is dedicated to earned value management (EVM). It describes the EVM fundamentals and demonstrates how it can be used as a performance measurement technique not only at the project but also at the portfolio level. Another chapter focuses on the role of PPM in resource planning and various related tools. The section ends with a discussion on the portfolio management office.

11

PROJECT EVALUATION

The evaluation of projects is a core portfolio management process. The objective is to facilitate their selection and prioritization in the portfolio, so the high value potential, strategically aligned projects can be pursued. Prior to evaluation, you must identify the criteria and metrics for project selection in the portfolio design phase. Project initiators must be encouraged to employ the required metrics to make the evaluation easy for the portfolio team. From an evaluation standpoint, the criteria may be grouped under two categories:

- Financials: Tangible and monetary in nature, these include financial costs and benefits. These can be measured using quantitative methods.
- Nonfinancials: These are intangibles (e.g., alignment, nonfinancial benefits, threats, opportunities) that cannot be seen, touched, or measured and are nonmonetary. Their evaluation tools are primarily scoring models.

This chapter is divided into two sections that discuss financial and nonfinancial metrics separately.

PROJECT EVALUATION: FINANCIALS

The evaluation of projects for their financial value is critical to portfolios that contain projects generating financial benefits. The project portfolio management (PPM) process must identify the financial metrics, tools, and techniques in the design phase of the portfolio. The portfolio team should work closely with the finance department of their business unit or the enterprise to establish guidelines as to how the metrics may be used, since there are so many variations to the models and calculations involved. The project initiators should be encouraged to employ the same metrics and models across the portfolio sponsoring organization (PSO). This creates consistency and makes it easier for the portfolio team to analyze the benefit-cost-risk equation of projects. In this section, I first start with a brief introduction to different components of shareholder value and how a project may contribute to this value. Then I delve into the basics of cash flow analysis, which you must understand before using any financial metric to quantify a project's financial worth. Most important, towards the end of this section I present commonly used financial metrics and models.

Shareholder Value

Shareholder value represents the market value of an organization and is applied to investor owned (publicly traded or privately owned) companies but not nonprofit organizations or the government. While the shareholder value of a privately owned company is not public information, the market value of a publicly traded company can be calculated using various techniques. A common technique simply involves multiplying the product of the company's share price by the number of outstanding shares:

Market Value = Company's Share Price × No. of Outstanding Shares

$$\text{(Eq. 11-1)}$$

This equation quantifies the monetary market value of an organization at a given time, also referred to as market capitalization. It conceptually represents the sum of the equity supplied by the owners of the organization and the market value added (MVA) due to the competitive position of the company in the marketplace as perceived by the market (Figure 11-1). Therefore, an organization's market value can be enhanced by increasing either the equity or the MVA. The former increases the "size" of the company, but an increase in the MVA results in higher returns and wealth for shareholders. The owners of the organization expect the executive management to maximize the MVA.

The MVA cannot be quantified easily and is a reflection of how the market sees the future potential of the organization. It is a function of the projected future earnings due to the current and expected future products and

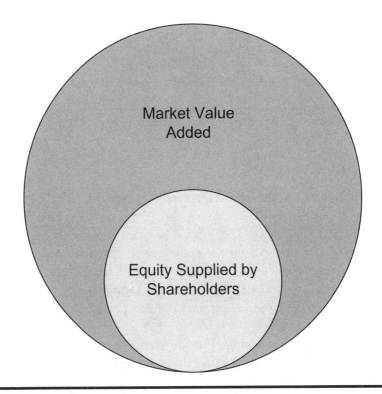

Figure 11-1 Market capitalization

services offered by the organization, the intellectual property it owns, its brand value, and its overall perception by the public. The larger the value of these factors, the larger the MVA is. To increase the MVA, executive management is expected to formulate a strategy to invest shareholder equity wisely in the right business initiatives. As the strategy is turned into a plan with clearly defined goals and in turn, into operational and tactical objectives, new projects are launched to achieve these goals. The portfolio team's job is to help the organization invest in the right projects that would ultimately result in maximizing the MVA, thereby maximizing shareholder value. The contribution of projects towards the MVA can be quantified in the form of two key components discussed below: net present value (NPV) and real option value (ROV). These two together will increase the MVA, which in turn as mentioned earlier, increases the shareholder value of the organization (Figure 11-2).

Figure 11-2   Project NPV and ROV drive shareholder value

Net Present Value

NPV is an indicator of the financial potential of a project. It reflects the difference between the projected earnings and the investment cost associated with the project's products or services. The calculation behind NPV is not precise. The value depends on the numerous assumptions that have to be made in making the calculation. The NPV method, more commonly known as discounted cash flow (DCF) analysis, is standard practice in corporate finance to calculate the projected earnings due to a project as well as the value of a company as a whole.

The NPV of a project is simply the difference, expressed in today's dollars, between the expected free cash flow to be generated by its products or services during their lifetime and the investment required to develop these products and services. Free cash flow is the expected revenue discounted (more on discounting later) back to today at a rate that reflects the risk of the project, after accounting for the cost of producing the products or services, operating expenses, interest, taxes, and capital expenditures:

Free Cash Flow = Net Sales Revenue − Cost of Production
− Operating Expenses − Interest − Taxes
− Capital Expenditures   (Eq. 11-2)

(The net sales revenue is the gross revenue
minus customer discounts and returns.)

Investment cost must also be discounted if the project development time is long, say, more than two years or so. The NPV represents the "take home" profit or the value added to the company because of the earnings generated by the products or services resulting from the project. A project is deemed to be worthy of investment, if its NPV is positive. The higher the NPV, the more attractive the project. Investment in high NPV projects will increase free cash flow, thereby increasing the MVA. (Further discussion on NPV is presented later.)

Real Option Value

The contribution of a project towards the MVA cannot always be captured by its projected earnings alone as calculated by the DCF method. This is because of two key limitations of the method:

- It takes a deterministic approach to generate just one value of NPV based on one set of input values. However, these values are rather probabilistic in the real world. Thus DCF does not consider the uncertainty of the future project outcome.
- It also does not take into account a manager's flexibility to change the project's course. For example, you may wait until some of the uncertainty clears before investing. Furthermore, after a small initial investment, you may terminate, contract, or expand the project depending upon how the project unfolds. DCF considers investment decisions as one-time decisions without valuing the managerial flexibility to alter the future project outcome.

ROV is a measure that accounts for the uncertainty of future earnings as well as the managerial flexibility to change the project's direction. It gives you the value of the project taking into consideration the initial as well as the future decisions management would make on the project. You can more accurately estimate the value of your investments based on the options you have as the project is implemented. The *real* option value denotes the underlying *non*financial asset, as opposed to the option value of a financial asset such as a stock. While standard methods to calculate project NPVs are relatively easy and widely available, methods for estimating project ROVs are more difficult and have become available only in recent years (Kodukula and Papudesu, 2006). If a project ROV is not considered in evaluating it for investment, it may not look attractive based on its NPV alone and be rejected, despite its significant potential to contribute to the MVA. The following box presents a more detailed discussion on real options and their role in PPM.

REAL OPTIONS

The standard financial tool for valuation of projects is DCF analysis. The major limitation of DCF is that it is deterministic, whereas the project outcomes are rather probabilistic. Furthermore, DCF assumes a fixed path and does not account for the managerial flexibility to change the course of the project. For example, you may defer the decision to start a new project until a later time, when the uncertainty of the outcome is diminished; or, you may terminate, expand, or contract an ongoing project. The value provided by these choices is not captured by the DCF analysis.

A simple example may illustrate these limitations. Let us say you have a chance to invest $100 in a project. In one scenario, the NPV is expected to be between $100 and $120 and in another between $70 and $150. The DCF analysis, which does not account for the uncertainty, will put the project NPV at $110 in either case. Assume that this return does not meet your standard; your decision will be not to invest in the project irrespective of the scenario. But what if an initial small investment (say $10) will help settle the uncertainty by giving you an option to fully invest in the project at a later date, if the return looks favorable, but abandon it otherwise? Your decision is likely to change now in favor of the second scenario. If your uncertainty has been cleared and the payoff is expected to be $150 (or relatively high), you will now invest in the project. If the payoff does not meet your requirements, you walk away. Thus, by considering the uncertainty and accounting for the managerial flexibility, you are able to make the right decisions to minimize losses and maximize returns. DCF analysis does not take such choices into account.

A real option is a right—not an obligation—to take action on an underlying nonfinancial asset, referred to as a real asset. This action may involve, for example, terminating, expanding, or contracting a project or even deferring the decision until a later time. It is called a *real* option, not a financial option, because the underlying asset is a real asset, not a financial one. Real option tools help you quantify the value of the option in terms of ROV. Several methods are available to calculate ROV, and the choice depends on the simplicity desired, available input data, and validity of the method for a given application. Calculation of ROV has its roots in financial options, thanks to the Nobel prize-winning work of MIT economists Fisher Black, Myron Scholes, and Robert Merton. Kodukula and Papudesu (2006) offer a practical guide for ROV calculation and project valuation in their book on real options.

When Do Real Options Provide Value?

The value of real options is a function of the project payoff uncertainty, the managerial flexibility with available alternative decision choices, and management's willingness to exercise the options. When there is little uncertainty, and there is not much room for managerial flexibility, ROV does not offer much value. Real options are most valuable when the uncertainty and managerial flexibility are both high and management is willing to exercise the options. Thus, ROV offers valuable additional information for "go/no-go" decisions. For example, your decision on a project with an NPV close to zero (positive or negative) and high option value may be a "go" when ROV is considered, whereas it would have been a "no-go" otherwise. But if the NPV is very high even in a worst-case situation, ROV does not provide additional value because your decision will be a "go" anyway. In a project portfolio, ROV offers additional value in comparing projects that are "equal" based on DCF alone, thereby acting as a "tie breaker." Real options should not be construed as a means to justify projects that should be turned down in the first place. If a project has a very high negative NPV, it probably should be rejected. ROV is not a substitute for the DCF method. It supplements and integrates DCF into a more sophisticated valuation technique.

Financial Metrics

Many financial metrics are available to evaluate a project's financial benefits and costs. Before discussing these metrics, it is important to review the building blocks common to many of them, keeping in mind the pre-project, project, and post-project phases from the funnel & filters[SM] model (Figure 11-3):

- Initiation cost (cash outflow) for evaluating new project candidates to be considered for investment by the portfolio
- Development or investment cost (cash outflow) for creating the project deliverables in the development phase
- Benefit or payoff (cash inflow) generated during the production phase after the project deliverables are launched

Initial cost is not considered as part of the investment and therefore not included in the business case analysis. The investment cost includes the total

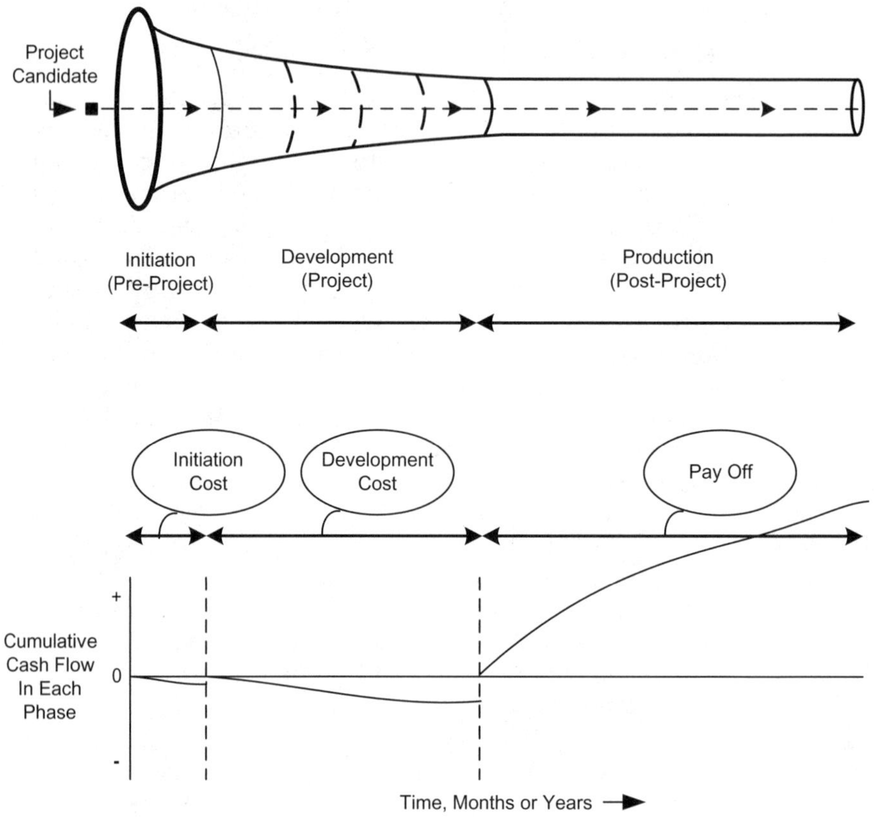

Figure 11-3   Cash inflows and outflows

investment needed to develop and launch the products/services to be delivered by the project. The total project benefit is the sum of the benefits calculated for different time periods (typically years) during the production phase. The benefit may be quantified in different ways depending upon the metric of interest and your organization's preference. It is expressed in different forms such as gross, operating or net profit, or free cash flow:

- Gross profit is the difference between net sales and cost of goods sold.
- Operating profit is the difference between the gross profit and the operating expense minus depreciation.
- Net profit is the operating profit minus taxes and interest.
- Free cash flow is equal to net profit plus depreciation.

The benefits can be expressed as either future or present values. A future value can be converted to a present value using the following equation:

$$PV = FV/(1 + i)^n \qquad \text{(Eq. 11-3)}$$

where:

FV = Future value

PV = Present value

i = Discount rate per time period

n = Number of time periods

Any financial metric typically uses one of the above forms of benefit as the building block in its calculation. The metrics basically fall into two categories: those that are expressed in terms of their magnitude and those that reflect efficiency. NPV and the payback period are standard metrics in the former category. Return on investment (ROI), benefit-to-cost ratio (BCR), and internal rate of return (IRR) are common in the efficiency category.

Net Present Value

As discussed earlier, NPV is the difference between the present values of expected cash inflows and outflows over the development and production phases. The reason the NPV method is also called DCF is that it involves the discounting of future cash flows back to today using an appropriate discount rate. The rate to be used is a function of the project risk; the higher the risk, the higher the rate. (Although NPV should mean that it has already been adjusted for risk, it is sometimes redundantly referred to as risk-adjusted NPV.) The adjustment presumably normalizes the risks associated with the competing projects, so that they can all be compared on a uniform basis. The advantages of NPV include: it is easy to understand, it gives you the bottom line "take home" value that takes into account revenues and costs, and, most important, it accounts for the time value of money. But one of its significant disadvantages (other disadvantages were discussed earlier) is that the discount rate to be used in the NPV calculation is subjective. Deciding on the appropriate rate is a challenge and is often referred to as the "discount rate dilemma." The reason for using a risk-adjusted rate is that investors expect returns higher than the "risk free rate" in order to compensate for the risks they are willing to take on projects. The risk free rate is the return you are guaranteed on an asset such as a U.S. Treasury bill or note that is considered completely risk free. The higher the risk involved in a project, the higher the expected return; therefore the higher the discount rate. The weighted average cost of capital (WACC) is typically used as a benchmark for the risk-adjusted discount rate, as discussed in the following box.

WEIGHTED AVERAGE COST OF CAPITAL

A bank will charge you a higher interest rate on your home mortgage, if your risk of default is higher as shown by your credit rating. Similarly, investors in a company expect returns in proportion to the risk they take with their investment. Since their investments fund projects, the future revenues from those projects have to be discounted at the expected rate of return. The challenge is to identify the appropriate rate that is commensurate with the risk involved. WACC is a benchmark that is often used in the calculation.

Cost of capital represents the cost of financing an organization's activities. If the credit and investment community sees the organization as more of a risk compared to the competition, the cost of capital is expected to be higher. Since an organization may be financed using different strategies (debt and equity) that carry different costs of capital, a weighted average is required. The WACC consists of the different cost components of issuing debt, preferred stock, and common equity. Typically the WACC is calculated for the enterprise as a whole based on the risk of the industry it operates in. If the enterprise is comprised of business units operating in different industries, separate WACCs are calculated for each unit depending upon the industry the unit is in. Although the WACC characterizes the cost of capital at the organizational level, it is used as a proxy to represent the risk of project investments. Your project must generate a return that is at least equivalent to the WACC, because it is what costs you to fund the project. Therefore, the WACC is used as the rate at which the project cash flows are discounted. The WACC inherently has risk premium to account for the risk perceived to be in the industry; however, an additional risk premium is often added to the WACC to arrive at the discount rate for higher risk projects. It is presumed that the organizational WACC represents "business as usual" projects, and higher risk projects warrant a higher rate.

WACC is also used as the "hurdle rate" or the "minimum acceptable rate of return" (MARR), which is the minimum rate of return the organization expects from a project before considering it investment worthy. If the NPV is greater than zero when the MARR is used as the discount rate, it means that the project is expected to produce at least a rate of return equivalent to the MARR; therefore the project is financially acceptable. The appropriate discount rates must be identified in the portfolio design phase and guidelines provided as to how to apply them in project cash flow calculations. For a detailed discussion on the discount rate dilemma, you may refer to Kodukula and Papudesu (2006).

Payback Period

The payback period (Figure 11-4) is the time expected to recover your investment. The point in time when that occurs is called the "break-even point." Conventionally, future values of cash flows are used in these calculations. For short payback periods, this may not make a big difference, but you may want to use present values when longer times are involved. The payback period is an important metric especially for investors that want quick returns on their investments because quick returns minimize long-term risk. For short periods, the calculation is relatively more reliable, because it is controlled by near-term cash flows. Long-term cash flow estimates tend to be less accurate because of their uncertainty. One disadvantage of this metric is that a

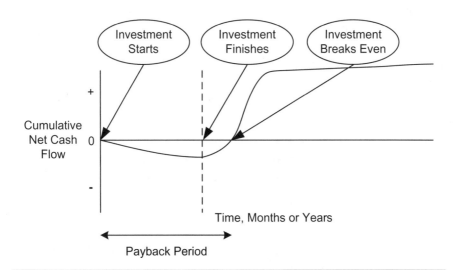

Figure 11-4 Payback period

seemingly unattractive payback time may still produce a project with highly profitable long-term cash flows.

Return On Investment

ROI is a measure of the efficiency of your investment and is given by the following equation:

ROI = (Benefit from Investment – Investment Cost)/Investment Cost

(Eq. 11-4)

As mentioned earlier, several different methods are available to calculate the benefit in the above formula. They vary in terms of: gross profit vs. free cash flow, future vs. present value, "lifetime" ROI vs. "annualized" ROI, and so on. A common method involves estimated net profit as a future value over the expected lifetime of the project's products and services. Because of numerous ways to calculate ROI, the portfolio team must provide clear guidelines as to how the ROI may be calculated for the projects in the portfolio. The major advantage of this metric is that it is simple to understand and can easily be compared to other projects and other types of investment. One disadvantage is that not everybody uses the same calculation to quantify the benefit from the project investment.

Benefit-to-Cost Ratio

The BCR is simply the ratio of the benefit to the cost of the project. The benefit is typically represented by the free cash flow (either future or present value). The cost part of the equation simply is the investment made in a project's development phase. The BCR is also called the profitability index. This metric is simple to understand and can also be easily employed for comparative purpose.

Internal Rate of Return

The IRR is the average annual rate of return a project will yield over its production phase, if the profits from each year are invested back in an asset giving the same return. It is equivalent to the annual compounded interest rate your investment will gain due to the project. It also translates to the "theoretical" discount rate at which the present value of the free cash flow during the production phase is equal to the present value of the investment cost. There is no discrete formula for this metric. It is calculated by an iterative process, where the discount rate in the present value calculation is changed until the cash flow from the production phase equals the investment cost.

Challenges with Financial Metrics

Figure 11-5 presents basic DCF calculations for a simple project example for which the metrics discussed above are applied. (Another example involving

---

Robo Tech is interested in developing and commercializing "robotic waiters" that can serve food and beverages in restaurants and at cocktail parties. The development and launch of the product is expected to cost $200 million. The estimated revenues, cost of goods sold, and other cash flow information (in millions of dollars) is provided below. A risk-adjusted discount rate of 20% is used in the free cash flow calculations. The building blocks for the financial metrics are calculated using the following formulas:

- Gross profit = Net sales revenue − Cost of good sold
- Operating profit = Gross profit − Operating expense − Depreciation
- Net profit = Operating profit − Taxes
- Free cash flow = Net profit + Depreciation

For the sake of simplicity and illustration purpose, interest and capital expenditures are ignored in the calculations.

	Time, Years						
	1	**2**	**3**	**4**	**5**	**6**	**7**
Net sales revenue	$250.00	$300.00	$375.00	$425.00	$300.00	$250.00	$120.00
Cost of goods sold	$125.00	$150.00	$187.50	$212.50	$150.00	$125.00	$60.00
Gross profit	$125.00	$150.00	$187.50	$212.50	$150.00	$125.00	$60.00
Operating expense	$25.00	$30.00	$37.50	$42.50	$30.00	$25.00	$12.00
Depreciation	$60.00	$30.00	$15.00	$10.00	$5.00	$0	$0
Operating profit	$40.00	$90.00	$135.00	$160.00	$115.00	$100.00	$48.00
Taxes	$14.00	$31.50	$47.25	$56.00	$40.25	$35.00	$16.80
Net profit	$26.00	$58.50	$87.75	$104.00	$74.75	$65.00	$31.20
Free cash flow FV	$86.00	$88.50	$102.75	$114.00	$79.75	$65.00	$31.20
Free cash flow PV	$71.67	$61.46	$59.46	$54.98	$32.05	$21.77	$8.71
Total free cash flow PV	$310.09						

The following conclusions can be made regarding the financial strength of the project:

- The NPV for the project is $110 million.
- Using the PVs of free cash flows, the pay back period is estimated to be less than four years.
- Return on investment over seven years based on net profit is 124%. This translates to an annualized ROI of 18%.
- The benefit-cost ratio, where the benefit is represented by the PVs of the free cash flows, is calculated to be 1.55.
- The IRR calculated by an iterative process is 40%.

Figure 11-5   Examples of financial metrics

DCF calculations and sensitivity analysis discussed in Chapter 13 is presented in Appendix A.) The biggest challenge with any of the models is the estimation of the input data. The other challenge is ensuring that the same calculation is used for a given metric for all the projects in a portfolio to create consistency. Input data is most often represented by single figures, which assume "certainty." However, many input variables such as revenues and costs are random. Therefore, you must make sure to account for uncertainty using proper tools such as those discussed in Chapter 13. The cash outflows are typically underestimated and inflows overestimated due to biases of project advocates. For better estimates:

- Develop comprehensive plans of project and post-project activities covering the development and production phases respectively.
- Include details of development, testing, marketing, design, engineering, manufacturing, finance, etc.
- Seek input from representative personnel from all facets of the development and production phases.
- Use peer reviews to increase the quality of the estimates.

PROJECT EVALUATION: NONFINANCIALS

Evaluation of a project for its potential to generate nonfinancial value needs an entirely different set of metrics, tools, and techniques. This form of value cannot be as easily quantified as financial value. Since we are dealing with intangibles, the tool set consists of primarily semiquantitative methods, which are more subjective. Scoring models are the most common tools in the PPM arena for project evaluation.

Scoring Models

A basic scoring model involves rating a project on each one of pre-selected evaluation criteria. The criteria depend on the PSO's business needs and the type of portfolio you are dealing with, as discussed in Chapter 8. The ratings from all the criteria are added in some fashion to arrive at a score, which represents the project's collective merit. Three types of scoring models are common: unweighted binary scoring models, unweighted scoring models, and weighted scoring models (Meredith and Mantel, 2008).

- **Unweighted Binary Scoring Model.** A list of positive or desirable project characteristics or attributes are first identified based on how each project is rated. The rating simply involves checking off on the list whether or not each individual attribute applies to the project under consideration; hence the name binary. The longer the checklist of applicable characteristics, the more attractive the project is. This method is simple but crude. It accounts for whether or not a project exhibits a desirable characteristic but does not rate its value. Furthermore, all characteristics are considered equal without accounting for any relative importance.

- **Unweighted Scoring Model.** This is similar to the above model, except that each project characteristic is rated on a scale, for example, 1-10 (1 represents the least desirable score in a project's favor and 10 the most desirable). The rating considers the merit on a given characteristic but does not account for that characteristic's relative importance compared to the rest.

- **Weighted Scoring Model.** It is an improvement over the unweighted scoring model because it considers the relative importance of each project characteristic by assigning a weightage factor to it. A weighted aggregate score for a project is obtained by adding up the weighted scores of all the characteristics. The higher the aggregate score, the more attractive the project is. The overall process involves the following steps:

  - ♦ Identify project characteristics that serve as criteria to evaluate projects in the portfolio design phase (Chapter 8).
  - ♦ Give a percentage weight to each characteristic, so that the total weight will add up to 100 (also performed in the portfolio design phase).
  - ♦ Score each project on every characteristic on a scale of 1-10.
  - ♦ Multiply the characteristic scores by their corresponding weights for the project.
  - ♦ Add up the scores to obtain the aggregate score that represents the project's merit.

The weighted scoring model is the most common tool for project evaluation (and prioritization). The biggest advantage of scoring models lies in their ease of use. But the real challenge is identifying the appropriate evaluation criteria and weightage factors that truly represent the organizational objectives and priorities. Application of sophisticated methods involving utility theory, analytic hierarchy process, and others will add a great deal of validity to the scoring models.

An example of the model is presented in Table 11-1. Any project characteristic used as an evaluation criterion can be rated with a weighted scoring

Table 11-1 Scoring model

No.	Criterion	Criterion Weight	Criterion Score (1-10)*	Weighted Score
1	Alignment	20%	8	1.6
2	Profitability	60%	6	3.6
3	Probability of timely completion	5%	6	0.3
4	Probability of technical success	5%	4	0.2
5	Probability of market success	5%	7	0.35
6	Future opportunities	5%	8	0.4
	Total:	100%		6.45

*Higher the score, the more attractive the project.

model. The ratings can be performed based on as little information as is available on the project's characteristics or preferably a rigorous business case analysis. The latter will obviously provide a stronger basis for the portfolio team to rate the project. Project initiators must be encouraged to include as much supporting evidence as possible in a clear and concise format in the project business plan to make the rating process easy for the portfolio team.

When dealing with projects that generate intangible value, organizations generally place significantly more emphasis on how strongly a candidate project is aligned with the strategy and goals compared to the other criteria. It means that in scoring models, the weightage factor for the alignment criteria would be higher. In order for the portfolio team to have a better understanding of the degree of alignment, the project initiators must provide sufficient information on their project's goals and how they align with the organizational strategy and goals. There are two tools that are effective in describing the alignment: graphical linkages and "if-then" statements.

Graphical Linkages

Graphical linkages are simple tools that show links between a candidate project's goals/objectives and the organizational goals/objectives (Figure 11-6). They can be effectively used only when the organizational goals and objectives are clearly made visible by the PSO and the project goals and objectives are clearly defined by the project initiators in the project business plans:

- **PSO's goals.** These goals must be articulated based on the strategic framework of the PSO that should be in alignment with that of the enterprise.

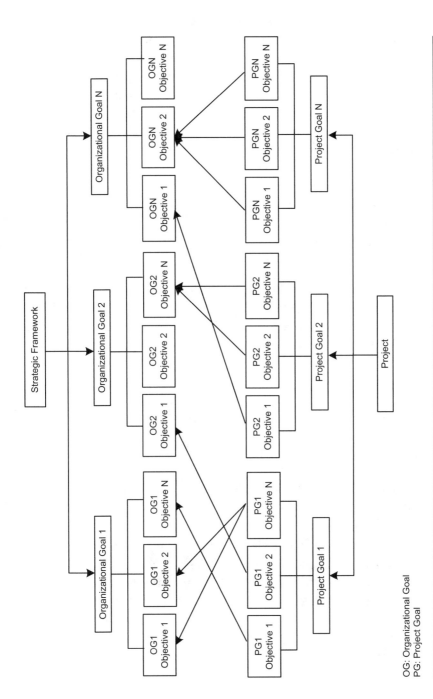

OG: Organizational Goal
PG: Project Goal

Figure 11-6 Graphical linkages

- **Objectives corresponding to each PSO goal.** These objectives must be SMART (specific, measurable, agreed-to, realistic, and time-bound) and should be expressed in terms of value metrics.
- **Project goals.** Project goals must be expressed as tangible deliverables (products, services, results) to be produced by a specified date and within a specified budget.
- **Project's "business" objectives corresponding to each project goal.** A project's business objectives define how they will help the business needs of the organization. The objectives must be SMART and should be expressed in terms of value metrics corresponding to the value the project deliverables are expected to generate.

If-Then Statements

If-then statements provide the same information as graphical linkages except that they are narrative rather than graphical. They are descriptions of how a project will help the organization achieve its goals. Multiple if-then statements may be needed to represent various scenarios through which multiple organizational goals may be achieved. As an example, a simple if-then statement and corresponding organizational and project goals/objectives are provided below.

- **Organizational goal:** Increase in organization-wide safety performance
- **Corresponding objective:** Decrease in safety incidents by 50% in the next year
- **Project goal:** Launch and complete an intense education campaign before the end of the year throughout the organization to increase the safety performance
- **Corresponding project objective:** Launch and complete the project on time and under budget to reduce "trip and falls" by 75% next year
- **If-then statement to describe goal alignment:** If the safety education campaign is completed under budget before the end of the year, then it will reduce trip and falls and directly contribute towards reducing the number of overall safety incidents which will enhance safety performance in the organization.

12

PROJECT PRIORITIZATION

Project prioritization is a key project portfolio management (PPM) process that involves the ranking of projects, so resources can be allocated based on those rankings. When there are relatively few projects that are also immensely large, and they are supported at the enterprise level, there may not be a need for a formal ranking, as long as each project demonstrates its investment worthiness. But in most organizations where there are many projects but resources are scant, project ranking has become a common practice. Ranking is based on the evaluation of projects using multiple quantitative and qualitative criteria often involving large amounts of project data. Since executives and senior managers associated with project go/no-go decisions prefer simple but powerful means of communication, numerous data presentation and visualization tools have emerged in recent years. Therefore, the subject of this chapter is not only project ranking but also data visualization tools. First, I start with ranking tools. For projects generating financial value, I show how the efficient frontier method can be applied for ranking. I touch on scoring models briefly, since we already discussed them in detail in Chapter 11. Forced ranking, paired comparison, and Q-Sort are some of the other ranking tools I illustrate in this chapter. The second part of the chapter is on data visualization tools. These tools can synthesize massive amounts of information and present it in a simple, intuitive, and visually appealing format.

PROJECT RANKING TOOLS

Project prioritization will be relatively simple, if you rank all the projects in the portfolio based on one single criterion representing one single project characteristic or attribute. You may identify a specific metric to measure that characteristic. If that metric can somehow be quantified, you can rank the projects, from best to worst, based on the actual value of that metric. You can then select projects on the ranked list in accordance with the resources available. Thus, you will be able to maximize the value of the portfolio with respect to whatever the sole criterion that you selected may be. For example, if your sole interest is in projects generating financial value, you may select benefit-to-cost ratio (BCR) as the metric to measure their financial merit and rank them starting with the highest BCR. In doing so, you are maximizing the financial value that the portfolio will create. Most projects, especially those that do not generate financial value, possess many characteristics that contribute towards a project's merit. Some of those characteristics are more important and some are less important. So to level the playing field, you may use a scoring model that takes into account multiple characteristics and appropriate weightage factors for each characteristic. (As mentioned in the previous chapter, sophisticated tools involving utility theory and analytic hierarchy, among others, are available to develop valid and reliable scoring models.)

None of the ranking tools can demonstrate that one project is unequivocally better than another because of the uncertainty in project data and the subjectivity associated with many of the tools. At minimum, the tools should give you excellent clues on projects that are strong, weak, or marginal in their merit. It can be a good starting point to have a debate and discussion around the go/no-go decisions.

Ranking the Benefit-to-Cost Ratio Using the Efficient Frontier

It may seem prudent on the surface to rank projects that generate financial value based on net present value (NPV), a key financial metric, in order to select the highest value-generating projects for the portfolio in accordance with the investment available. But according to the efficient frontier principle discussed in Chapter 5, you may be suboptimizing the portfolio. Optimal portfolios lie on the so-called efficient frontier and likely include a different mix of projects than those obtained by the NPV ranking. You will be destroying value for the organization by not selecting the optimized portfolio. While sophisticated mathematical programming tools are available for portfolio optimization (Bayney and Chakra-varti, 2012), a simple ranking of projects based on their BCR can produce the efficient frontier marking the optimum portfolios associated with different investment levels. The technique involves identifying every single theoretically possible combination of competing projects to form a portfolio and selecting the one and only portfolio with the right project mix that would produce the maximum financial value for a given level of investment. Whereas you may require a fast computer to identify the numerous possible portfolios, a simplified method that needs no more than a calculator is available. However, a spreadsheet is preferable, especially if the number of projects is relatively large. You can generate the efficient frontier by simply plotting the "cumulative" BCRs of the competing projects, where benefit is represented by the NPV (the cash flows must be adjusted for risk), vs. the corresponding total investment for those projects. As an example, Table 12-1 shows a list of 25 projects that are ranked according to their BCRs from the highest to the lowest, and Figure 12-1 presents the efficient frontier for these projects (except those with a BCR less than 1.0). The calculations in Table 12-1 involve the following steps:

- Estimate the cost and the NPV for each competing project.
- Compute the BCR of each project.

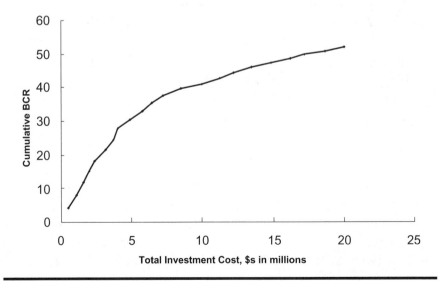

Figure 12-1   Efficient frontier curve

Table 12-1 List of projects

Project ID	Cost	Benefit	Descending BCR	Cumulative Cost	Cumulative BCR
11	557,657	2,284,584	4.10	557,657	4.10
1	546,846	2,124,381	3.88	1,104,503	7.98
6	473,533	1,801,917	3.81	1,578,036	11.79
20	465,502	1,501,761	3.23	2,043,538	15.01
17	373,138	1,195,650	3.20	2,416,676	18.22
19	732,088	2,338,347	3.19	3,148,764	21.41
7	547,635	1,744,401	3.19	3,696,399	24.60
15	372,350	1,171,577	3.15	4,068,748	27.74
16	850,940	2,244,128	2.64	4,919,689	30.38
13	869,969	2,254,094	2.59	5,789,658	32.97
14	711,566	1,717,228	2.41	6,501,224	35.38
23	725,401	1,654,142	2.28	7,226,624	37.66
9	1,279,143	2,278,628	1.78	8,505,767	39.45
18	1,514,746	2,559,467	1.69	10,020,514	41.14
22	1,249,797	2,104,847	1.68	11,270,311	42.82
21	906,649	1,512,290	1.67	12,176,960	44.49
10	1,318,790	1,952,749	1.48	13,495,750	45.97
25	1,381,673	1,704,111	1.23	14,877,423	47.20
5	1,320,046	1,619,634	1.23	16,197,468	48.43
12	1,011,730	1,227,030	1.21	17,209,199	49.64
2	1,481,124	1,691,119	1.14	18,690,322	50.78
24	1,311,985	1,438,845	1.10	20,002,307	51.88
4	1,058,819	1,039,880	0.98	21,061,127	52.86
8	1,193,978	1,053,459	0.88	22,255,105	53.74
3	1,665,676	1,267,437	0.76	23,920,781	54.51

- Rank the projects starting from the highest BCR to the lowest.
- Add the BCRs cumulatively, one project at a time, from the top to the bottom of the list. (Please note that this cumulative BCR of a group of projects is not the same cumulative BCR for all those projects, if you used their cumulative benefits and costs in the BCR calculation. The former is just a mathematical operation required to generate the frontier.)

- Similarly, add the cost of the projects cumulatively, one project at a time, from the top to the bottom of the list. Each cumulative cost represents the corresponding total cost of the component projects of the mix.

If you plot the cumulative BCRs against the corresponding cumulative project costs as in Figure 12-1, the resulting curve is the efficient frontier representing portfolios containing projects with the highest BCRs. As shown in Chapter 5, the efficient frontier is useful in many different ways: 1) For a given amount of investment, you can identify the right mix of projects with the highest BCRs. 2) The decreasing slope of the curve shows that for each additional dollar of investment added to the portfolio, the benefit in return decreases. You can define a "cut off" point for your investment, beyond which projects have marginal returns. That point can be translated to a BCR-based benchmark for investment decisions. 3) You can apply the frontier curve to an existing portfolio and identify low value projects, which you may want to terminate.

Scoring Models

Scoring models, already discussed in Chapter 11, are simple, easy, and the most common tools for ranking projects. Once an aggregate score is obtained for each competing project reflecting their individual merit, they can be ranked starting with the highest scoring project as the most attractive one for investment. An example of a weighted scoring model for project ranking is shown in Table 12-2.

Forced Ranking

In a forced ranking method, each member of a group of subject matter experts (or decision makers) independently ranks the competing projects giving them numerical values 1, 2, 3, etc., where 1 represents the most attractive project, 2, the second most attractive, and so on. For each project, the rankings of the group members are added up, and the projects are re-ranked based on their rank sums. The example in Table 12-3 shows 10 projects (A through J) force ranked from 1 to 10 by five experts. Project I received the lowest rank sum (11) gaining first place on the list as the most attractive project.

Table 12-2 Weighted scoring model

Project		Criteria (% Weightage)					Sum of Weighted Scores	Rank
		Strategic Fit (5%)	Goal Alignment (10%)	Value Generation Potential (65%)	Threats (10%)	Opportunities (10%)		
A	Score*	8	2	8	5	7	7.0	5
	Weighted Score	0.4	0.2	5.2	0.5	0.7		
B	Score	8	3	8	7	3	6.9	6
	Weighted Score	0.4	0.3	5.2	0.7	0.3		
C	Score	8	6	8	8	6	7.6	3
	Weighted Score	0.4	0.6	5.2	0.8	0.6		
D	Score	6	4	4	6	5	4.4	9
	Weighted Score	0.3	0.4	2.6	0.6	0.5		
E	Score	3	6	5	8	5	5.3	8
	Weighted Score	0.15	0.6	3.25	0.8	0.5		
F	Score	5	7	9	9	6	8.3	1
	Weighted Score	0.25	0.7	5.85	0.9	0.6		
G	Score	7	4	8	5	6	7.1	4
	Weighted Score	0.35	0.4	5.2	0.5	0.6		
H	Score	10	5	9	6	7	8.2	2
	Weighted Score	0.5	0.5	5.85	0.6	0.7		
I	Score	5	8	7	8	4	6.8	7
	Weighted Score	0.25	0.8	4.55	0.8	0.4		

*On a scale of 1–10; higher the score, the more attractive the project

Table 12-3   Forced ranking of projects

Project	Ranking Person					Total Score	Project Rank
	ADE	RCS	PDS	ROL	CFK		
A	3	1	5	2	2	13	2
B	8	7	9	8	10	42	9
C	4	6	2	5	4	21	5
D	9	10	8	7	5	39	8
E	1	2	7	4	6	20	4
F	6	8	4	9	8	35	7
G	10	9	10	10	9	48	10
H	7	5	6	6	7	31	6
I	2	4	3	1	1	11	1
J	5	3	1	3	3	15	3

Paired Comparison

In paired comparison, every project is compared with every other project as a pair. The better project between the two receives a score of 1 while the other receives a score of 0. The scores for each project are added. The projects are ranked in descending order with the project having the highest total score ranked as No. 1. In Table 12-4, 10 projects are compared one against the other in pairs. The scores for each project are added horizontally in rows. Project I was picked to be superior more often that any others (eight times out of the nine comparisons). Therefore it was ranked as No. 1. Projects D and E are tied by receiving the same number of scores (5 each). The tie is broken by the specific pair-comparison, where Project D is rated superior to Project E. If there are several people performing the comparison, the scores (0s and 1s) from each person can be added and tallied to determine the rankings. Paired comparison is easier when you have a small number of projects. It becomes increasingly cumbersome and inconsistent as the number of projects increase. For example, if you have rated A as better than B and B better than C, to be logically consistent you must rate A as better than C, but this can become difficult as the number of comparisons grows. Paired comparison is a highly simplified version of a sophisticated prioritization and decision-making tool called the analytic hierarchy process pioneered by Thomas Saaty (Saaty, 2001).

Table 12-4 Paired comparison of projects

Project	A	B	C	D	E	F	G	H	I	J	Sum	Rank
A		0	0	1	0	1	1	1	1	1	6	3
B	1		1	1	1	0	1	1	0	1	7	2
C	1	0		0	0	0	1	0	0	1	3	8
D	0	0	1		1	1	1	0	1	0	5	4
E	1	0	1	0		1	0	1	0	1	5	5
F	0	1	1	0	0		0	0	0	0	2	9
G	0	0	0	0	1	1		1	0	1	4	6
H	0	0	1	1	0	1	0		0	1	4	7
I	0	1	1	1	1	1	1	1		1	8	1
J	0	0	0	0	0	1	0	0	0		1	10

Q-Sort

When you are faced with a relatively large number of projects for ranking, you may find it difficult to compare and rank them using the tools such as forced ranking and paired comparison discussed above. Q-Sort is a technique that can help you divide the projects into a number of groups based on their relative merit (e.g., high, medium, and low), so ranking can be more easily done within each group containing a smaller number of projects. First you divide the projects on your list into two groups, those that exhibit high vs. low merit based on the business case information provided in their project business plans (PBPs). Then you divide the "high" group into two groups with projects showing high vs medium merit. Similarly, you divide the "low" group into medium and low groups. As shown in Figure 12-2, you carry on the division until you reach the desired level. It is generally recommended that the division should continue until you have approximately no more than eight projects in any one group.

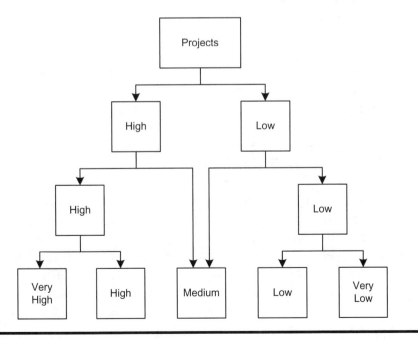

Figure 12-2 Q-Sort

DATA VISUALIZATION TOOLS

Data visualization tools have exploded in the market within the last ten years. The goal of these tools is to convey complex information clearly and effectively in a visually appealing fashion. They can especially help you synthesize massive amounts of data and express them in a simple and intuitive format. You can easily get carried away with the capability of some of the highly sophisticated visualization tools, but the key to remember is the function they serve rather than their form. The intention of this section is not to review the commercial applications in the market, but to point out the most common generic tools used in the PPM arena.

Scorecards

The purpose of a scorecard is to display the key performance indicators of a process, system, or an organization. A PPM scorecard shows how the portfolio and the component projects are performing. The performance record gives you an indication of whether you are on track with the expected performance. Typically a scorecard is presented as a spreadsheet. You can keep it simple by including only high-level information by keeping the number of cells in the spreadsheet to a minimum. For details related to each cell, you can drill down through links to other spreadsheets, documents, web pages, and other sources. Since scorecards provide detailed performance data, they are meant for operational purposes rather than executive decision making. An example PPM scorecard is shown in Table 12-5. It shows a list of projects in the portfolio rated on predefined criteria with weightage factors and the latest weighted scores. It also displays the current as well as the expected future schedule and cost performance data for each component project. In addition, it summarizes key portfolio requirements such as portfolio budget needs, value to be generated by the portfolio, remaining contingencies, and so on. For details, you may create links to each project's project request form, PBP, project performance report, and other important documentation. The scorecard can be made simple or sophisticated depending upon the available project data and the level of analysis that goes into the evaluation of each project in the portfolio. It ties the tools related to the criteria that form the basis for screening, ranking, and selection of projects.

Table 12-5   Portfolio scorecard

A. Project Metrics

Project ID	Current Performance								Expected Future Performance		
	% Completion		Critical Path Status			Schedule Variance (SV)	Cost Variance (CV)	% Contingencies Used	Estimate To Complete (ETC)	Estimate At Completion (EAC)	Variance At Completion (VAC)
	Plan	Actual	On Track	Ahead	Behind						
Alpha											
Bravo											
Charlie											
Delta											
Etc.											

Business Case Status

Project ID	Alignment Score		Financials						Non-Financial Value Score		Threat Score		Opportunity Score		Overall Score	
	Initial	Current	NPV		ROI		Payback Period		Initial	Current	Initial	Current	Initial	Current	Initial	Current
			Initial	Current	Initial	Current	Initial	Current								
Alpha																
Bravo																
Charlie																
Delta																
Etc.																

Table 12-5   *Continued*

B. Portfolio Metrics

Total Budgeted Cost of Work Planned
Total Budgeted Cost of Work Completed
Actual Cost of Work Completed
Schedule Variance (SV)
Schedule Performance Index (SPI)
% Total Milestones Completed
Cost Variance (CV)
Cost Performance Index (CPI)
Budget Remaining
Budget Required
% Contingencies Used
Contingencies Remaining
Total NPV

Project Category Allocation		
Category	Design, %	Actual, %
1		
2		
3		
N		

Dashboards

Dashboards are charts or spreadsheets showing the status of processes, systems, or organizations. Most of them display the status using red-amber-green symbols. Dashboards contain high-level information for senior and executive management review and are often used to facilitate decision making. They show most critical high-level performance indicators using simple, easily understandable, and visually appealing graphics. They have become common management tools in recent years because of their simplicity. Dashboards displaying real-time data are increasing in popularity. A typical portfolio dashboard includes a red-amber-green status indicator reflecting the performance of each component project relative to key criteria such as cost and schedule. An example portfolio dashboard is presented in Table 12-6.

Radar Charts

Radar charts, also called spider charts, are visual and easy-to-understand tools that depict ratings on various project characteristics. Figure 12-3 is an example where ratings for a project on key evaluation criteria are displayed. The chart shows the project's areas of strengths and weaknesses.

Table 12-6   Portfolio dashboard

Projects Status				
Project ID	Status		Major Issues	Major Risks
	Red	Amber	Green	
Alpha				
Bravo				
Charlie				
Delta				
Etc.				

Portfolio Status							
Status			Schedule Performance Index (SPI)	Cost Performance Index (CPI)	Budget Avaialble	Budget Required	Major Issues
Red	Amber	Green					

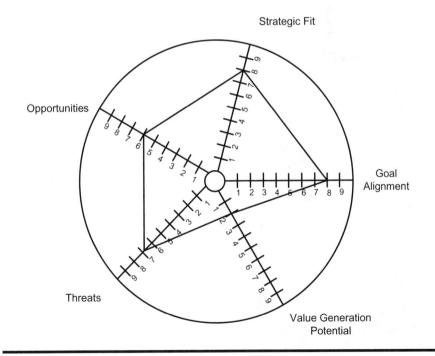

Figure 12-3   Radar chart

Pie Charts and Stack Charts

Pie charts have been used for many decades, while stack charts have become more common in recent years. Figure 8-1 in Chapter 8 is a stack chart showing the design percent investment allocation to be achieved for a portfolio and the actual allocations for two consecutive years.

Bubble Diagrams

Bubble diagrams are basically X-Y plots that enable you to display information on numerous variables. Dye and Pennypacker (1999) illustrate the use of various bubble diagrams, and Figure 12-4 is an example summarizing the

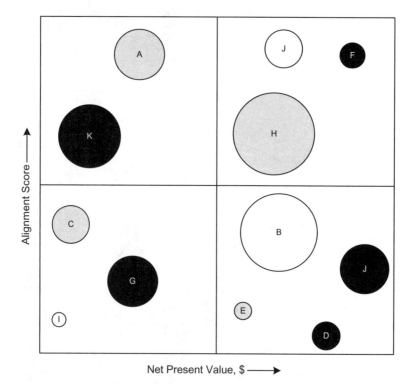

Net Present Value, $ ⟶

A thru M: Project ID
Size: Larger means higher cost
Shading: Darker means higher success probability
Color (not shown): Payback period

Figure 12-4   Bubble diagram

project evaluation information for a small portfolio. This figure presents data from a 12 × 5 matrix in an easily understandable and visually appealing way. Twelve projects in a small portfolio are compared on five different project characteristics. Bubble diagrams can be employed in numerous ways to present PPM information and have become the most common tools in this arena. Several commercial PPM software packages have the capability to produce such diagrams.

13

UNCERTAINTY AND RISK

Decision making is at the core of portfolio management. Making the right investment decisions consistently will help you achieve long-term organizational success. Poor decisions, on the other hand, will result in wasting organizational resources and undermining or even destroying your long-term competitiveness. It is not likely that every single project go/no-go decision you will make will be the right one, nor is it likely that they all will be wrong either. It is often said about bets that: "You win some, you lose some." In a project portfolio, you want to maximize your wins and minimize your losses.

When you are making the decision, you obviously don't know what the outcome will be. For most projects, you won't know the outcome until far into the future. Project decisions always have to be made with no guaranteed positive outcome. Most often decisions have to be made with uncertain information. Once you implement the decision, sooner or later you will face the consequence, which also has its own uncertainty (Figure 13-1). This uncertainty is part of the risk you face in making the decision. Uncertainty and risk are two of the biggest unknowns management has to understand and deal with in making project decisions. By identifying and analyzing them and implementing appropriate proactive measures, you are more likely to make the right project bets where your wins will far outweigh your losses.

Decision analysis is a discipline that offers a structured process and tools for decision making, so you can identify the best course of action. In particular, the tools will help you identify and analyze the uncertainty and risk associated with the decisions and the outcomes. The decisions made after rigorous analysis may not always result in the best outcomes. In fact, some

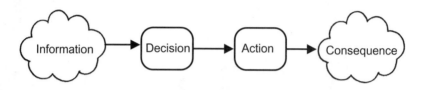

Figure 13-1   Risk and uncertainty in decision making (Kodukula & Papudesu, 2006)

hasty decisions made with little or no analysis *can* result in highly desired outcomes. This should not be taken as evidence against the benefits of rigorous analysis. Such decisions are unlikely to produce consistent positive outcomes in the long run, but decisions based on sound principles and under the rigor of decision analysis will often yield superior outcomes.

It is not my intention to delve into a detailed discourse on decision analysis in this chapter. My objective is to focus on the role and influence of uncertainty and risk in decision making. In this chapter, I will first define uncertainty and risk for the context of this book. Their definitions are varied in the literature, so it is paramount that you understand what they mean in the project and portfolio management context. I will differentiate project and portfolio risks and present different approaches to mitigating the latter. I will briefly describe our common biases that we must overcome in making sound decisions. Finally, I will discuss various tools and techniques that can help us understand and evaluate uncertainty and risk, so we can make better project go/no-go decisions.

UNCERTAINTY

Uncertainty exists when the information is not certain, definitive, or perfect. For example, as you embark on a project involving development of a new product, you don't know exactly how much revenue it will generate. Among other things, you also don't know exactly what the development cost will be, although you expect that uncertainty to be relatively less compared with that of future revenues. There are different ranges of uncertainty for the variables we normally consider in evaluating projects. Furthermore, the range of uncertainty also varies between projects in a portfolio. Therefore, it is important that we understand uncertainty, so we can gain a better insight into a project's own merit as well as its relative merit compared to competing projects and make better project investment decisions. Uncertainty is most commonly measured in terms of probabilities.

For example, using deterministic analysis, you may conclude that Projects Alpha and Beta in a portfolio will produce an average net present value (NPV) of $1 million. However, it does not say anything about the uncertainty around the NPV. If you were to choose between Alpha and Beta, your decision might be indifferent, because both are equally attractive from an NPV standpoint, considering all other factors to be equal. But what if the uncertainty analysis reveals that there is a 5% and 15% probability that the NPV of Projects Alpha and Beta will be less than zero, respectively? What if the analysis also shows that there is a 10% and 30% probability that the NPV will be greater than $5 million, respectively? If you are risk averse, you might select Project Alpha because of its lesser chance of being in the negative NPV territory. On the other hand, if you want to take advantage of the potential upside, you might select Project Beta.

RISK

Different definitions of risk exist in the literature. In the project management arena, risk is defined as an uncertain event that if it occurs, has either a positive or negative impact on the outcome. It is measured as a set of events, with each event's probability of occurrence and impact. Events with positive impact are called opportunities and events with negative impact are called threats. Risks are categorized in many different ways, but one important categorization separates them as controllable vs. uncontrollable. The former are within your organization's control. For instance, you may assign more resources to a project to mitigate the risk of project delay. In the case of a portfolio, you may establish higher financial thresholds (for example, hurdle rate) for selecting projects to minimize the risk of investing in marginal projects. Uncontrollable risks are those that you have little or no control over. An example of an uncontrollable project risk is whether a new technology will be effective. Another example is an unforeseen change in the regulatory environment. For a portfolio, a general economic downturn is an uncontrollable risk.

PROJECT RISK MANAGEMENT

Project risks are associated with the project development phase and primarily related to the project triple constraint. They impact the fundamental objective of completing a project's entire scope of work on time and on budget. Examples of threat impacts are: the entire scope is not delivered, the project is delayed, or the project cost has exceeded the allocated budget. Finishing the project ahead of time and under budget are examples of opportunities. Project risk management is a well-established process. It basically involves the following steps:

1. Start with an overall plan for managing risks.
2. Identify the risks.
3. Analyze the probability and impact of each risk.
4. Prioritize the risks.
5. Identify and assess response strategies for each risk.
6. Implement appropriate strategies.
7. Monitor, control, and manage risks throughout the project life cycle.

You may refer to many books available on the subject including the Project Management Institute's *PMBOK® Guide* (PMI, 2013a). The project manager and the team are responsible for managing this process. Although the portfolio team is not directly involved in project risk management, it needs to understand and monitor the risks closely because they will impact portfolio performance. Project risks must be considered in making project go/no-go decisions at the portfolio level.

PORTFOLIO RISK MANAGEMENT

Portfolio risks are primarily related to the portfolio triple constraint. They impact the achievement of organizational goals. Examples of negative impact are: not all the organizational goals are achieved; value generation is less than expected; unnecessary projects are funded wasting organizational resources; projects are failing to finish on time and on budget; resources are not utilized to the optimum level. Examples of positive impact include: organizational goals are exceeded; greater value is generated compared to the plan; projects are finishing ahead of time and under budget; higher resource efficiencies are realized. The basic approach for managing project risks outlined earlier in this chapter can also be applied for managing portfolio risks. You may first identify, analyze, and prioritize the risks, assess different response measures, implement the best measure, and repeat the overall process at regular intervals. One of the major differences between project and portfolio risks is that the impact of the latter is not seen until far into the future after the component projects are completed and their deliverables are launched. The long timeline increases the uncertainty of the information and the risk associated with go/no-go decisions. To maximize the upside and reduce the threats, every portfolio can implement a few mitigation actions presented below.

Implement a Formal Project Portfolio Management Process

A formal project portfolio management (PPM) process will increase the efficiency and the effectiveness of a portfolio and will reduce the chances of failure. As part of this process, first and foremost, the organizational strategic framework and the organizational goals must be articulated. The organizational risk preferences must be taken into account in formulating the strategy and the goals. The portfolio design specifications accounting for the risk preferences must be defined in advance and followed thoroughly in making project go/no-go decisions. The consistent use of appropriate tools and techniques must be promoted throughout the organization to facilitate effective decision making.

Implement Governance with Phase-Gates and Funnel & Filters^{SM}

Phase-gates help you control the project development process and reduce individual project investment risk. A well-structured PPM process with funnel & filters^{SM} helps you balance the risk of the portfolio by investing in the right mix of projects.

Overcome Judgment Biases in Decision Making

The role of quick judgment and intuition in decision making has received increasing attention in leadership and management circles in recent years thanks to Malcolm Gladwell's (2005) best-selling book *Blink*. Gladwell's narrative in the book makes a case for spontaneous decisions. The author claims that decisions based on intuition are often as good as or even better than those based on rigorous analysis. More recently, in his groundbreaking book *Thinking, Fast and Slow*, Nobel Prize winner Daniel Kahneman (2011), describes the errors and biases in our decision making and explains that there are two systems that shape our judgments and decisions: System 1 is fast, intuitive, and emotional; and System 2 is slower, more deliberative, and more logical. Making project selection decisions requires System 2 thinking. It should involve rational analysis of data using proper decision and risk management tools. The quality of decision making can be improved by understanding the biases in judgment and overcoming them. (Please see the following box.)

MAJOR BIASES IN DECISION MAKING

Comfort zone bias is the preference by people to maintain the status quo rather than try anything new or different. They are afraid to take risks because they are concerned about the possibility of failure, the possibility of increased responsibility, the idea of being held accountable for potential future problems, and a host of other reasons.

Sunk cost bias (discussed in Chapter 10) arises because many people consider what has already been spent (sunk) on a project in making future decisions. But rational decisions should not be based on sunk cost.

Supporting evidence bias is favoring what we already believe is the right choice and gathering evidence to support that choice.

Framing bias is created based on how the problem is stated or framed. Outcomes framed as gains are more favored than those framed as losses, although both outcomes are equivalent, one being the flip side of the other. For example, a new product launch decision is more likely when it is offered as a "30% chance of success," as opposed to a "70% chance of failure."

Overconfidence bias relates to our belief that we are better at estimation than we really are. For example, a majority of people believe that they are better than average drivers, although mathematically only half of them should be better. Similarly, more people rate themselves as better looking, more popular and healthier than half the population.

Anchoring bias is created when people use initial impressions as an anchor to subsequent judgments. Preliminary project cost and revenue estimates can become anchors and cloud the decisions to be made based on subsequent estimates that are more accurate. Also, dramatic events can be powerful anchors. For instance, September 11, 2001, became an anchor for many people to consider air travel too risky, although air travel has never been more safe.

Probability bias, also called probability neglect, occurs when people's emotions are intense. Due to this bias, people disregard the probability of an event happening. When an extraordinary outcome, especially a bad one, is vivid in people's minds, they tend not to think about the likelihood of it happening. A terrorist event is a good example, where people are more focused on the outcome itself rather than the probability of its occurrence.

Select "Stronger" Projects

You may select projects that are significantly more attractive and have a higher likelihood of success by incorporating elevated project acceptance thresholds. For example, higher thresholds on aggregate scores for selecting projects that generate intangible value and higher hurdle rates for selecting projects that generate financial value will increase the likelihood of more successful projects.

Create and Maintain a Balanced Portfolio

Portfolio risk can be minimized by investing in a diverse group of projects. Create proper project categories and subcategories to invest in projects of different characteristics. Consistently follow the predefined relative investment allocations between the categories to maintain a balanced portfolio.

Establish Management Contingencies

Create contingencies for "unknown" project threats at the portfolio level (discussed in Chapter 8), so that adequate funds are promptly available when such threats materialize. These contingencies may not reduce the actual threats, but they might help you manage them more effectively.

Decrease Uncertainty

Through "active learning," that is, by actively spending time and effort up front, you may reduce the uncertainty and improve the accuracy of information. Performing market research on the demand for a new product will decrease the uncertainty with sales forecasts. Prototype testing will increase confidence in new technologies. Statistical modeling can help you gain better insight into uncertainty. Peer reviews of project cost, benefit, and risk estimates by independent subject matter experts can minimize errors and omissions and increase the accuracy of the estimates.

Understand Measurements

Uncertainty, risk, and other project evaluation data consist of many estimates and measurements. The portfolio team and the decision makers must understand the characteristics of measurements as defined in the following box.

CHARACTERISTICS OF MEASUREMENTS

Accuracy vs. Precision. Accuracy represents the degree of closeness of a measurement to its true value; the closer the measurement, the more accurate it is. Precision represents the degree to which repeated measurements under the exact conditions give the same result. Figure 13-2 shows different possibilities.

Valid vs. Invalid. The concept of validity is applied in different ways. It generally refers to the degree a measurement, a piece of information, a conclusion, or an argument accurately corresponds to the real world.

Subjective vs. Objective. A measurement is considered objective if it is taken against an external standard. If a standard that is internal to the system is used, it is subjective. Measuring weight using a scale is objective and measuring weight by an experienced judge is subjective. Objective is often considered to be fact, while subjective is thought of as opinion; facts and opinions are frequently equated as true and false, respectively. This is not necessarily true. A defective scale that always weighs your travel bag 10 pounds heavier would give you an inaccurate measurement, whereas an experienced person can lift it and give you a more accurate measurement.

Quantitative vs. qualitative. Quantitative and qualitative are generally considered numeric and nonnumeric, but this is not a good criterion for differentiation. The number of M&Ms in a bag is quantitatively measured, whereas their color is qualitatively described as red, blue, or another color. But the color can also be measured quantitatively in microns using a wavelength measurement. The true difference between quantitative and qualitative measurements is that the law of addition applies to the former but not the latter. The number of M&Ms in multiple bags can be added, but the color is a description of quality that cannot be added.

Deterministic vs. Stochastic. In applying a deterministic model, an output variable is estimated using single values for each input variable. There is only one output value corresponding to a given set of single values for the input variables. In a stochastic model, a range of values (in the form of a probability distribution) is used for each input variable to represent the input's random variation. The resulting output will have a range of values represented by its own probability distribution.

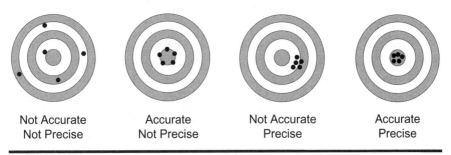

| Not Accurate | Accurate | Not Accurate | Accurate |
| Not Precise | Not Precise | Precise | Precise |

Figure 13-2   Accuracy and precision

TOOLS AND TECHNIQUES FOR UNCERTAINTY AND RISK

Several tools are available for quantifying and analyzing uncertainty and risk, but most of them are applied in evaluating projects that generate financial value. Therefore, they are limited to portfolios containing such projects.

Decision Tree Analysis

As discussed in Chapter 11, the commonly used discounted cash flow (DCF) approach for project valuation is deterministic. It does not take into account the uncertainty associated with the cash flow estimates. Nor does it consider the managerial flexibility in changing the project's course by making contingent decisions as the project goes through different phase-gates. The decision may be to continue the investment as planned; abandon, expand, or contract the project; defer the investment for a while; and so on. There is great strategic value imbedded in these decisions which can be taken advantage of, if management recognizes it and is willing to exercise the decisions. Decision tree analysis (DTA), a tool that quantifies that value, has been used for nearly half a century in the decision analysis science and has proven effective in the valuation of projects that involve contingent decisions. It can be applied effectively especially when a phase-gate process is used as part of project governance. A decision tree shows a strategic road map depicting alternative decisions, the implementation costs of the decisions, possible outcomes, and the probability and payoff of the outcomes. It involves the calculation of "expected value," also referred to as expected monetary value. It is simply the product of a cash flow (revenue or cost) and its probability of occurrence. For example, if there is a 70% probability that a revenue of $1 million will be realized, the expected value is 0.7*$1,000,000 = $700,000.

The accompanying box (page 179) gives an example of a classic DTA application. In the course of developing and commercializing a new product (or technology), you are frequently faced with two major decisions: 1) To develop or not to develop the new product at the time of initiating the project, and 2) to launch or not to launch the product, if and when the product development has turned out to be successful. Figure 13-3 shows the decision tree including these two decisions and other DTA information for the example. As illustrated in the box, EVs of each decision alternative at a given decision point starting at the far right-hand side of the decision tree are first compared. The alternative with the highest EV is selected as the right decision choice. Its EV is then folded back to the next decision point moving toward the left on the decision tree and then further EV calculations are made. Again, the alternative decision with the highest EV is

DECISION TREE ANALYSIS

TerminaTerror, Inc. (TTI) is a start-up company involved in developing technologies for homeland security applications. One of their new patent-pending products is an early warning system that detects poison which may have been introduced by terrorists into municipal drinking water supplies and distribution systems. The technical effectiveness of the product has to be proven first through development effort, which is expected to cost $1 million and take one year. Successful development will be followed by commercialization of the technology, which is estimated to take an additional year and cost $2 million. Estimates also show a project payoff of $15 million over the project horizon. Although this payoff is attractive compared to the investment costs, TTI is not certain about the technical and commercial success of the project, because the success probabilities are estimated to be 0.5 and 0.7, respectively. Figure 13-3 presents the decision tree for this scenario. The expected value calculations and the decision choices are summarized in Table 13-1. (For the sake of simplicity and illustration purposes, discounting of cash flows is ignored.)

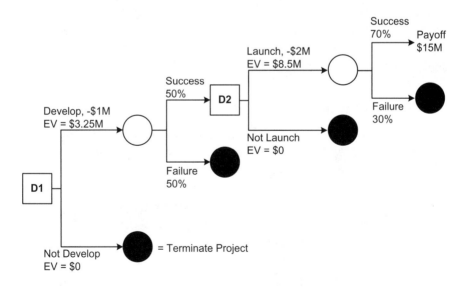

EV = Expected Value

Figure 13-3   Decision tree

Table 13-1   Decisions tree calculations

Decision Point	Alternatives	Expected Value Calculations	Total Expected Value	Decision Choice
D2	Launch	$15M(0.7) + $0M(0.3) − $2M	$8.5M	Launch
	Not Launch	$0	$0	
D1	Develop	$8.5M(0.5) + $0M(0.5) − $1M	$3.25M	Develop
	Not Develop	$0	$0	

selected. When multiple contingent decisions are available, the EVs are rolled sequentially all the way back to the first decision point to make the go/no-go decision at the beginning of the project. For the example in the box, the initial decision would be to develop the product ("go"), because its EV is higher than the "no-go" decision's EV. If the product development is pursued and proven successful one year from now, the decision will then be to launch the product, unless the most current data at that time shows otherwise.

By aggregating the EVs of the component projects, a portfolio EV can be obtained. A comparison of the EV with the deterministic NPV indicates the collective risk associated with the component projects of the portfolio. EV translates to a risk-adjusted value based on the success/failure probabilities of future contingent decisions, as opposed to the deterministic value that does not take into consideration the uncertainty.

Scenario Analysis

Using the DTA results, you can also gain further insight by considering the best, worst, and most likely case scenarios. Best case represents the scenario where only the best outcomes are experienced and worst case represents the scenario with only the worst outcomes using the rational decisions shown by the DTA. For the example in the box, the best case is where both product development and commercialization efforts are successful, while the worst case involves successful development followed by commercial failure. The most likely case is represented by the project's EV today.

- Best case = $12 M (– $1M – $2M + $15 M)
- Worst case = – $3M (– $1M – $2M)
- Most likely case = $3.25M

The advantage of the scenario analysis is that it gives you a perspective on the relative upside and downside to the project. If the most likely EV is close to the best case and is significantly higher than the worst case, there is an excellent chance of success and vice versa. This analysis provides a simple summary of the decision tree calculations that management can easily understand.

Sensitivity Analysis

Any financial estimates related to the project business case are influenced by the input variables. For example, NPV is impacted by the estimated project cost, sales revenue, cost of sales, the discount factor, etc. In fact, each one of these variables, in turn, is impacted by other variables. For instance, sales revenue is influenced by selling price, sales volume, and profit margin. Among the numerous input variables, there may be just a few that have the highest impact on the output variable you are estimating. By identifying such variables, you can gain a better understanding of a project's viability. You can increase project viability through proactive measures by identifying the most important inputs as shown below:

- **One-dimensional sensitivity analysis.** You may perform a simple one-dimensional analysis, where you change one of the input variables by plus or minus x%, and observe the impact on the output variable.
- **Multidimensional sensitivity analysis.** This is an extension of the one-dimensional analysis. It involves studying the effect of a few selected important input variables on the output. The results are generally shown in the form of a tornado diagram. For the DCF example presented in Appendix A, a sensitivity analysis is performed, where the effect of peak annual revenue, investment cost, the discount rate, and peak annual cost are displayed in the form of a tornado as shown in Figure 13-4. Each "base case" input variable is adjusted by +/– 20% to examine the impact on the base case NPV of $3.23 million, as shown in the appendix.

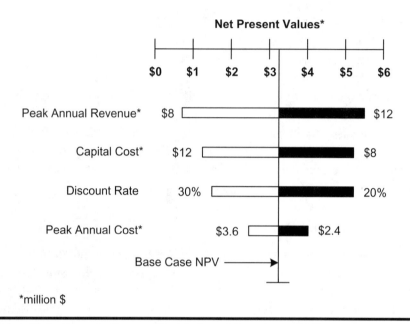

Figure 13-4   Tornado diagram (Kodukula and Papudesu, 2006)

Monte Carlo Simulation

Project financial estimates (cost, benefit, NPV, etc.) are deterministic. They represent the "base case" deterministic scenario that utilizes one set of input variables resulting in one value of the output variable. However, each input has its own uncertainty and may vary with its own probability distribution. Using the Monte Carlo technique—named after the famous gambling city in Monaco—you can account for all the possible values of each input variable, so that you can estimate the probability distribution of the output variable. For example, applying this technique to NPV, it will involve the simulation of thousands of possible project scenarios, calculation of the project NPV for each scenario using the DCF method, and analyzing the probability distribution of the NPV results. Figure 13-5A is an example of the "point" probability distribution (called the probability distribution function) of a project's NPV, and Figure 13-5B is the corresponding cumulative probability distribution function. The latter figure shows that the probability of the project's NPV being greater than zero is 80%. Such information is extremely valuable in not only evaluating the merit of a given project, but in comparing it with competing projects (especially with the same or similar NPV) in a portfolio.

A. Probability Distribution

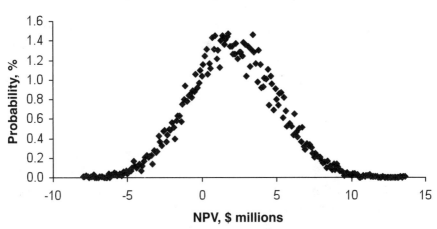

B. Cumulative Probability Distribution

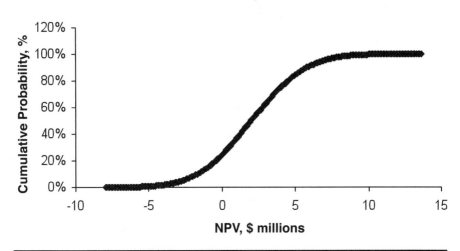

Figure 13-5 Monte Carlo simulation—Probability curves (Kodukula and Papudesu, 2006)

Real Options Analysis

Real options analysis (ROA), discussed in Chapter 11, is a relatively new, novel technique to quantify the real option value of a project. It accounts for future uncertainty related to project success and quantifies the value of management's flexibility in changing the project course. This flexibility is created by the availability of contingent decisions such as termination, continuation, contraction, expansion, or delay of the project. Rather than assuming a fixed path as in the case of NPV, ROA accounts for the value of the future contingent decisions that management would presumably exercise as the project uncertainty is cleared. For example, uncertainty may be cleared simply by the passage of time or by deliberate action by management such as technology testing, product introduction on a small scale, or an initial market survey. ROA is based on the Nobel Prize winning financial options valuation framework developed by three MIT economists in 1973, namely, Fisher Black, Myron Scholes, and Robert Merton. While being highly complex in theory, ROA accounts for uncertainty, considers managerial flexibility, builds on NPV and decision trees, and can differentiate projects with similar NPV. You may refer to the book by Kodukula and Papudesu (2006) for detailed calculations involving how to apply the ROA technique for project valuation.

14

EARNED VALUE
MANAGEMENT

When I started teaching and speaking on project management in 1995—after more than 10 years of going to the "School of Hard Knocks"—there was hardly anybody in my audience that had heard of earned value management (EVM). About five years into my new career, I began to notice an increasing number of people being aware of the technique, but there were just a few practitioners. Today almost everybody I come across in the profession has heard of EVM, and about half of them have been exposed to the framework, while about 10% have actually used it. My observations by no means are based on a scientific study, but the trend is real. Thanks to the Project Management Institute (PMI®) and its PMP® certification test that includes many EVM related questions, the technique has recently gained tremendous visibility.

EVM is a project performance monitoring and controlling technique that provides an objective evaluation of a project's cost and schedule status to date and forecasts its future performance. It helps you quantify the cost and schedule variance compared to the plan. At the portfolio level, it is a quantitative tool to compare the health of different projects with the same metrics. It also provides you with an objective assessment of the cost performance of the portfolio as a whole. EVM offers the objectivity the project portfolio management process seeks in order to make the go/no-go decisions more rational.

Numerous books, chapters, and articles have been published on EVM including PMI's second and latest edition of *Practice Standard for Earned Value Management* (PMI, 2011). These works address not only the theory but also the application and many of the nuances associated with the technique. My intention in this chapter is not to delve into details, but to explain how EVM can be applied at the portfolio level to evaluate an individual project status to facilitate go/no-go decisions and gauge the cost performance of the portfolio as a whole. I fear that digging right into the application aspects may confuse the reader without first reviewing a few basics. Therefore, my objective for the earlier sections of this chapter is to provide a quick history and background and elucidate the conceptual framework of EVM. In the later sections, I will demonstrate its application to a single project as an example. I will illustrate how a project's cost and schedule performance to date can be evaluated and a forecast made on future budget requirements. Towards the end of the chapter, I will show how EVM can help you with a broader view of multiple projects in a portfolio and evaluate the cost performance of the portfolio as a whole and forecast its future budget needs.

BACKGROUND

EVM was first introduced by the U.S. Department of Defense in 1967. Since then the U.S. government has mandated its use on major defense acquisition projects. The defense industry has successfully employed EVM for more than four decades. PMI has been promoting it for more than 20 years and issued the first edition of *Practice Standard for Earned Value Management* in 2004. However, its use in the commercial sector has been slow for many reasons. First, most organizations have not reached the minimum level of project management maturity needed for its effective use. Second, they are not willing to spend the resources to build and maintain the required project management information systems infrastructure that is especially capable of collecting the "true" actual costs incurred on project tasks. Third, a few that attempted to implement the technique failed—for reasons that had nothing to do with the technique's effectiveness—and simply gave up. And finally, many practitioners are intimidated by the formulas and calculations involved and are not too eager to embrace the technique. As more organizations are reaching higher project management maturity levels and increasingly sophisticated project information management systems are becoming available, EVM is slowly catching on. Most of today's advanced project and portfolio planning software tools have EVM modules that can generate EVM reports for easy review and analysis.

At the core, EVM compares the actual cost of work completed with the budgeted cost for that work to evaluate the cost status, and the value of actual work performed with the value of planned work to determine the schedule status. The future is predicted based on the actual performance to date and the expected future project conditions. The conceptual framework of EVM is intuitive and based on sound management principles. The technique is not project- or industry-specific, and it can be applied universally because of its robust conceptual foundation. The metrics are the same whether you are applying them to a one thousand dollar task, a one million dollar project, a one billion dollar program, or a portfolio consisting of any of these components. Once you have the detailed EVM data at the desired work breakdown structure (WBS) (preferably "work package") level of each project, you can roll it up to the individual project and then to the portfolio level to evaluate the cost and schedule performance of each of the component projects as well as the entire portfolio. The key EVM metrics will help you determine the cost variance and the cost efficiency of the portfolio as a whole at any given time. The metrics will also show how much you need to budget in the future to complete all the component projects. EVM shows you the schedule efficiency of the ongoing projects as an aggregate in completing the planned work within the entire portfolio. Tracking the cost and schedule efficiency over time gives you an indication of the historical portfolio performance.

EVM FOUNDATION: PROJECT BASELINES

A baseline is a reference plan against which you compare a project's actual performance. The comparison reveals whether the project is performing on target or deviating from the plan. If there is significant and unacceptable deviation, its cause may be investigated and proper corrective action taken. EVM's foundation consists of scope, time, and cost baselines. The proven tools for these, respectively, are the WBS, Gantt chart, and the bottom-up cost estimate, which are discussed below.

Work Breakdown Structure

The WBS is the foundation of any project plan. It is a tool that outlines all the tasks that must be performed in order to complete the project. The WBS basically creates a list of things to do with a structure built around them. It is a hierarchical decomposition of the project's scope of work into increasingly smaller components of work. It breaks the project down to manageable "chunks." Each chunk is a self-contained unit with a clearly defined work output that can be assigned to an individual, a small team, or can be contracted out. Whatever work is included on the WBS is considered to be within the project's scope of work. If it is not on the WBS, it is outside the scope. The tasks at the bottommost level of the WBS, referred to as "work packages," are critical components of project planning. Schedule, cost, and resource estimates are made on the work packages as part of the project plan. Resources are assigned to work packages where the actual work is performed. A WBS schematic is shown in Figure 14-1 for Project Delta, a hypothetical case

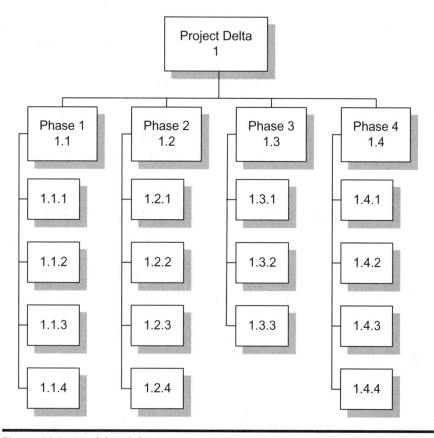

Figure 14-1　Work breakdown structure—Project Delta

example used to illustrate EVM in this chapter. It shows only three levels (project, phase, work package), but more levels may be necessary depending on the project size. When a phase-gate process is used to manage the project as part of a portfolio, the WBS lends itself to breaking down the project into phases at the second level, as is shown in Figure 14-1.

Gantt Chart

The Gantt chart, also called a bar chart, is probably the most universal project scheduling tool. Named after its inventor Henry Gantt, the chart simply shows the project work packages or tasks and their corresponding timelines along the time axis. Once the WBS is built, you can estimate durations for the work packages, define the workflow with appropriate predecessor/successor dependencies of the work packages and develop a project schedule using a Gantt chart. A common practice is to use a planning tool such as Microsoft's Project to create the chart. However, it may be difficult to ensure that all the task dependencies have been accurately accounted for with this approach. If they are not, the tool may calculate an incorrect project duration that is shorter than what it should be. A better practice is to create a "network diagram" first and ensure that all the task dependencies are accurately established. (Irrespective of whether you use a Gantt chart or a network diagram to determine your project duration, the key is to confirm that all the task dependencies have been accurately identified.)

A network diagram shows the sequence in which you plan to perform the work packages on the WBS. (If you prefer to make it more detailed, you may break down the work packages into smaller activities and build the network using those activities.) By using a network diagram, you can more easily ensure that the task predecessor and successor relationships are logically correct. You can also make sure that there are no "hanging" tasks—tasks without at least one predecessor and one successor—which otherwise could create an incorrect "critical path" and give you a wrong project duration estimate. As an example, Figure 14-2 shows a network diagram developed for Project Delta. You can identify the critical path, which is the longest path on the network and represents the project duration. A path includes successive tasks on the network from start to finish following from the predecessor to the next successor. For Project Delta, the critical path and the tasks on that path, called critical tasks, are highlighted in Figure 14-2. The project duration for Project Delta is 75 workdays (or 15 weeks). The critical path is so named, because it is considered "critical" from the schedule standpoint. A delay on any

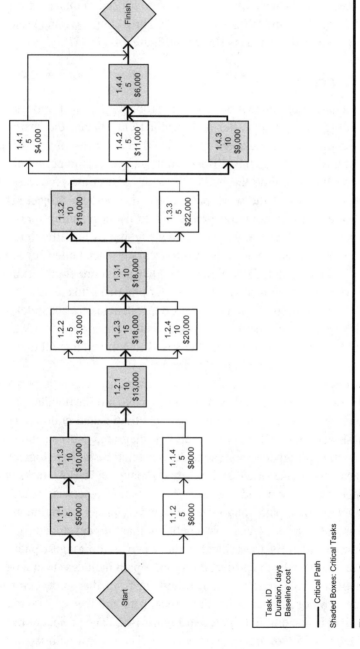

Task ID
Duration, days
Baseline cost

—— Critical Path

Shaded Boxes: Critical Tasks

Figure 14-2   Network diagram—Project Delta

task on that path will result in a project delay—unless the future plan is modified to prevent the project delay. For example, if Task 1.1.3 on Project Delta's critical path takes longer than the expected 10 days and no action is taken to compress the future schedule, the project will be delayed. On the other hand, Task 1.1.4, which is not on the critical path, can be delayed up to a maximum of five days without impacting the project finish date. The amount of time a task can be delayed (from its earliest possible finish date) without impacting the project finish date is called float or slack. Therefore, Task 1.1.4 has a float of five days. By definition, critical tasks have zero or the least float.

You may need to go through a few iterations of the network diagram until it meets your schedule needs and constraints. Once the network diagram is ready, you can allocate the required resources to the work packages. This allocation is normally made in a way to achieve optimum resource utilization by taking advantage of the float of the noncritical tasks, while making sure that the project will be completed on time. You may finalize the schedule in the form of a Gantt chart showing the work packages and the corresponding timelines (Figure 14-3). A Gantt chart is simpler and easier to understand and, therefore, more commonly used to show the schedule baseline than the network diagram.

Bottom-Up Cost Estimate

The bottom-up cost estimate, as the name implies, starts with the estimation of costs at the work package level of the WBS, that is, the bottom of the WBS. You may estimate the detailed costs of each work package and roll them up to the next higher level of the WBS and all the way up to the project level. The costs should include the internal material and labor costs as well as the subcontractor costs. The labor costs are estimated based on person hours for different resource types (or specific resources, if they have already been identified) needed to complete each work package and their corresponding unit rates. In many organizations, however, the internal labor costs are not included as part of the project budget. But EVM is most effective when the labor costs are also accounted for. (If your organization does not monitor and track human resource costs on projects, it is essential that you develop a baseline for the human resources using estimates on their required labor effort [hours] at the work package level. You can apply the EVM technique using labor hours instead of monetary units.)

Table 14-1 presents a bottom-up cost estimate for Project Delta. It shows the work package costs as well as the rolled up phase and project costs. These costs include material, internal labor, and external contracting costs.

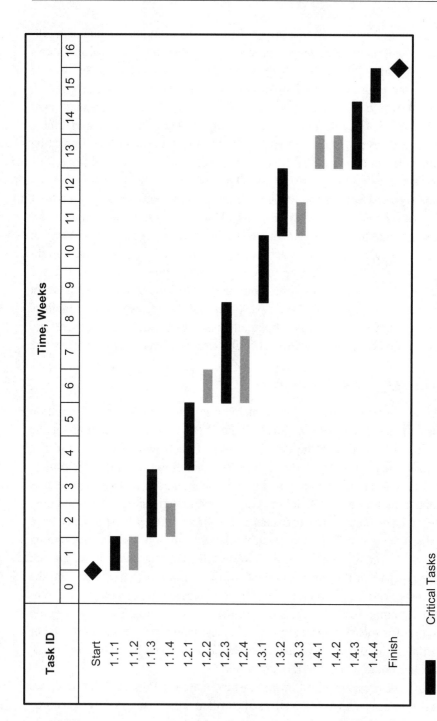

Figure 14-3   Gantt chart—Project Delta

Table 14-1 Bottom-up cost estimate—Project Delta

Project/Phase	WBS Code			Cost Estimate		
Project Delta	1					$182,000
Phase 1	1.1			$29,000		
		1.1.1	$5,000			
		1.1.2	$6,000			
		1.1.3	$10,000			
		1.1.4	$8,000			
Phase 2	1.2			$64,000		
		1.2.1	$13,000			
		1.2.2	$13,000			
		1.2.3	$18,000			
		1.2.4	$20,000			
Phase 3	1.3			$59,000		
		1.3.1	$18,000			
		1.3.2	$19,000			
		1.3.3	$22,000			
Phase 4	1.4			$30,000		
		1.4.1	$4,000			
		1.4.2	$11,000			
		1.4.3	$9,000			
		1.4.4	$6,000			

(To keep the example simple for illustration purposes, it is assumed that the estimates include project management costs, presumably taken as x percent of the total cost of each task.) The total budget needed for this project is $182,000, which is called the budget at completion (BAC).

Contingencies

Project and portfolio budgets should include contingencies to account for cost impacts due to risks that may materialize. As discussed in Chapter 8, guidelines to estimate these contingencies must be provided as part of the portfolio design. Project contingency is meant for threats that have been identified and analyzed by the project team. Management contingency held at the portfolio level is for unidentified risks. Different approaches exist depending upon organizational preferences, as to how the two contingencies are estimated, tracked, and managed. Typically the project contingency is not part of the BAC, but is under the project manager's control, whereas the other is held at the portfolio level under management's control. Irrespective of the approach, the contingencies should be tracked and managed just as any other cost element of the project budget.

Performance Measurement Baseline

Once the WBS, Gantt chart, and the bottom-up cost estimate are approved by the project sponsor or the customer, they become the baselines for the project's scope, time, and cost, respectively. It is paramount that the three baselines are in balance. It means that for a given scope of work, an adequate amount of time and budget (including financial and labor resources) must be available. The individual baselines can be integrated into a time-based project budget as shown in Table 14-2 for Project Delta. A cumulative cost curve, also known as the performance measurement baseline (PMB) (Figure 14-4), can be developed from this budget information. The curve shows how the project budget is expected to be spent from its start to the finish. The PMB serves as the reference for comparing the actual progress and evaluating the project's cost and schedule performance. The PMB should not change as long as the scope, time, and cost baselines do not. If any one of the individual baselines changes, appropriate changes to the other two must be made to keep the balance. Accordingly, the PMB should be revised as well. The individual baselines and the PMB form the foundation for EVM analysis.

Variance from Baselines

One of the primary objectives of the EVM method is to gauge a project's health by comparing the actual performance with the baselines. It helps you determine if the project is on plan or showing variance. If there is variance, you may take appropriate action, especially when it is not acceptable. As discussed in Chapter 8, it is important to specify in advance as part of the portfolio design how much project and portfolio variances are acceptable for cost and schedule, particularly when they are negative. The limits of acceptance, referred to as variance thresholds or tolerance limits, are generally expressed as +/– x% deviation from the baselines. The thresholds should be primarily a function of the accuracy range of the baseline estimates of project activities. For example, if the cost estimates have a +/– 5% accuracy, it makes sense to

Table 14-2   Time-based budget—Project Delta

WBS Code	Week							
	1	2	3	4	5	6	7	8
1.1.1	$5,000							
1.1.2	$6,000							
1.1.3		$5,000	$5,000					
1.1.4		$8,000						
1.2.1				$6,500	$6,500	$13,000		
1.2.2						$6,000	$6,000	$6,000
1.2.3						$10,000	$10,000	
1.2.4								
1.3.1								
1.3.2								
1.3.3								
1.4.1								
1.4.2								
1.4.3								
1.4.4								
Total	$11,000	$13,000	$5,000	$6,500	$6,500	$29,000	$16,000	$6,000
Cumulative	$11,000	$24,000	$29,000	$35,500	$42,000	$71,000	$87,000	$93,000

WBS Code	Week							
	9	10	11	12	13	14	15	
1.1.1								
1.1.2								
1.1.3								
1.1.4								
1.2.1								
1.2.2								
1.2.3								
1.2.4	$9,000	$9,000						
1.3.1			$9,500	$9,500				
1.3.2			$22,000					
1.3.3					$4,000			
1.4.1					$11,000			
1.4.2					$4,500			
1.4.3						$4,500		
1.4.4							$6,000	
Total	$9,000	$9,000	$31,500	$9,500	$19,500	$4,500	$6,000	
Cumulative	$102,000	$111,000	$142,500	$152,000	$171,500	$176,000	$182,000	

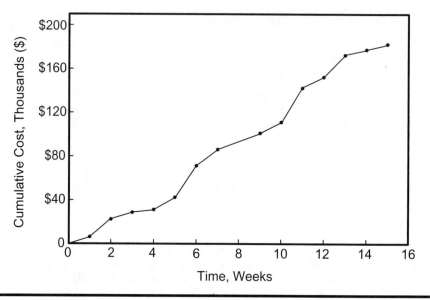

Figure 14-4   Performance measurement baseline—Project Delta

use the same or a wider range as your threshold. The range also depends on your organizational tolerance, the nature of the projects, whether a project is implemented for an internal or an external client, and other reasons. In many professional service firms, no negative variance is tolerated on projects performed for external clients. The reason is that a negative schedule variance may be unacceptable to or even penalized by their clients. Negative cost variance may decrease the profit for the firms and even yield losses, depending upon the contracting terms. For internal projects, especially in the research and development (R&D) arena, some companies may allow up to a 15% or even greater negative cost variance but not as much negative schedule variance. Variance thresholds, if exceeded, should trigger further action by the project manager and team. This action may involve investigation of reasons for the variance and follow-up action, if necessary. If a negative cost variance exists at approximately the 20% project completion mark, it has been shown that it is unlikely that the project will be completed under budget. This can be a powerful guideline or rule of thumb to evaluate the project health in making a go/no-go decision. Even when the variance is in the positive territory, you may want to understand the reasons in order to leverage any lessons learned for the remainder of the project or other current and future projects in the portfolio.

LEVEL OF DETAIL IN PLANNING

If the entire scope of a project is well-defined to begin with, your baseline estimates can be more detailed and realistic. The EVM technique will be most effective with such estimates, but obtaining detailed estimates for the entire project from start to finish may sometimes be difficult. The scope may not be clear at the start of the project, or it may need to be defined, as the project unfolds. The scope of the later phases of the project may be dependent on the results of the earlier ones. The customer may learn more about the project requirements with the progression of time. In these scenarios, detailed baselines may be developed for phase after phase using the "rolling wave" planning described in more detail in the following box. Using this technique, the scope is progressively elaborated from one phase to the next; hence another name for this technique is "progressive elaboration." The immediate next phase of the project is planned in detail, while subsequent phases are planned at a lower level of detail. EVM can be applied for each phase at a time where the same level of planning detail is used for all the baselines.

ROLLING WAVE PLANNING

You or your project sponsor may want to know at the start of a project exactly how much it costs, how many resources it will need, and how long it will take to complete. But it may not be possible to obtain that information for certain projects. For instance, the scope of the later phases of a project may depend on the results from the earlier ones, as in some R&D projects. A proven practice, "rolling wave" planning helps you plan such uncertain projects in waves through an iterative process. As you are planning for a new project, the first phase of the project is closer to the "shore" and more clearly visible. Therefore, you develop detailed estimates for this phase. For the distant later phases, you may create high-level plans with lesser detail. This is generally referred to as 30,000 feet level planning with an airplane view—not to mix metaphors. At this level the view or the scope is wide and fuzzy, and accordingly the plans are broad and preliminary. As the "waves" approach the shore (that is, as you near the completion of one phase with the next phase about to begin), you descend from the airplane view to the ground view, which is clear but narrow. Therefore, the plans will be focused on discreet portions of work and detail. The appropriate time for turning to the next level of greater detail is when you transition from one phase to the next going through the phase-gate process.

There are no hard and fast rules as to how many levels of detail are necessary. The simple guideline is however many it takes. Two levels are typical and are called preliminary and detailed. Table 14-3 provides guidance on differentiating preliminary vs. detailed estimates for scope, schedule, resources, and cost. The difference between the preliminary and detailed definition of scope is related to the number of WBS levels. More levels reflect a detailed scope definition from which you can derive detailed estimates of other components. The preliminary schedule, resource, and cost estimates are based on higher-level WBS tasks (for example, one level above the work package level), while the detailed estimates are on the work packages.

Figure 14-5 illustrates the rolling wave planning for a phase-gate-based project. It shows how you first begin with preliminary estimates and sharpen them with a higher level of detail, as you go from one phase to the next. The rolling wave planning fits well with the phase-gate process that is integral to portfolio management, where the decisions are made from phase to phase. In the initiation phase of the project, you may start with preliminary estimates. You do not need to commit the budget and all the resources required for the whole project at this time. You may approve only the next phase of the project for which you would have detailed estimates. Subsequently, you will follow the same process from phase to phase. Having the detailed estimate for the next immediate phase helps you with planning the budgets and resources more effectively for the immediate future. A standardized rolling wave method across all "uncertain" projects in the portfolio will create a uniform level of accuracy for the estimates. To keep it consistent for any given phase, you should apply the same level of detail in developing the baselines. EVM will be most effective when all the estimates are at the same level of accuracy. You should be cautious in applying the current performance EVM metrics to forecast performance in future phases that have estimates at a lower accuracy level and involve an intrinsically different nature of work.

Table 14-3   Preliminary and detailed estimates

	Preliminary	Detailed
Scope	WBS - less levels (e.g., 2 or 3)	WBS - more levels (e.g., 3 or 4)
Time*	Milestones (Milestone chart)	Task durations (Network diagram, Gantt chart)
Resources*	FTEs, Resource types	Labor effort, Specific resources
Cost*	+25%/−20%	+10%/−5%

*Preliminary estimates are based on preliminary scope and detailed ones on detailed scope.

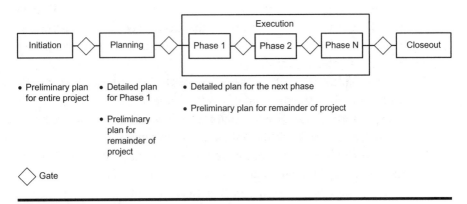

Figure 14-5   Rolling wave planning

EARNED VALUE MANAGEMENT BUILDING BLOCKS

There are four parameters that form the building blocks of the EVM method: planned value, budget at completion, actual cost, and earned value. The data for these parameters is collected at regular intervals, preferably weekly, at the work package level. These task parameters are then aggregated up to the phase and project levels. By adding the respective parameters of individual projects in a portfolio, you can obtain the portfolio parameters. When EVM data is collected at the work package level, you can analyze the cost and schedule performance not only at that level, but also at the phase, project, and portfolio levels. It makes the EVM analysis more accurate and meaningful and gives you a better control over project costs and schedule.

1. **Planned Value (PV).** It is the value of the work planned or scheduled to date (or up to a reference point of time, known as the "data date"). It is the same as the budgeted cost of work scheduled up to the data date. The project PV is shown as the cumulative cost curve or the PMB.

2. **Budget at Completion (BAC).** It is the total planned budget for a given amount of work. For a task, it is called Task BAC. For a project, it is simply referred to as BAC. It is the summation of budgeted costs of all the work packages. It is also the same as the PV at the time of project completion or at the end of the cumulative cost curve.

3. **Actual Cost (AC).** It is the actual cost of work completed by the data date. It is how much you paid for the work you have completed. It is measured as the material, sub-contractor, and internal human resource expenses incurred.

4. **Earned Value (EV).** It is the value of the work performed or the value earned by the data date. It is the same as the budgeted cost of work performed. EV is calculated for each work package as the product of the Task BAC (obtained from the bottom-up baseline cost estimates) and its percent completion. For example, if the Task BAC is $200 and it is 70% completed by today, the current EV is: $200*0.70 = $140. There are other approaches to calculating EV, which are described in more detail in the PMI's EVM standard (PMI, 2011) and other references.

The building blocks of EVM defined above are typically expressed in terms of monetary units (e.g., dollars). They can also be expressed in resource units, as resource hours. This will be particularly applicable on projects that are highly resource intensive (e.g., R&D projects), where resources are managed more closely than the monetary costs.

Example

Let's continue to use the Project Delta example. Let's say that after completing the project planning phase, you started implementing the project activities and three weeks have passed. By today you have completed 100% of all Phase 1 tasks and 50% of Task 1.2.1 in Phase 2. Table 14-4 presents the EVM building blocks data for each task from which project EVM metrics are calculated as follows:

Table 14-4   EVM Data: Project Delta

WBS Code	Task BAC	PV	% Completion	AC	EV	CV	%CV	CPI	SV	%SV*	SPI*
1.1.1	$5,000	$5,000	100%	$5,500	$5,000	-$500	-10%	0.91	$0	0%	1
1.1.2	$6,000	$6,000	100%	$5,900	$6,000	$100	2%	1.02	$0	0%	1
1.1.3	$10,000	$10,000	100%	$11,000	$10,000	-$1,000	-10%	0.91	$0	0%	1
1.1.4	$8,000	$8,000	100%	$8,300	$8,000	-$300	-4%	0.96	$0	0%	1
1.2.1	$13,000	$0	50%	$6,400	$6,500	$100	2%	1.02	$6,500	—	—
1.2.2	$13,000	$0	0%								
1.2.3	$18,000	$0	0%								
1.2.4	$20,000	$0	0%								
1.3.1	$18,000	$0	0%								
1.3.2	$19,000	$0	0%								
1.3.3	$22,000	$0	0%								
1.4.1	$4,000	$0	0%								
1.4.2	$11,000	$0	0%								
1.4.3	$9,000	$0	0%								
1.4.4	$6,000	$0	0%								
Total Project	$182,000	$29,000		$37,100	$35,500	-$1,600	-5%	0.96	$6,500	22%	1.22

*Cannot be estimated for Task 1.2.1, because PV in the denominator is $0.

1. **BAC:** The BAC or the total planned budget for the project, which is the sum of the baseline cost estimates of all the work packages, is $182,000.
2. **PV:** According to the schedule baseline, the planned work by today consists of completion of all Phase 1 tasks; therefore, the PV or the budgeted cost of work scheduled is the total of all the Phase 1 Task BACs, that is, $29,000.
3. **AC:** The AC of work completed is given as $37,100. This is the cost incurred in completing 100% of Phase 1 tasks and 50% of Task 1.2.1 in Phase 2.
4. **EV:** The EV or the budgeted cost of work performed is the sum of all the Task BACs in Phase 1 ($29,000) and 50% of the budgeted cost of Task 1.2.1 (50%*$13,000 = $6,500), which is $35,500.

CURRENT PROJECT PERFORMANCE INDICATORS

Project performance evaluation involves comparison of the actual performance to date with the baselines. The time and cost estimates reflected in the baselines are presumably accurate, and any significant deviations from them (for example, those exceeding the predefined +/− x% tolerance limits) warrant investigation and possible corrective action. The key project performance indicators related to cost and schedule can be calculated using the formulas provided in Table 14-5 and are briefly explained below:

1. **Cost Variance (CV).** CV is the difference between EV and AC, or the budgeted cost of work performed and the actual cost of work performed up to the data date. It shows whether you have spent more, less, or the same as you budgeted for the work completed by the data date. A positive variance means you are under cost and a negative one denotes an overrun compared to the cost baseline.
2. **% Cost Variance (%CV).** Whereas the variance shows the magnitude in monetary units (say, dollars) of cost deviation from the baseline, % variance is relative. It is a metric to measure the performance efficiency. %CV is the cost variance divided by the earned value. Depending upon CV, %CV can be either positive or negative.

Table 14-5 Formulas for EVM performance indicators

Performance Indicators	Abbreviation	Formula
Current Performance		
Cost Variance	CV	EV – AC
% Cost Variance	%CV	%(CV/EV)
Cost Performance Index	CPI	EV/AC
Schedule Variance	SV	EV – PV
% Schedule Variance	%SV	%(SV/PV)
Schedule Performance Index	SPI	EV/PV
% Completion	—	EV/BAC
Future Performance		
Estimate to Complete*	ETC	—
Estimate at Completion	EAC	ETC + AC
Variance at Completion	VAC	BAC – EAC
%Variance at Completion	%VAC	%(VAC/BAC)

*ETC formulas are provided in Table 14-6.

3. **Cost Performance Index (CPI).** CPI, the ratio of EV to AC, is another indicator for cost performance efficiency. It represents the "bang for the buck." It is the value that you have earned for the money you have spent. A CPI of greater than 1.0 means that you have received higher value for the money you have spent and you are under baseline cost. A CPI of less than 1.0 indicates that you have received lower value and you have exceeded the baseline cost.

4. **Schedule Variance (SV).** Most of us are used to expressing schedule variance in terms of time units, for instance, days or weeks. But the EVM measures it in monetary units. SV is the difference between EV and PV or the budgeted cost of work performed and the budgeted cost of work scheduled to date. A positive variance means that you are ahead of schedule compared to the baseline and a negative one denotes schedule slippage. SV indicates the value, in monetary units, of work that you are supposed to have completed, but have not completed as of today. SV does not reveal the project's critical path status but considers the combined schedule performance of both critical and noncritical tasks. It is possible that the overall SV may be positive, while the critical path is delayed giving us the false illusion of being ahead of schedule. To determine whether the project is on

track with the critical path, you may determine the SV on the critical path tasks only. It will be the difference between EV and PV of the critical tasks. A positive variance on the critical path means that the project will be completed ahead of time, as long as the remainder of the project performs according to the plan. On the other hand, a negative variance denotes a delay of the project's finish date, unless necessary changes are made to bring the project back on track.

5. **% Schedule Variance (%SV).** %SV is a metric for schedule performance efficiency. It is the ratio of SV to PV. The positive and negative variances are reflected in the same fashion in the percentage metric also. %SV shows the schedule variance compared to the budgeted cost of work scheduled by the data date. Once the project is complete, SV will be shown as zero, even if the finish date has been delayed.

6. **Schedule Performance Index (SPI).** SPI is another indicator of schedule performance efficiency. It is the ratio of EV to PV, or the budgeted cost of work performed to the budgeted cost of work scheduled. An SPI of greater than 1.0 means you have performed more work than you have scheduled. An SPI of less than 1.0 means you have performed less work than you have scheduled. For example, an SPI of 0.80 means that you have performed only 80 units of work as opposed to the 100 units that you have scheduled up to the data date. Once the project is complete and past its scheduled completion date, its SPI will be 1.0, even if the project finish date has slipped.

7. **Percent Completion.** Task % completion information is collected from the project team members, but the % completion for the entire project can be calculated by comparing the budgeted cost of work performed by the data date, with the project's total baseline cost. It is obtained by dividing EV by the project BAC.

Example

Continuing on with the same example, CV for Project Delta as of today is −$1,600 (= $35,500 − $37,100), as shown in Table 14-4. It means there is an overrun of $1,600 at this time compared to the baseline cost. %CV is −5% (= 100*(−$1,600/$35,500)) indicating that there is a $5 overrun on every $100 worth of work completed. The CPI is 0.96 (= $35,500/$37,100) indicating that the organization has received only 96 cents for every dollar spent by the data date. (There may be minor discrepancies between % variance and the performance index due to rounding off errors in the calculations.) Despite the negative variance, it does not mean at this point that the project will not have enough funds to cover the overrun to date. You need to track the negative variance vs. the project contingency throughout the project life cycle. At project completion, if the variance exceeds the contingency, you would not have enough funds. It may have to be absorbed by the portfolio contingency or other sources.

The SV, %SV, and SPI for Project Delta are: \$6,500 (= \$35,500 − \$29,000), 22% (= 100*(\$6,500/\$29,000)), and 1.22 (= \$35,500/\$29,000), respectively. It means that you are ahead of schedule and have completed an extra \$6,500 worth of work that is not in the plan as of today. It indicates that you have performed 22% more work than scheduled to date. This does not necessarily mean that you are ahead on the critical path and therefore, will finish the project early. You can, however, determine this by drilling further down to the task level to examine where the variance has occurred. Such an examination will reveal that Task 1.2.1, which is on the critical path but not part of the PV at this point, has been 50% completed. Thus, it indicates that if the rest of the project goes according to plan, the project will be completed ahead of time. If you assume that the effort involved is uniformly spread out during the 10 days of Task 1.2.1's duration, it appears that you will complete the project five days early,

While the data date EVM information provides you with a snapshot of the project status at a given time, it is important to follow the trends to gauge the overall health of the project. Figure 14-6 is a schematic showing the trends of key EVM metrics and their relationships. (This figure reflects the approach where the project contingency is not part of the BAC.)

FUTURE PROJECT PERFORMANCE INDICATORS

The EVM technique also helps you forecast the future budget and resource needs of a project. The required budget to complete the remainder of an ongoing project, referred to as the estimate to complete (ETC), is a key future performance estimator. It depends on the project's expected cost performance from today until its completion. The estimate will be dependent on

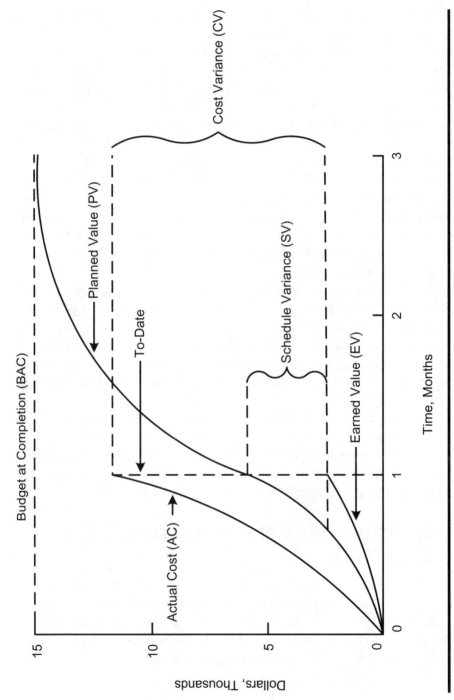

Figure 14-6 Earned value management relationships

the assumptions you need to make to represent the future project conditions. The following scenarios may apply:

1. The project will continue until the end at the same level of performance as it is today. It means that the future CPI for the remainder of the project will be the same as the current CPI.
2. Irrespective of the project performance to date or the current CPI, the cost performance during the remainder of the project will be exactly on track with the baseline plan. It means that the expected future CPI for the remainder of the project is 1.0.
3. Irrespective of past performance, you must finish the project at or under the current BAC.
4. None of the three previous scenarios is applicable. The original baseline estimates have turned out to be flawed, or the assumptions behind them are no longer relevant. Therefore, you need to develop a new cost estimate for the work remaining on the project.

Looking down the remaining project life cycle, you must identify the likely future conditions and make appropriate assumptions in estimating the new ETCs. You may assume the same scenario for the rest of the project or different scenarios for different phases/tasks of the project. Scenario 1 is more likely when future project activities are similar to past activities. For instance, if you are in the early stages of a design phase, it is highly probable that the performance trend to date may continue through the rest of that phase. But the same trend may not apply to another future phase such as testing. Scenario 2 may be more applicable for the testing phase in this case. (As mentioned before, if you are using the rolling wave planning method, you should be cautious in applying EVM data from the current phase to a future phase because of the differences between these phases regarding not only the nature of the work, but also the level of detail involved in planning.) If the original conditions assumed for the rest of the project are no longer valid, you might consider Scenario 4. If the project must be completed within the original BAC as in Scenario 3, the project scope may need to be reduced.

Table 14-6 shows the formulas for calculating the ETC for the above scenarios. Once the ETC is calculated for the appropriate scenario, a new *total* budget estimate for the project, referred to as the estimate at completion

Table 14-6 ETC formulas & project delta's ETCs and EACs

No.	Scenario	ETC Formula	ETC	Project Delta		
				EAC*	VAC	%VAC
1	Future cost performance will be at same level as current performance	(BAC – EV)/CPI	$152,600	$189,700	–$7,700	–4.2%
2	Future performance will be on target with original plan, irrespective of current performance	BAC – EV	$146,500	$183,600	–$1,600	–0.9%
3	Project must be completed at or under the baseline budget (BAC)	BAC – AC	$144,900	$182,000	$0	0.0%
4**	New cost estimates need to be made for remainder of project	ETC	—	—	—	—

*EAC = ETC + AC; AC = $37,100 (Table 14-4)
**No formula for ETC because new cost estimates are to be made for each individual task.
Therefore, EAC, VAC, and %VAC are also not available.

(EAC), can be obtained by adding its ETC to the AC that has been incurred by the data date. Adding the ETC and AC gives the EAC for any of the scenarios. Variance at completion (VAC) can be calculated as the difference between the BAC and the new EAC. %VAC is simply represented by the ratio of the VAC to the BAC. The formulas for future performance indicators are included in Table 14-5 (except ETC in Table 14-6).

Example

Table 14-6 includes the ETC and the EAC estimates for Project Delta for the four scenarios mentioned above. In the first two scenarios, EAC (the estimated final budget) is $189,700 and $183,600, respectively. Compared to the original BAC of $182,000, it translates to a negative %VAC of 4.2% and 0.9%, respectively. This would not be a cause for concern, if at least a 5% project contingency is available. Scenario 3 calls for project completion under the original BAC. For the last scenario, you do not know what the EAC will be until you go back and reestimate the costs for the remainder of the project.

It may be evident from the forgoing discussion that EV plays a critical role in the EVM method, hence the name. The use of the word "value" in EV can be misleading in the context of a portfolio, where "value" represents the benefit-cost-risk equation, as we have discussed over many previous chapters. EVM methodology was developed for evaluating project performance, and the value in this context represents the budgeted cost of work completed. You may not have generated true value for the stakeholders, although according to EVM, you may have "earned" value. It may be misinterpreted as value generated against the actual cost incurred, which is also called the sunk cost. This can promote the so-called sunk cost fallacy discussed in Chapter 10, where project advocates may use the value "earned," rather than the potential to generate true value, to justify the continuation of the project.

PORTFOLIO PERFORMANCE

The same task and project EVM parameters (PV, BAC, AC, and EV) can also be applied to a portfolio. They will simply be the respective aggregates of those of the individual component projects. As an example, Table 14-7 includes the portfolio EVM building blocks obtained by summing up the data for Project Delta and the other hypothetical projects in the portfolio. (To

Table 14-7   Portfolio EVM data

Project	BAC	PV	AC	EV	CV
Delta	$182,000	$29,000	$37,100	$35,500	–$1,600
Echo	$250,000	$220,000	$220,000	$225,000	$5,000
Golf	$345,000	$57,000	$54,000	$55,000	$1,000
Hotel	$176,000	$158,000	$164,000	$162,000	–$2,000
November	$459,000	$242,000	$225,000	$220,000	–$5,000
Quebec	$610,000	$250,000	$220,000	$190,000	–$30,000
Portfolio	$2,022,000	$956,000	$920,100	$887,500	–$32,600

Project	CPI	SV	%SV	SPI	%Completion
Delta	0.96	$6,500	22%	1.22	20%
Echo	1.02	$5,000	2%	1.02	90%
Golf	1.02	–$2,000	–4%	0.96	16%
Hotel	0.99	$4,000	3%	1.03	92%
November	0.98	–$22,000	–9%	0.91	48%
Quebec	0.86	–$60,000	–24%	0.76	31%
Portfolio	0.96	–$68,500	–7%	0.93	—

keep the illustration simple, only a small number of projects are included in the example portfolio.) The data given in this table reflects the portfolio status at a given point of time (say, the data date). Since the individual project baseline information is presumably available over their respective timelines, a portfolio cumulative cost curve (a portfolio PMB) can be obtained by integrating the time-based PVs or the PMBs of the projects in the portfolio. Thus, portfolio EVM relationships can also be tracked as in Figure 14-6. A portfolio PMB is tricky to generate and update, since the portfolio is in a state of constant flux with incoming and outgoing projects. Furthermore, the portfolio does not have a start and finish as a project. Therefore, it would be easier—and more meaningful—to prepare the portfolio PMB at the beginning of a year and track and update it regularly through the end of the year.

The portfolio cost and schedule performance indicators (portfolio CV, %CV, CPI, SV, %SV, and SPI) can be calculated from the portfolio PV, AC, and EV. An examination of the portfolio metrics should quickly reveal its general health. The cost performance indicators will provide an objective status of the portfolio budget relative to ongoing projects. For example, you can determine how much of the portfolio budget has been spent on these projects and whether there has been a cost overrun. The schedule performance indicators, on the other hand, will show the schedule efficiency with which the overall project work in the portfolio is being performed. If the portfolio variance is in an unacceptable territory, you may drill down to the project level to investigate and identify the culprit projects. Consistent variance across many projects is an indication that the portfolio may be facing structural issues related to project management maturity, organizational culture, management structure, etc. On the other hand, if the variance is related to only a limited number of projects, those particular projects need to be examined closely.

Any negative cost variance at the portfolio must first be compared against the total sum of project contingencies available at the time. If you do not have adequate project contingencies, then you need to compare the excess vs. the management contingency. An ongoing analysis of cost variances vs. contingencies will give you an advance warning of any serious deficiencies of funding at the portfolio level. Significant deviations and long-lasting trends in the negative direction are early warning signals for corrective action. A rebalancing of the portfolio triple constraint may be in order. It may involve postponing some organizational goals, terminating or suspending some projects, seeking more investment, altering resource allocations, and so on.

Positive cost variance means that the portfolio is spending less than what has been budgeted for the work that has been completed on the component projects. Whereas this may seem to be a good sign, excessive positive variance indicates that investment is unnecessarily tied up causing lost opportunities. The extra funds available could have been used on other high performing ongoing projects or attractive new projects.

The EVM metrics for the hypothetical portfolio are summarized in the last row of Table 14-7. The following conclusions may be made:

- The total budget for all ongoing projects in the portfolio is $2.022 million. The actual cost incurred to date is $920,100. An excess of $32,600 has been spent compared to the budgeted cost of work performed to date of $887,500.
- The portfolio is exhibiting a CPI of 0.96 or %CV of −4% as of today. This may or may not be cause for alarm, depending upon the tolerance limits presumably predefined for the component projects and the portfolio. The portfolio's negative cost variance at this point may not be

considered a true cost overrun. This is a variance from the aggregate PMBs of the projects that do not include the project contingencies. Further examination is warranted to identify what projects are responsible for the variance. You need to investigate whether the cause is due to known or unknown risks. Depending on the findings, the variance may be covered by the contingencies of the corresponding culprit projects or those of other projects containing unused contingency or by the management contingency. Analysis of variance vis-à-vis the individual project and management contingencies will reveal insights into the true cost performance of the portfolio.

- It appears that Project Quebec, the largest project in the portfolio, is responsible for the negative cost variance. If the individual project tolerance limit is +/− 5%, Project Quebec is exhibiting a significant negative cost and schedule variance, while the other projects are within the acceptable range. At 31% completion, Project Quebec has a CPI and an SPI of 0.86 and 0.76, respectively. It is more than likely that this project will experience serious cost overruns, based on the "20% completion" rule of thumb introduced earlier in this chapter. The portfolio team needs to assess the status of this project closely. Upon further evaluation and recalculation of the benefit-cost-risk equation for its business case, this project has to be reprioritized in the portfolio. A quick decision needs to be made as to whether the project should be terminated or continued with reduced scope or the infusion of more resources.

- The portfolio schedule performance indicators may not be quite meaningful, but they may reveal a few insights. The portfolio schedule efficiency is 93%, which is also reflected in the negative %SV (−7%). It indicates that a less amount of work is being performed compared to the baseline plan. Only 93 units of project work are performed for every 100 units scheduled to date in the portfolio.

- The component projects seem to be at various stages of their life cycle as shown by a range of percent completions.

Portfolio EVM "Bull's-Eye" Chart

A portfolio bull's-eye chart is an effective snapshot to examine the health of the portfolio as a whole as well as its component projects. The percent variance metrics for cost and schedule from the portfolio EVM data in Table

14-7 are presented in the form of a bull's-eye chart in Figure 14-7. The center point of the chart is where %SV and %CV are exactly zero. The small square around the center point represents the bull's-eye covered by the performance boundaries of +/– 5% variance for both cost and schedule. If the portfolio's position is inside the bull's-eye, its variances are negligible and acceptable. If it is outside the eye, you may need to examine each one of the component project's performance more closely. The upper right quadrant indicates positive performance in both cost and schedule. Even if the performance is extremely positive, you may want to explore the reasons further. Negative performance in both areas is reflected in the lower left-hand quadrant. A

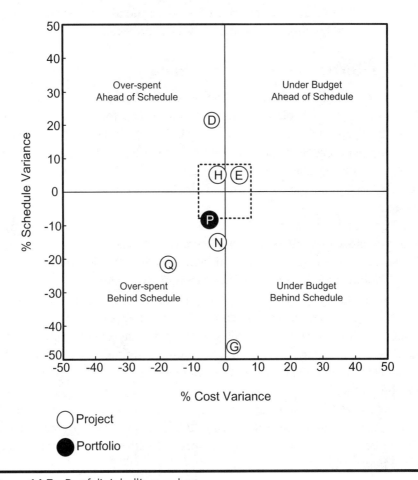

Figure 14-7 Portfolio's bull's-eye chart

position in any of the other two quadrants means negative performance in either cost or schedule.

The bull's-eye chart can also be plotted as the CPI vs. the SPI in lieu of %CV vs. %SV. Percent variances are probably easier to understand especially for those that may not have any EVM background. The chart is an excellent tool for management reporting because of its ability to convey key messages in a simple format. It gives a snapshot of the health of the portfolio and can also show the performance of the component projects in a simple fashion. In addition, the moving trends of the portfolio metrics (%CV vs. %SV) can also be tracked in the same figure. You must be cautious in interpreting the SV at the portfolio level. It is only an indicator of the schedule efficiency of the component projects of the portfolio as a whole and does not say much about the timely completion of those projects.

Future Portfolio Cost Performance

At the time of phase-gate and funnel & filters[SM] reviews, the project CPI and the ETC are key pieces of information needed for the go/no-go decisions. EVM analysis offers powerful insight into the future cost performance once a project reaches approximately 20% completion. If the cost variance is negative and significant at this stage, as mentioned before, that variance is expected to continue and the project is highly unlikely to be finished under budget.

ETCs must be incorporated into the benefit-cost equation of the project business cases that are periodically revalidated. The new ETC may alter the business case leading to a possible termination decision for the project. The CPI and the ETC analysis along with other pertinent information can help you make early and timely project termination decisions to overcome the "sunk cost dilemma" discussed in Chapter 10. Once decisions are made at the reviews, the combined ETCs of the surviving ongoing projects and the BACs of the approved new projects would form the new portfolio ETC, which is the total budget required to complete all the current projects in the portfolio.

The project EAC equivalent for the portfolio will be the sum of all the EACs of the ongoing projects and the BACs of the new arriving projects. This represents the total investment associated with the component projects of the portfolio at any given time.

EVM'S POTENTIAL

It must be clearly evident from this chapter that EVM is data intensive. First, you need detailed bottom-up project cost estimates to determine the PVs. For accurate estimates, you must have internal labor costs based on the labor hours associated with each specific resource or resource type and corresponding labor rates. Every team member must document the amount of time spent each week on each work package by using "time sheets" to account for accurate ACs. EVs must be calculated using the right techniques to accurately capture the value of the work completed. All this requires proper infrastructure involving the right input data, effective tools and techniques, and robust information management systems. In addition, there must be discipline and commitment to make the EVM work. With the structure and discipline in place, EVM offers great value. First, you will have a solid project plan with detailed baselines to monitor your progress. Every team member will have a better understanding of how much effort is expected of them. You can objectively quantify variances, so you can take proper proactive measures to prevent the project from going out of control. No other tool is as capable of providing quantitative and objective evaluation as EVM. You will have a better historical record of the actual effort involved in performing a task. This information is also useful in schedule and cost estimates on future projects. You can evaluate portfolio performance as a whole based on the performance of the component projects and forecast the investment needs for the future.

Some of the common arguments against EVM are: 1) it involves "time sheeting"—a practice where every project team member reports the amount of time spent each week on every project, preferably at the work package level—and many people loathe it; 2) it creates unnecessary overhead; and 3) there is excessive number crunching that may not add value. These arguments may hold some merit, but today's highly sophisticated information management systems have made collection and processing of the required data increasingly easier. Moreover, the benefits certainly outweigh the extra effort involved. Time sheeting is a standard practice in consulting organizations such as engineering, legal, and design firms and has been proven to be effective. Having realized the power of metrics, many organizations in various industries are moving towards time sheeting. Once you are used to it, it becomes a habit. The performance measurement baseline data at each individual project level gives powerful information to the portfolio in planning and managing the portfolio budget, as well as the common pool of resources shared within the portfolio effectively. With the increasingly ubiquitous "Big Data" and supercomputing power, creating the necessary infrastructure and tools should not be a concern. EVM systems, used in the right fashion, can help you improve the project and portfolio management processes as a whole in your organization, adding tremendous value.

15

RESOURCE PLANNING

In the lectures I deliver in various parts of the world, I frequently ask the project managers in the audience this question, "What's your number one challenge?" Everywhere the answer invariably centers around human resources: "We don't have enough people." "We don't have the right skilled people." "We can't get the right people at the right time." "We keep losing good people, and the boss doesn't want to hire new people." And so on. I reframe their challenge as too many projects rather than too few resources. Let us consider this a supply (resources)/demand (projects) problem, where the supply is rather fixed or limited (the resource supply is often referred to as "capacity"). The solution then lies in decreasing the demand and increasing the supply efficiency. And that's where portfolio management comes in.

In the absence of effective project portfolio management (PPM), you may be faced with an enormous demand for project work, all of which may not be aligned with your organizational goals or may not generate value. PPM helps you focus on strategically aligned, value-generating projects, thereby reducing the demand. You can prioritize such projects based on their merit and select as many projects as your resources will allow thus focusing on projects with higher merit. At the same time, you can increase the supply efficiency by using proper resource planning and management tools and techniques. This is part of the portfolio triple constraint balancing act we introduced in Chapter 2.

Resources include money and people as well as materials and equipment. The latter are of less concern from the portfolio standpoint. Money and people are most important to PPM and the portfolio triple constraint. Previous chapters dealt with organizational goals, projects, and financial resources of the triple constraint. In this chapter we will turn our attention to the human resource part of the constraint. (In the rest of the chapter, resources always refer to people.) Human resource management is a vast and complex topic. It is not my intention in this chapter to delve into that area. However, my objective is to address resource *planning*, which is important to the portfolio. There are no simple and easy solutions to the resource challenges we face every day. I will make a modest attempt in this chapter to present important concepts regarding resource planning and allocation and offer a few simple tools.

WHY PROJECT PORTFOLIO MANAGEMENT FOR RESOURCE PLANNING?

Portfolio management's roots lie in capital project portfolios, which involve major investments typically related to infrastructure and construction. Project examples include building a chemical processing unit, adding a new assembly line, and retrofitting a manufacturing plant. (Examples in the public sector include construction of roads, highways, and dams.) Most of the project work is usually outsourced. Internal human resource requirements are relatively low compared to the contractor and equipment cost. Once completed, the projects are expected to generate revenues with acceptable return on investment and payback times. PPM, equipped with the right financial tools, has been employed for a long time to evaluate and prioritize capital project investments. In recent years, however, projects requiring human resources have exploded, thanks in part to the technology revolution and global competitiveness. IT, R&D, and product development are a few examples of projects with a strong demand for human resources. With an increasing number of matrix organizations and cross-functional projects, where the resources are shared across the functions, a need for efficient allocation of those resources has soared. PPM again turns out to be the right mechanism. Just as it can facilitate efficient allocation of investment money to the right projects, it can also do the same with human resources.

In a "projectized" environment, the resources on a project are solely dedicated to that project alone. They do not have any other projects assigned to them. Responsibility for non-project work including operations, administration, and other routine activity is minimal. If all the projects in a portfolio are based on such a structure, resource planning is relatively easy, because there would be hardly any conflict for a given resource between projects and other non-project activities. On the other hand, if your project and non-project activities share resources from a common pool provided by different functions, planning can be particularly daunting. Commonly referred to as a matrix structure, this scenario has become increasingly common in today's organizations. In this scenario, any resource may have multiple "bosses" with varying levels of authority making it difficult to decide on the priorities. It is this shared authority between the functional and project managers that causes immense conflict in deciding on resource allocations and priorities. PPM offers a central hub from where the resource supply-demand equation can be effectively managed. This is typically done through a portfolio management office (PMO), while the portfolio team is held responsible for deciding on the project priorities and the functional managers for non-project work.

The PPM's most important objective in resource planning is to ensure that the right skilled people are available at the right time for all the projects in the portfolio. It also aims to achieve optimum resource utilization by avoiding or minimizing over or under allocation of resources for extended periods of time. Several processes and related tools discussed in the rest of this chapter can help PPM achieve these objectives.

ROLLING WAVE PLANNING

Introduced in Chapter 14, rolling wave planning is an effective method to manage resources at the portfolio level. First, you plan the resource needs for each project in the portfolio at a preliminary level for the long term. This is typically done in terms of full-time equivalents (FTEs) for the next four quarters or so. The FTE requirements are estimated for different resource *types*, since the specific resources (that is, individual team members) may not have been identified for the long term. At the same time, near-term planning is performed for the next 13 weeks (equivalent to a quarter), using resource estimates in labor hours. These detailed estimates are for specific individuals allocated to the project activities. The long, as well as near-term plans, are regularly revised based on the latest information available on a rolling basis. The functional needs of the resources supporting the projects in the portfolio must also be included in these plans. In Chapter 14 we discussed rolling wave planning based on project phases where each phase represents a wave. But in resource planning each quarter represents a wave, where you translate the preliminary plans into detailed estimates each week for the next thirteen weeks in a rolling fashion.

BOTTLENECK ANALYSIS

The rate of outflow of water from a bottle is limited by the size of its neck. As the neck gets bigger, more water can flow out. The bottleneck metaphor is used in project resource management where a single or a small number of resources allocated to a task can restrict the performance of the entire project causing schedule slippage and cost overrun. A bottleneck is nothing but a constraint created due to the shortage of a resource. For example, a project may be constrained by a highly skilled, highly paid subject matter expert (SME), who is needed by multiple projects in a portfolio. Removal of one bottleneck will lead to another bottleneck at some other place. According to the "theory of constraints" (Goldratt, 1990), any system will have at least one constraint. For instance, if you removed the SME bottleneck by hiring several of them, a low-wage team member may become the new bottleneck. This may not be the most efficient way of utilizing resources because you may not have enough work for the highly paid SMEs, who may end up doing the low-level tasks. Proper project planning facilitated by PPM can identify bottlenecks and the tradeoffs between project priorities and resource utilization. The portfolio should track and manage the bottlenecks in the long term as well as the immediate term using many of the tools and techniques discussed in this chapter.

RESOURCE LEVELING

Sometimes a resource may be over allocated due to excessive demands by a project or other support work or under allocated because of insufficient work. The level of allocation is represented by the "resource loading factor," which is the ratio of the time required for a given resource by his/her allocated project and non-project activities and the time available for that resource to perform those activities. This basically translates to the demand/supply ratio. High resource loading factors mean over allocation and low factors mean under allocation. The former can lead to burnout and loss of motivation of the individual. They also extend the time required to complete a project task compared to its original plan because of the "queuing" phenomenon illustrated in the accompanying box. On the other hand, if under allocation persists for long periods of time, organizational resources are wasted. Resource leveling is an activity in which you smooth out the peaks and valleys of the workload allocation to achieve optimal resource utilization.

RESOURCE LOADING FACTOR AND QUEUING THEORY

If a resource has the capacity to finish an activity in one hour and similar activities are allocated to the resource at a rate of one per hour, you might think that all the activities will be completed on time with no need for any one of them to "wait" in a queue. You might consider this a situation where the supply is exactly the same as the demand and therefore, demand will be met on time. However, according to the "queuing theory," the wait time for an activity will increase exponentially, as the demand for the resource reaches the same level as the supply. This relationship is shown conceptually in Figure 15-1, where the vertical axis shows the completion time of an activity (which includes the waiting time) and the horizontal axis shows the ratio of the demand to the supply, which is the resource loading factor. Each resource will have its own loading factor. This factor can change from week to week depending upon the resource needs for the allocated project and non-project work.

To illustrate the above relationship, let's consider the following: You are working at 80% capacity and fall sick for one day. To catch up, you will need to work for five days at an extra 20% every day. Similarly, if you are working at 90% capacity and fall sick for one day, you will need nine days to catch up; at 95% capacity, 20 days; and at 99% capacity, 99 days. At 100% capacity, you can never catch up. You may decide to work overtime, paid or not, to catch up faster, which often happens in the real world.

The implications of queuing theory are quite important in resource allocation. If we consistently match our projects with resources available for project work (after accounting for their non-project work, non-utilizable time, and non-productive time, discussed later) at parity for every single resource, the probability of project delays will be high and most of the projects in the portfolio will be completing late. It seems that below 70% resource loading, that probability is relatively small with little impact. Overtime work, a common remedy for resource shortages, may alleviate part of the problem, but you may still experience significant project delays. However, long periods of overtime have been shown to result in productivity loss that can become counterproductive.

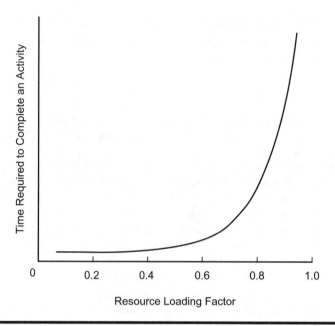

Figure 15-1   Effect of resource loading factor on time required to complete an activity

   If a resource is allocated to only one project, as in a projectized environment, the leveling of his/her work load may not be so easy. The reason is that there may not be additional suitable work for the resource during the "under" periods. Similarly, to lessen the load during the "over" periods, other resources with the right skill set may not be available. Alternatively, if you want to move the "over" work to an "under" period, it may result in project delays if that work happens to be on the critical path. However, in a multi-project portfolio environment, there are multiple projects to fill the valleys and a larger resource pool to remove the peaks. For resource leveling, you first need to have a clear picture of the loading profile of every resource to identify the peaks and valleys. Further, you need to identify every single activity on the critical path of every project and also how much float is available on every noncritical activity. This information will help you move the noncritical work around to remove the peaks and fill the valleys without impacting the critical path schedules. Resource leveling should be practiced considering both long- and near-term planning horizons.

ESTIMATES OF EFFORT VS. LAPSE TIME IN RESOURCE PLANNING

Effective planning at the portfolio level starts with effective planning at the work activity level. It requires accurate estimates of resource requirements for each activity associated with the project and non-project work for every resource associated with the portfolio. As mentioned before, for long-term planning, you may start with estimates of FTE requirements for both project and non-project activities. But for the near term, you need more detailed estimates of resource effort in labor hours. Proper and timely communication between the portfolio team and the functional managers is especially important in making better estimates of the near-term effort.

When you ask a team member for an estimate on how long a given project task takes to be completed, the answer is typically in terms of lapse time. This is the expected start-to-finish time for the task, expressed as workdays or calendar weeks or months, irrespective of how many actuals hours will be spent on the task. The estimates are presumably based on several assumptions, which are most often not made explicit. Although this may be a common practice, the best practice calls for making the estimates as effort in labor hours to begin with. This is the number of hours the resource is expected to spend from start-to-finish of the task. Assuming "average" skill(s) for the resource(s) to be allocated to the task, you may convert the effort to lapse time based on the number of resources to be allocated to the task and their availability to work on the task. The labor hour estimates for various tasks on the project (and other non-project work) become the building blocks of resource planning for the entire portfolio. Starting with labor hours rather than lapse time will give you better estimates of resource needs. As resource needs for various projects in the portfolio and other non-project work change, it is easier to convert the labor hours to lapse time accounting for those needs. Furthermore, monitoring labor effort in hours is more effective in evaluating project performance (for example, using earned value management) and estimating future needs of ongoing as well as new future projects. (This requires "time sheeting," where every resource documents how much actual effort in labor hours is spent in performing each task on every assigned project as well as other activities.)

With the building blocks for resource needs clearly defined in terms of labor effort, resources can be better planned and utilized across the organization using the tools presented in the next section. I have seen many organizations struggle and get frustrated at the portfolio level in managing resource allocations because of poor planning at the individual project level to begin with. Unless project management has matured in your organization, resource planning at the portfolio level will likely be ineffective.

FACTORS AFFECTING RESOURCE AVAILABILITY

The amount of time a resource is available to work on a given project is far less than it may appear at first sight. On the surface you may think that there are eight hours in a day or about 20 person-days in a month for a resource to work on your project. But the various competing demands on the resource, which if not accounted for, will make your task and project duration estimates inaccurate and overly optimistic. Ignoring or underestimating the other demands is one of the most common reasons for project schedule slippage. I have come across many organizations where the operational support activity is completely omitted in developing the project plans. Unfortunately, in the implementation phase of the projects, resources are often pulled out of the projects when the operational demands for those resources arise. With operations being the profit centers, they typically receive higher priority over project work. As a result, project plans become unrealistic. When the actual work is performed, resource availability turns out to be far less than was expected in the original plan. Resources invariably use overtime to make up for the initial low estimates, but they often still come up short in meeting the milestones. This causes negative schedule variances compared to the original plan and ultimate project delays.

Estimation of resource needs for various demands and balancing the supply against that demand is not an exact science. A structured approach coupled with proper tools can give you a close approximation. Let's start with a clear definition of the various demands and the factors that should be considered in quantifying resource availability:

- Resource utilization rate
- Resource productivity factor
- Project and non-project availability factors
- Project timeshare

Resource Utilization Rate

No resource can be utilized for productive work 100% of the work time available on the standard calendar (that is, 2,080 hours in 52 weeks based on a 40 hour work week). This is because of the time taken for holidays, vacation, education and training, sickness, and other such reasons. The resource utilization rate is the fraction of time a resource can be utilized for productive work. The amount of time that is not utilized can easily be more than 15% depending upon the resource's country of residence and the employer's policies that dictate vacation time, sick time, and the number of holidays the workers are entitled to. This will be an important consideration, especially for global teams. Table 15-1 presents a sample calculation where the utilization rate is shown to be 0.85.

Resource Productivity Factor

Even after accounting for non-utilization time, the remaining time available for productive work is not 100%. People are not robots. We cannot work continuously for hours. We take lunch, coffee, bathroom, and other breaks. We have to attend to personal matters frequently while at work. We indulge in social chat. We also spend time on special social activities (for example, organizing or attending special events such as birthdays and office parties). This is all time taken away from productive work. Such nonproductive time amounts to at least 10% and may even be as high as 30%, corresponding to a productivity factor of 90% and 70%, respectively. Productivity decreases

Table 15-1   Example calculation for resource utilization rate

Standard work hours in a day	8
Standard work hours in a week	40
Work hours in a year	2,080
Non-utilizable time, hrs:	
Holidays (12 days/year)	96
Vacation (12 days/year)	96
Education & Training (10 days/ year)	80
Sick time (5 days/year)	40
Utilizable time, hrs (2,080 hrs - 312 hrs)	1,768
Utilization rate (1,768 hrs/2,080 hrs)	0.85

dramatically when an organization is going through a major change such as a merger, an acquisition, or a structural reorganization. As productivity decreases, the time it takes to complete project tasks increases. For example, if a task requires 10 hours of effort by an average skilled individual, the task duration would be approximately 11 hours (10 hours/0.90) and 13 hours (10 hours/0.70) for a productivity factor of 90% and 70%, respectively. Determining the productivity factor for every individual in the organization is difficult and time consuming. Moreover, it is a highly sensitive issue with potential legal and political ramifications. Therefore, you may use the same productivity factor for everybody knowing fully that we all exhibit different productivities.

Availability Factors

After you have accounted for the utilization rate and productivity, the remaining time is the "total available productive time" a resource can use for either project or non-project work. The specific availability factors determine how much time is available for each type of work.

Project Availability Factor

This is the fraction of the total available productive time a resource can use for project work. Project work may involve multiple projects. The project availability factor will increase as the responsibility for operations, administration, and other routine work decreases.

Non-project Availability Factor

This is the fraction of the total available productive time a resource can use for non-project work, which may involve operational, administrative, and other routine activities. By definition, the summation of the project and non-project availability factors should be equal to 1.0.

Project Time Share

Taking into account the utilization rate, productivity factor, and project availability factor, you can estimate how much time a resource can spend on project work. However, if that resource is sharing his/her time among multiple projects, the time available for a particular project is obviously influenced by what I call the "project time share." It is defined as the fraction of time a resource can be allocated to a specific project out of the total productive time available for all project work. For example, if a resource is assigned to only one project at a time as in a projectized organization, the project time share is 100%. On the other hand, if he/she is assigned to a total of two projects, Alpha and Bravo, and only 25% of the project work time is spent on Alpha and the rest on Bravo, the project time shares for the two projects are 25% and 75%, respectively. By definition, the summation of the time shares of a resource for all the assigned projects at any given time should be 1.0.

Example

Table 15-2 shows a breakdown of 100 hours of a resource's time for the following conditions:

- Resource utilization rate = 0.8
- Resource productivity factor = 0.85
- Project availability factor = 0.7
- Non-project availability factor = 0.3
- Project Tango time share = 0.6
- Project Yankee time share = 0.4

It can be seen from the table that only 20 hours are available for Project Yankee out of the total 100 hours of a resource's time. Alternatively, if a task on Project Tango requires an effort of 20 hours by a resource exhibiting the above characteristics, the lapse time to complete the task will be 100 hours,

Table 15-2 Example of a resource's time breakdown (hours)

Total resource time	100			
Non-utilizable time		**20**		
Utilizable time		80		
Non-productive time			**8**	
Productive available time			72	
Productive available time for non-project work				**22**
Productive available time for project work				50
Productive available time for Project Tango					**30**
Productive avaialble time for Project Yankee					**20**

*The numbers in bold add up to the total time of 100 hrs.

which will translate to two and a half weeks (or 12 and a half workdays), assuming 8 work hours in a day and 5 workdays in a week. This can simply be calculated by dividing 20 hours by all of the above factors ($20/[0.4*0.7*0.9*0.8]$). On the surface, the 20 hour effort may seem to be half a week's (or two and a half days) duration. But when you systematically and quantitatively consider the other demands on the resource's time, the expected task duration turns out to be five times longer. This small example should illustrate the importance of the resource utilization rate, the resource productivity factor, the project availability factor, and the project time share in resource planning.

RESOURCE PLANNING TOOLS

Several resource planning tools are available for portfolio managers. These tools can be incorporated and automated as part of your organization's enterprise resource planning systems as well as portfolio management software. A few tools that can easily be integrated into any project information management system are presented below. Many are based on the rolling wave planning process and the factors affecting resource availability discussed above. Although the tools are conceptually simple, the most difficult part is to generate the critical input data to make them work effectively.

Resource Requirements Plan

Resource planning is an iterative process and is commonly done in waves. It does not involve precise estimates especially for long-term needs. It is a process where a continuous refining of estimates is paramount. You may start with high-level estimates for the long term and refine them into more accurate estimates as time passes. Table 15-3 is a sample project resource requirements plan that shows long-term resource needs on every project in the portfolio including ongoing projects and new projects on the horizon. It identifies only the resource types or functional roles but not specific individuals. The needs are expressed in terms of FTEs for every calendar quarter of each project's remaining lifetime. They must be identified in the individual project plans and continuously updated. These plans help the PPM team understand the long-term resource needs of every project in the portfolio. The resource requirement plan can also include resource supply information showing the FTEs available for all the projects in the portfolio. This FTE information should reflect their availability for project work only, after excluding the other demands (non-project work) of the resources. Otherwise the supply will be shown as optimistically too high. A comparison of the demand vs. supply (resource loading factors) will give advance indications as to where the resource bottlenecks are. Proactive measures can be taken to manage those bottlenecks effectively. The first such measure you want to attempt is resource leveling. It may break periodic bottlenecks, but is not effective for long lasting ones. When the project demand is consistently heavy compared to the resource supply, the supply has to be increased or the demand reduced. If the demand is reduced by suspending or terminating low-ranking projects, all the current organizational goals may not be achieved. It means the goals have to be adjusted also. Thus, the portfolio triple constraint has to be rebalanced.

Resource Skills Matrix

The objective of the resource skills matrix is to make the resource skill set and competency level information easily available, so that the right people can be matched with the right projects. The skill matrix includes a list of all the individuals that can be allocated to the projects in the portfolio and their functional roles, skills, and competence levels for each skill. The role refers to functions such as project manager, system architect, database manager, developer, etc., and the skills denote the resource's capability to fulfill his/her role. The more specific the role and the skills are defined, the more effective the matrix will be. The resource's competence level in each skill is rated on a numerical (for example, 1 through 5), alphabetical (A, B, C, D, etc.), or some other scale. Table 15-4 is an example of a skills matrix for web application developers. It shows just a few skills for illustration purposes, but depending upon the functional role and its breadth, many more skills may need to be added.

Many other resource characteristics can be included in this matrix, but you have to be cautious about the information made visible for "public" use, due to the different laws in various parts of the world. Some of the challenges with the matrix include who provides the skill/competency information, how often it should be updated, who should update it, and so on. Typically the individual resource and his/her manager are responsible for keeping the information current. Hiring people with the skills required for projects is usually not under the purview of the PPM process. This is done at the functional level. But PPM is responsible for keeping the functions abreast regarding the long-term skill requirements for the projects.

Table 15-3   Example resource requirements plan*

Project	Project Managers				Architects				Design Engineers				Developers				Others			
	Q1	Q2	Q3	Q4	Q1	Q2	Q3	Q4	Q1	Q2	Q3	Q4	Q1	Q2	Q3	Q4	Q1	Q2	Q3	Q4
Alpha																				
Bravo																				
Charlie																				
Delta																				
Total Project Demand																				
Total Resource Supply																				
Demand/Supply																				

*Resource requirements are to be expressed in FTEs.

Table 15-4   Example resource skills matrix: Functional role—web application developer*

Resource Name	Skill						
	Advanced .NET	Microsoft SQL Server	Microsoft SharePoint	Business Intelligence Tools	Mobile Application Development	Java Script	Microsoft Project
Joseph Smith							
Jane Williams							
Raoul Gonzales							

*The competence level of each resource for each skill is to be rated on a numerical or alphabetical scale.

Resource Loading Chart

The objective of a resource loading chart is to understand the long-term work load of an individual resource. Specifically, it displays all the projects a person is assigned to and the effort expected from the resource in FTEs for each project as well as non-project work. Since it includes long-term preliminary estimates, it typically does not specify the resource's time allocated for vacation, training, and any other such activities. The non-utilizable time is presumably accounted for in the FTE estimates. Table 15-5 is an example chart. The estimates on the chart reflect the future resource loading factors, which can be adjusted to remove over and under allocations through resource leveling. For example, the resource's loading factors shown in Table 15-5 are relatively higher for the first two quarters. It indicates that the resource is over allocated for an extended period and schedule slippages for his/her projects are likely, unless necessary changes are made. Through iterative updates of the long-term plans, the near-term resource loadings can be captured in the resource management plan as illustrated below.

Resource Management Plan

As shown in Table 15-6, the resource management plan is a detailed resource loading chart that matches the resource supply with the demand for the immediate future and near term. It presents detailed resource allocations from week to week in discrete labor hours for each resource assigned to the various projects in the portfolio for the next 13 weeks. The allocations should also include other specific demands such as non-project work (operational, administrative, etc.) and non-utilizable time commitments (vacation, training,

Table 15-5   Example resource loading chart*—Name: Joseph Smith

	Q1	Q2	Q3	Q4
Non-project work	0.2	0.2	0.3	0.3
Project Alpha	0.5	0.5	—	—
Project Charlie	0.2	0.2	0.1	0.1
Project Sierra	0.2	0.2	0.2	—
Project Tango	—	0.1	0.1	0.1
Resource Loading Factor	1.1	1.2	0.7	0.5

*The numbers in the chart are in FTEs.

Table 15-6   Example resource management plan

Resource Name	Allocation	Allocated Hours Each Week					Notes
		1	2	3	N	13	
Joseph Smith							
	Holidays						
	Vacation						
	Education & Training						
	Operations						
	Administration						
	Project Alpha						
	Project Delta						
	Project Tango						
	Other						
	Total						
Jane Williams							
	Holidays						
	Vacation						
	Education & Training						
	Operations						
	Administration						
	Project Alpha						
	Project Delta						
	Project Zulu						
	Other						
	Total						
Raoul Gonzales							
	Holidays						
	Vacation						
	Education & Training						
	Operations						
	Administration						
	Project Charlie						
	Project Delta						
	Project Yankee						
	Other						
	Total						

etc.). For every project, if the effort involves an activity on the critical path, it must be highlighted to indicate its impact on the project's finish date. The effort and critical task information is provided by individual project managers every week for the next 13 weeks and the plan is updated accordingly. The functional managers are responsible for providing the non-project requirements. The individual resource is expected to furnish vacation and training time information. The PPM team can perform the following important activities aided by the resource management plan:

- Match the near-term resource demand vs. supply for ongoing as well as new projects and maintain balance.
- Identify bottlenecks where demand for a particular resource is consistently higher than his/her available time and determine ways to relieve the constraint.
- Level the resources by adjusting over and under allocations particularly to prevent excessively high resource loadings.
- Ensure that resources are not removed from activities on the critical path in the process of resource leveling.
- Shift resources from one project to another as project priorities change based on the portfolio analysis.

Maintenance and management of this plan on your organization's computer systems can be facilitated through a PMO. A detailed discussion of PMOs is presented in the next chapter.

16

PMO

"PMO" has recently become a well-known acronym in the project management vernacular. The "P" in the abbreviation may stand for project, program, or portfolio. A PMO is sometimes referred to as a center of excellence, among other names. Project and program management offices are more common and have been around longer. Portfolio management offices are relatively new and rather rare. Defense contractors have been using program management offices on large government programs for more than two decades. Project management offices, on the other hand, have become more common in the last decade and are particularly prevalent in the IT sector. They have higher value-adding responsibilities and morphed out of project offices (POs), which basically serve administrative functions. PO can also mean—the terminology is probably getting confusing by now—program or portfolio office, which deals with administrative functions of a program or portfolio, respectively.

The PMO term may even have a prefix to denote a particular characteristic. For example, an IT PMO refers to the department it is associated with. The scope of such a PMO is usually defined by the characteristic represented by the prefix. Another term that has become increasingly common, especially in the IT sector, is EPMO where the "E" stands for "enterprise." An EPMO is typically at the higher levels of an organization, such as a business unit or enterprise. EPMO is sometimes also called the strategic project office, which has become the next step in the PMO evolutionary process, since it supports strategic activities such as investing in the right projects, maintaining a balanced portfolio, managing portfolio risks, executing the organizational strategy, and so on. These are clearly project portfolio management (PPM) functions and are increasingly being supported at the EPMO level. A more recent trend seems to integrate the EPMO into the office of strategy management or some other office responsible for innovation initiatives. The overall notion of PMO is hot and evolving. What the future brings remains to be seen.

My intention at the outset of this chapter is not to beleaguer the terminology, but to point out the terms that are in common usage today. It is rather easy to clearly spell out the abbreviation to avoid any misunderstanding, but the real challenge lies in defining the PMO's role and creating real value for the organization in the long run. Projects and programs are already taking advantage of the PMO to support their activities. As portfolio management is being increasingly adopted in recent times, the PMO has offered itself as the right tool to support the PPM process also. In this chapter I will briefly describe the current state of the PMO practice and discuss the PMO scope and functions. I will also comment on the PMO maturity models and close the chapter with the PMO's role in portfolio management.

CURRENT STATE OF PRACTICE

The PMO literature is replete with studies (ESI International, 2013; PM Solutions, 2012) that have surveyed numerous PMOs across several industries. Typical findings of most recent surveys include:

- No standard terminology or nomenclature is used to describe a PMO.
- No uniform standards are available to describe the maturity level of a PMO. There is plenty of discussion around maturity models, but there does not seem to be an emerging leader.
- Many organizations still question the value of a PMO. Executives and senior managers in such organizations believe that the PMO is an overhead activity and does not positively contribute to the organization's bottom line.
- Many PMOs fail in less than four years from their inception. The failure rate was higher in the past but is getting better recently. The reasons for failure are the usual suspects related to the failure of any new major business process initiative:
  - ◆ Implementing the PMO in one big leap
  - ◆ Not enough time given for the PMO to prove its worthiness

- ◆ No real value generation
- ◆ Lack of commitment from upper management or loss of the PMO champion
- There is no consensus on what constitutes PMO success. Some link it to completing the projects meeting its triple constraint. Some relate it to gaining efficiencies by providing common services to multiple projects in a program. Others claim success when the PMOs deliver value and improve continuously. Still others consider effectiveness in executing the organizational strategy and achieving long-term performance in conjunction with portfolio management as the key determinant of a PMO's success.
- The role of the PMO is expanding. Traditional PMOs focused on a single project or a group of projects (program). But the trend shows PMOs taking the responsibility of supporting portfolio management as well as management of resources shared across multiple projects, programs, and operations.
- PMOs in large organizations are being placed at a high level reporting directly to a C-level executive.

Some of the findings may paint an image of the PMO being in disarray, which could further negatively influence potential PMO sponsors and perpetuate the negative image. The truth is that the whole notion of the PMO was born relatively recently and is probably experiencing growing pains. Whereas a snapshot of the current status of the PMO may look bleak for some, a motion picture of recent trends should reveal a brighter picture. We are learning from our past failures as well as successes and improving the status of PMOs.

PMO SCOPE

Traditionally PMOs started with a relatively narrow scope of supporting a single large project or multiple related projects managed in a coordinated fashion as a program. They were more commonly employed in projectized organizations (e.g., defense contractors), where teams are dedicated to only one program with no responsibilities for operational work. The basic objective of a PMO in such organizations is to provide shared services to improve consistency, quality, and efficiency across the projects in the program. The services, also referred to as functions, involved simple administrative and tactical activities.

As projects became more cross-functional and organizations adopted a matrix structure, a need emerged to support the project activities more efficiently across the functional silos through a PMO. Furthermore, due to global competitive pressures, technology innovation, the "great recession," and various other factors, demand for projects and resources soared, while available resources shrank. This warranted better resource management, and the PMO's scope crept into the functional realm that controls the project resources. In a relatively new trend, the PMO has extended its tentacles into operations, since some of the project resources also have operational responsibility. Thus, the PMO scope expanded from program and cross-functional projects into functions and operations.

The PMO scope has escalated vertically as well in the organizational hierarchy, thanks in part to the portfolio management process. As project management maturity has evolved, organizations are executing their strategic project initiatives and managing their investment priorities through a high-level PPM process, and the PMO has turned out to be the right tool to support it. Expansion of the PMO scope brings more business processes, organizations, and stakeholders into its purview, thereby multiplying its functions. This has increased the PMO's visibility and performance expectations. However, its level of authority has been weakened, since it has more "customers" (projects, programs, portfolio, and functions) to serve with little control over them.

PMO FUNCTIONS

The PMO is a support function akin to HR, marketing, and IT—functions needed to support the core business of the organization. While the need for the latter functions are taken for granted, the PMO's value is often challenged by management. As alluded to before, it may be because the PMO is a relatively new kid on the block and still needs to prove its value unequivocally before being accepted as an important support function. In recent years, more PMOs have become sophisticated and are serving higher level strategic needs. They are showing an impact on organizational performance as a whole. It is likely that in the not too distant future PMOs may become accepted as an essential business function. This would especially be true in organizations that are becoming increasingly project-centric.

The functions of a PMO can be placed into three major groups: operational, tactical, and strategic. Operational functions are related to day-to-day project, program, and portfolio activities. Administrative tasks, such as scheduling meetings, recording minutes, printing reports, etc., may also be included in the operational category. Tactical functions are related to methodologies, processes, and tools, among others, that are common across many or all of the projects, programs, or portfolios associated with the PMO. Strategic functions involve higher level activities that primarily serve the PPM process. They may include facilitating project investment decisions, portfolio risk management, improving PPM process, etc. Table 16-1 provides a list of various PMO activities grouped under the three broad functions.

PMO MATURITY

Measuring and modeling the maturity of business processes has become fashionable since Carnegie Mellon University introduced the Capability Maturity Model (CMM®) in 1993 for software development. The objective is to assess the capability of a given business process to successfully achieve the desired outcomes vis-à-vis the industry standards (or best practices) captured in the form of a model. The model provides a benchmark against which a business process can be assessed. Its premise is that the process performance is directly related to the process capability. The closer your business process is to the standards, the better its expected performance and more likely its success. The capability is translated into a maturity scale that may be continuous or "staged." Four or five stages are common, where each stage indicates a certain level of capability. Assessments are normally made not just merely to evaluate where your process stands on the maturity scale. They also help you set a target level to improve its capability and execute a plan to reach that level. For overall project management capability, the Project Management Institute published the Organizational Project Management Maturity Model (OPM3®), and the United Kingdom's Office of Government and Commerce developed the Portfolio, Programme, and Project Management Maturity Model (P3M3®). There is no one single well-recognized maturity model specifically tailored for PMOs at this time.

It has often been said that there are no uniform standards for a PMO except: one size does not fit all. The key reason is that PMOs are considered to be of different types (e.g., a PMO for projects, programs, and portfolios; an IT PMO; an EPMO) depending upon the scope of the domain they cover. Each type is considered to have different goals, which translates to different

Table 16-1   PMO functions

Operational Functions
1.   Provide administrative support for P3*
2.   Report project and program status to upper management
3.   Manage archives of P3 documentation
4.   Conduct P3 audits
5.   Perform post-project and program reviews
6.   Manage staffing of P3
Tactical Functions
7.   Develop and implement P3 methodologies, process maps, tools and techniques
8.   Maintain P3 information management system
9.   Manage contracts associated with P3
10. Facilitate procurement associated with P3
11. Implement, control and improve P3M** processes
12. Translate lessons learned into P3 standards
13. Facilitate customer (internal and external) interfaces
14. Manage risk database
15. Facilitate resource planning between projects and functions
16. Offer training and development in P3M and capability/competency models
17. Promote and facilitate mentoring of P3 managers
18. Manage projects and programs
19. Manage lessons learned database
20. Facilitate P3 governance
Strategic Functions
21. Interface between the portfolio management and upper management
22. Promote P3M within the organization
23. Maintain P3 dashboards and scorecards
24. Monitor and control performance of P3 and the PMO
25. Manage portfolios
26. Advise upper management in P3M
27. Interface with P3 and functional managers
28. Manage benefits validation process
29. Participate in or facilitate strategic planning
30. Ensure portfolio team has the current, appropriate organizational strategic plans available
31. Develop capability and competency models for P3M
32. Establish project management career path
*P3: Project(s), program(s), and portfolio(s)   **P3M: Project, program, and portfolio management

standards, which in turn warrants different maturity models. It is argued that, for example, a *project* management office's goal may be to simply increase the number of projects in your organization that are completed on time, on budget, and meet scope requirements. Then your maturity model will focus on standards related to how you can achieve better project performance related to scope, cost, and time targets. On the other hand, the argument goes, a *portfolio* management office may aim to ensure the right project investments, a balanced portfolio, and achievement of strategic goals. Therefore, the model will focus on different standards accordingly.

Instead of considering the PMOs to be of distinct types with different goals, I propose that we consider them as only one type, wherein every PMO serves to achieve the same goals. These would be higher level goals that are linked to the ultimate organizational success. A unified model eliminates the need to have different models or different maturity scales within the same model for the three domains. It directly links PMO goals to organizational goals. It will include operational, tactical, as well as strategic functions that projects, programs, and portfolios are expected to serve. You may call it a project, program, or portfolio management office or by some other name, but there would only be one standard to measure its capability. The same model should be applicable, irrespective of the PMO location, that is, a department, business unit, division, or enterprise.

Maturity models will likely become more widespread as organizations show a positive correlation between the PMO maturity and overall organizational performance. A recent PMO survey (PMSolutions, 2012) of 554 organizations in numerous industries spanning various parts of the world demonstrated that organizational effectiveness improved with PMO maturity. Organizational effectiveness was measured in terms of shareholder satisfaction, financial success, strategy execution to plan, and other indicators. Other organizational performance improvements reported in the survey are summarized in Table 16-2. The same survey also showed that the PMOs contributed towards a cost savings of $411,000 per project.

PMO ORGANIZATIONAL STRUCTURE

Depending upon the maturity level of the PMO, the organizational structure of the PMO can range from bare bones to elaborate. A simple PMO may

Table 16-2　PMO's impact on organizational performance improvements (PMSolutions, 2012)

Decrease in failed projects	30%
Projects delivered under budget	25%
Improvement in productivity	22%
Increase in customer satisfaction	31%
Projects delivered ahead of schedule	19%
Improvement in projects aligned with objectives	39%
Cost savings per project, % of total project cost	15%
Cost savings per project	US $411,000

have a director with only part-time responsibility receiving ad hoc help from the staff assigned from functions and operations. A highly mature PMO may, on the other hand, house a full-time director as well as administrative staff (Figure 16-1). It may also have full-time planners and schedulers to assist the project, program, and portfolio managers. One survey (cited in Durbin and Doerscher, 2010) indicates that an effective PMO, on the average, has a minimum of four or five staff members. The PMO may even include full-time portfolio managers and project/program managers that are "loaned" to business functions to manage projects/programs. Subject matter experts are typically assigned to the PMO on a part-time basis, and the functional managers liaise with the PMO regarding the resources (shown as the dotted relationship in Figure 16-1). Advanced PMOs are generally sponsored by and report directly to the executive management team.

Organizational Structure: Portfolio vs. PMO

Figure 1-4 in Chapter 1 outlines a portfolio organizational structure. A portfolio can be placed at a functional, division, business unit, or enterprise level. You may have a PMO to serve each individual portfolio or a mix of them, depending on the number of projects in the portfolio, skill sets of the resources, number of resources shared across projects, and so on. The common practice is to have an individual PMO associated with each portfolio. The PMO can be highly effective by focusing on the needs of the portfolio it is associated with. For instance, an IT department would benefit from its own PMO with the responsibility to serve IT projects rather than one that focuses on non-IT functions.

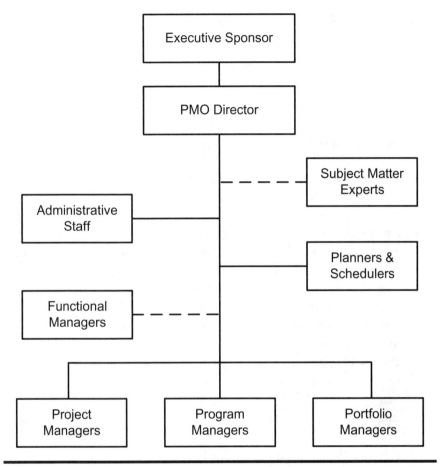

Figure 16-1   PMO organizational structure

Superimposing the PPM team organizational structure (Figure 7-3) over Figure 16-1 helps us better understand the relationship between the portfolio and the PMO. Depending on the size of the portfolio and the required effort to manage it, the portfolio manager and the team may be full-time inside the PMO or part-time outside it. The portfolio review team which consists of subject matter experts is typically outside the PMO. The portfolio executive board, project initiators, and the project sponsors are always outside the PMO. The project managers may be full-time either inside or outside the PMO.

THE PMO'S ROLE IN PPM

It is not a coincidence that the PMO's functions have evolved along the same lines as portfolio management, as organizations started to embrace PPM as a critical strategy execution process. For many of the key PPM processes that encompass projects and programs, the PMO is the natural support tool, since its scope already includes the same domains. The PMO can play a key role in numerous ways in facilitating the PPM process:

- **Portfolio standards.** The PMO can be responsible for identifying the right PPM methodologies, processes, and tools. It can promote their consistent use across the organization.
- **Integration of portfolio, program, and project processes.** PPM is not a stand-alone process. Its success is strongly tied to the success of its component projects and programs. A unified approach must be used wherein project, program, and portfolio processes are synchronized. Integration is paramount along the lines of methodologies, governance, tools, information management systems, communications, and many others. The PMO can be the vehicle to make all this happen.
- **Portfolio information management systems.** The PMO can be responsible for hosting, maintaining, and updating the portfolio information management systems. PPM needs a tremendous amount of information related to pre-project, project, and post-project phases of the portfolio process. The documentation requirements include the project inventory of the portfolio, the project request form, the project business plan, project dashboards, among others. The PMO can be a repository for these documents. Furthermore, there is enormous data related to individual projects, which can be hosted by the same system. For example, project scope, schedule, cost, risk, and resource related information and all the project plans can be part of this repository. All the tools associated with project planning, monitoring, and controlling can also be part of the same information management system. Required links to other systems must be created for efficient integration of overall organizational information management infrastructure.
- **Resource management.** As mentioned before, an evolving PPM trend is that resources shared across the projects as well as operations are managed at the portfolio level. The PMO can be the conduit in collect-

ing the resource information and making it available for the portfolio team. Working with project and functional managers, it can maintain and update the resource management database in its systems. The database can include the skills matrix as well as many other resource planning tools discussed in Chapter 15. As the project priorities shift based on portfolio decisions, the PMO can facilitate the resource reshuffling, updating of the resources databases, and stakeholder communications. All the resource planning and management data and tools can be included as part of the same information management system mentioned above.

- **Strategic alignment.** The foundation for effective PPM lies in understanding the strategic framework and organizational goals, so that the projects in the portfolio can be aligned accordingly. The PMO can facilitate the strategic planning for the organization and make sure the organizational strategy and goals are clearly articulated for the portfolio team. It can update and keep the organization's current strategic plan available for the portfolio team. This will ensure that new as well as ongoing projects are assessed for their alignment with the current, but not the outdated organizational strategy and goals.

- **Governance.** The PMO is the central conduit for facilitating the overall project and portfolio governance. It formalizes the decision support processes that assist the executives to make project go/no-go decisions. PMOs can clearly define accountability at various levels of the project and portfolio organizational structures.

- **Benefits realization and validation.** The true success of the portfolio in large part lies in delivering the value it promised in the business cases of its component projects. It is a vital responsibility of the PPM process to validate a project's original business case by comparing the promised value against the actual value delivered. The PMO can be the responsible party in collecting the information on value delivered by the projects long after they are completed, and it can validate their original business cases.

- **Communications management.** A portfolio is a critical interface between the project managers, project sponsors, project steering committees, resource managers, and the senior/executive managers. There is a tremendous amount of communication activity among these parties. The PMO can be an excellent channel for these communications.

- **Centralized services.** The PMO can facilitate any portfolio service that is also common to the projects and the programs in the portfolio. The service can range from basic administrative to operational support.
- **Training and education.** As with project and program management, the PMO can take the added responsibility of educating the portfolio as well as the project initiators, sponsors, and managers in the PPM process.
- **Implementation of PPM.** The PMO can be responsible for planning, initiation, and execution of a new PPM process in the organization. In addition, it can monitor the performance of the process and help with future improvements.
- **Leveraging lessons learned.** Capturing lessons learned from past experience has become common business practice, but what is not common is effectively leveraging those lessons for the future. This is primarily due to the lack of their easy access. A PMO can facilitate this process. For example, it can look for common themes and translate them into standards and tools made available for everybody to use.

SECTION 4

PROJECT PORTFOLIO MANAGEMENT CASE STUDIES/EXERCISES

Section 4 contains several mini case studies, presented in the form of exercises, to show how the methodology and the key tools presented in this book can be applied to manage a portfolio. A total of seven exercises are presented. The first six are related to portfolio foundation, design, construction, and balancing; and project ranking. The last exercise focuses on the evaluation of a specific project candidate and a final go/no-go decision.

17

CASE STUDIES/EXERCISES*

This chapter presents several mini case studies that simulate real-world scenarios. They are presented in the form of exercises. The scenarios behind the exercises are built as part of a fictitious biotechnology company that is in the process of streamlining more than 25 ongoing and new projects under a new project portfolio. You are presented with background information on the company and the projects in the form of "exhibits." In each exercise you are asked to perform certain tasks by applying key portfolio management processes and tools discussed in the book. The exercises basically follow the different phases of the PPM methodology. Out of a total of seven exercises, the first six focus on how to:

- Build the portfolio foundation
- Develop the design specifications for the portfolio
- Construct the new portfolio
- Balance the portfolio
- Rank the projects in the portfolio

The last exercise is related to evaluating a new project for its merit and making a go/no-go recommendation. The mini case studies presented herein do not have one obvious solution. It is hoped that they create a stimulating discussion on many possible solutions. Solutions to each exercise may be found in the appendix—just one solution for each question posed in the exercises, among the many possible. The solutions are brief and to the point without elaborate explanations.

* © Prasad Kodukula, 2014. For permission to use the case studies and other inquiries, please contact: prasad@kodukula.com.

I developed the case studies based on my own entrepreneurial experience with founding and managing small companies as well as working as a project management coach and consultant with more than 40 Fortune 100 companies. These cases have been peer reviewed by subject matter experts and "pilot-tested" four times in workshops attended by senior and portfolio managers in many parts of the world. I tried to keep the industry-specific jargon and details to a minimum and focus on the portfolio aspects. My hope is that you will not get intimidated with the technology details. I also tried to keep the financial aspects at a relatively high level, so you do not need to get too bogged down with the nitty-gritty. I made the size of the portfolio relatively small to avoid complexity and confusion, yet included a diverse mix of projects. Notwithstanding the small size, the principles and tools you would apply to a larger portfolio are still reflected. My overall objective is to give you a flavor for how the methodology and the tools can be applied to design, build, and manage a real-world portfolio.

EXERCISES

Exercise 1: Portfolio Foundation

An effective portfolio contains only those projects that are aligned with the organization's mission, vision, strategy, goals, and objectives that form its strategic framework. The portfolio manager and team are not responsible for creating the strategic framework for the organization supporting the portfolio, but must clearly understand it. The objective of this exercise is to identify the strategic framework of the protagonist organization that drives the portfolio. Exhibit 1* presents a profile of a fictitious company named GeneMatrix (GMX), a genomics-based biotechnology company located in San Diego, California. Exhibit 2 provides you the latest information on the company's plans and outlook. The tasks for this exercise are:

- Describe, in your own words, GMX's strategic framework.
- Articulate the company's strategic goals along the four perspectives of the balanced scorecard (BSC) framework.
- For each goal, develop at least one corresponding objective. Make sure the objectives are specific, measurable, agreed-to, realistic, and time-bound.

*Exhibits are presented starting on page 254.

Exercise 2: Portfolio Design

Every portfolio must be constructed and managed in accordance with the predefined design specifications. The specifications identify the project categories to be used in balancing the portfolio, relative allocations of resources to these project categories, criteria for evaluating projects in each category, weightage factors, discount rates, contingencies, and tolerance limits, among others. The objective of this exercise is to develop the design specifications for the portfolio. Based on the information provided so far on GMX, your task is to develop the design specifications for the new portfolio. The exercise involves the following tasks:

- Categorize the portfolio along the four perspectives of the BSC framework.
- For each project category, specify the target percent investment allocations.
- For each project category, list evaluation criteria that will be used to evaluate and select projects for investment.
- For each evaluation criterion, specify a weightage factor.
- Recommend discount rates to calculate net present value (NPV), project and management contingencies, and tolerance limits for project schedule/cost performance and portfolio cost performance.

Exercise 3: Portfolio Construction

Building the new portfolio involves bringing ongoing projects into the new portfolio, which most likely does not meet the design specifications. In this exercise you will evaluate each ongoing project in the newly formed portfolio vis-à-vis the portfolio design specifications. You will identify projects that are not aligned with the organizational strategic framework, that do not show potential to generate value, that exhibit unacceptable levels of risk, that are redundant, and so on. Finally, you will make project termination and consolidation recommendations. The objective of this exercise is to build and begin the calibration of the initial portfolio so that it contains only those projects that meet the portfolio design specifications (except for the mix of projects to achieve balance). Table 17-1* is a listing of ongoing as well as new projects that are being considered for inclusion in the new portfolio. It also provides a brief description of each project. Table 17-2 shows preliminary business case

---

*All tables are included at the end of this chapter.

information on all the projects and the current status of the ongoing ones. Your task is to build the initial portfolio and start the calibration process by performing the following activities:

- Categorize the projects and place them in the categories you identified in the previous exercise.
- Evaluate each project for its alignment with GMX's strategy and its goals. Trace and identify the goal(s) each project is aligned with, if you see alignment to begin with.
- Based on your evaluation of their alignment, value-generation potential, and risk characteristics, recommend which projects should be consolidated, continued, suspended, or terminated. Justify your recommendations.

Exercise 4: Portfolio Balancing

A balanced portfolio supports diverse categories of projects in desired proportions. It also must be in balance with respect to its triple constraint. In this exercise you will compute the relative proportion of the different project categories in the portfolio and recommend actions to bring it into balance. You will also evaluate whether there are sufficient and necessary projects in the portfolio to help achieve GMX's goals and objectives. The objective of this exercise is to identify the actions needed to transform the initial portfolio to a balanced portfolio. In the previous exercise you built the initial portfolio for GMX and started the calibration process. Assuming that GMX's executive management team has authorized your consolidation/termination recommendations from the previous exercise, please perform the following tasks:

- Map out organizational goals vs. projects and evaluate whether the projects in the portfolio are necessary and sufficient to achieve the goals.
- Compute how much total investment will be needed to complete the projects in each category.
- Calculate the relative percent investment needs for each category.
- Identify the likely differences between the current relative category allocation and the design allocation you specified in your solution to Exercise 2.
- Recommend actions to turn the new portfolio into a balanced one that will be effective in achieving GMX's goals.

Exercise 5: Project Ranking by Efficient Frontier Method

Projects that generate financial value can be ranked using their benefit-cost ratios in accordance with the efficient frontier principle commonly used in financial portfolio management. The objective of this exercise is to rank projects (only those that survived your recommendations) that are expected to generate financial benefits using the efficient frontier principle. Table 17-3 provides benefit-cost information on those projects. Your task in this exercise is to:

- Develop the efficient frontier for the portfolio.
- Recommend any actions based on this analysis.

Exercise 6: Project Ranking by Paired Comparison and Forced Ranking

It is generally difficult to rank projects that generate intangible benefits using quantitative methods. Paired comparison and forced ranking are qualitative techniques that are commonly used for ranking purposes. The objective of this exercise is to rank projects that are expected to generate nonfinancial benefits using these two methods:

- Rank surviving business process and employee value projects within their own categories using paired comparison and forced ranking techniques, respectively.
- Recommend any actions based on these rankings.

Exercise 7: Project Go/No-Go

The objective of this exercise is to evaluate a new project for its investment worthiness to make a go/no-go recommendation. Exhibit 3 presents portions of a proposal and business case analysis of a new project that is being considered at GMX. Your task is to:

- Evaluate the project for its strategic fit, value-generation potential, risks, and other criteria you identified as part of the portfolio design in Exercise 2.
- Make a go/no-go recommendation for the project.
- Justify your recommendation.

EXHIBIT 1: GENEMATRIX PROFILE

GeneMatrix (GMX) is a San Diego, California-based biotechnology company founded by two MIT molecular biology PhDs, who met at Stanford while doing their executive MBAs. The founders' mission is to save lives and improve the quality of life through human genomics, a relatively new science, sparked by the "human genome" project and the exponential growth of computing power. They envision GMX to become the most innovative company in this area. The guiding principles of the company are product innovation, technology excellence, and customer focus. GMX was started in 2010 with seed capital from "angel" investors and in the last few years received a series of investments from venture capitalists. This year it is expected to have operating revenues of approximately $15 million. The company is contemplating an initial public offering (IPO) in the next few years. A major player in this industry attempted an unsuccessful acquisition last year.

GMX's core competence is the development of products related to DNA microarray technology. It owns a few patents in this area with many others pending. The products sold by the company are marketed under two different divisions, namely, Arrays and Reagents. The former includes various models of DNA microarrays, also known as gene chips. Each array is similar to a tray, where test samples that have been treated with special reagents are placed and processed by an instrument, known as a DNA sequencer. While GMX has so far worked with third-party sequencer manufacturers through strategic partnerships, there has recently been debate within upper management about entering the sequencer market itself. GMX's flagship product is the AcuChip 1000, a state-of-the-art low-density array with the highest market share in its product class with a list price of $20,000. Variations of this model are available to fit sequencers made by different vendors and for different applications ultimately to be used by end users. Other arrays (mid-density and high-density) with far superior processing speed and throughput compared to the AcuChip 1000 are under development. GMX's arrays are manufactured at a highly advanced, robotics-controlled facility in China using their patented technology.

GMX's second division offers several reagents needed to prepare the samples before loading them using the arrays. The reagents are made at a plant in San Diego, California. The list price of reagents is approximately $250 per kit. A kit contains a few different reagents needed for a given array.

A third division of the company, Info Tech, is responsible for software application development, implementation, and customer support associated with the arrays. The primary software product, known as AcuTrack (current version 2.0), allows you to store, retrieve, download, upload, report, and track massive amounts of data related to AcuChip. It is scalable and can easily be configured to a variety of customer systems. Info Tech houses a call center with 10 highly skilled biotechnologists on staff who can help the customers with genome-based data analysis, presentation, and reporting. It owns most of the hardware, networks, and the storage required to support AcuTrack users. GMX is also capable of providing access to public as well as commercial genome databases through its licensing agreements with vendors carrying such databases. Although AcuTrack was created originally for GMX's own arrays, due to customer requests, different versions of this product were developed and marketed for use with products from other array makers.

Technology Description

DNA microarrays or gene chips are a revolutionary technology that is transforming molecular biology. A typical array consists of a plastic tray (e.g., 3" × 3") made of three parts: a barcode that identifies the tray, a spare area that is left "blank" for future use, and a sample area that carries an array of dots. Each dot contains a well to hold the test sample. The larger the number of dots, the more samples you can run through the sequencing instrument. (The AcuChip 1000 has 1,000 dots and is considered a low-density array.)

Microarray technology helps you determine the exact composition of genes, which carry the information to build and maintain an organism's cells, and pass it on to the next generation. Genes consist of DNA molecules, which in turn are made up of the building blocks named nucleotides. There are four nucleotides (A, C, T, and G) that are arranged in a unique sequence in each DNA molecule. It is this unique sequence that makes a particular gene exhibit certain characteristics, which manifest as specific traits in living organisms. A typical test to determine the sequence involves the following steps:

1. Prepare the test sample using the necessary reagents for the extraction of DNA, which is then chopped into pieces with the help of enzymes.
2. Add the chopped DNA pieces to the arrays.
3. Run the arrays through a gene sequencing instrument, which reads the sequence of A, C, T, and G nucleotides.
4. Analyze the data using advanced software tools.

A deluge of information is generated, as you use this technology for various applications, creating a need for its storage, organization, and indexing. The theory and practical aspects of analysis and management of this information has evolved into a new area of science called bioinformatics.

Technology Applications

Knowing the sequence of the building blocks of the DNA molecules and the composition of genes not only unravels the mystery of life, but it can also provide cures to many of our health problems. A few examples, among numerous applications for gene chip technology are:

1. To identify the genome of humans, plants, and animals for research.
2. To detect the presence of a mutation responsible for a specific disease (e.g., a particular type of cancer).
3. To evaluate a subject's response to a drug including its side effects.
4. To develop customized therapies based on the genome of a person.
5. To develop preventive care habits in accordance with a person's genome.
6. To test unknown samples against known DNA to determine if someone was present at the scene of a crime and was responsible for that crime.
7. To set up a genetic clock to identify when various traits emerged; along the same lines, to predict when an organism first appeared on earth and what it looked like at various points in its evolutionary lifetime.
8. To test material from outer space for life.

EXHIBIT 2: GENEMATRIX'S FUTURE PLAN

The executive team of GeneMatrix recently met at a retreat for their annual strategy planning. At this meeting, the owners reiterated the company's focus on its core competence involving product innovations in microarray technology, strategic partnerships with current and new third-party sequencer makers, and seamless integration of GMX's products with sequencers. It was revealed at the meeting that a few prospective acquirers had contacted GMX's owners, who apparently are still interested in an IPO in the near future. As part of its strategic planning, and with the help of an outside consultant, the team first performed a strengths, weaknesses, opportunities, and threats analysis (the results are shown below). It also identified broad goals for the near future:

- Expand revenue streams through new product development and entry into emerging markets.
- Increase customer satisfaction.
- Improve current business processes.
- Enhance skills of project and product managers.

Strengths
- Technical excellence
- Intellectual property
- Motivated staff
- Capital funding

Weaknesses
- Crisis management
- Weak business processes
- Poor project management
- Slow decision making

Opportunities
- Expanding markets
- Emerging countries
- New technologies
- High revenue growth

Threats
- Growing domestic competition
- Low-cost competition from China and India (especially for reagents)
- Fast-growing technology
- Regulations

EXHIBIT 3: NEW PROJECT REQUEST— NANOPORE TECHNOLOGY AND NEXT GENERATION SEQUENCER

There has been a lot of excitement lately at GMX, especially in its product development group, about a breakthrough technology. GMX recently applied for a patent for a chip containing nanopores that makes sequencing of genes faster and cheaper by several orders of magnitude, compared to the state of the art. The development process started about a year ago and was expected to take a total of two years. Since it has missed a few key milestones, its launch has been extended by six months. Although the new chip offers fast through-puts that could not even have been imagined before, there are no compatible sequencing instruments in the market today. However, third-party sequencer manufacturers recognize the power of nanopore technology and are already gearing up to develop next generation products.

Whereas GMX's core competence has been development and marketing of cutting-edge microarrays, there has been some talk among senior managers about entering the gene sequencing instrumentation market. Currently GMX does not make any sequencers but works very closely with third-party manufacturers through strategic partnerships. The product development team at GMX sees an opportunity in the next generation sequencer (NGS) and is interested in exploring entry into this market. A multidisciplinary team consisting of managers from product development and marketing, among others, was formed to put together the business case for developing the NGS. Code named Omega, the project is off to a great start!

As part of the business case, GMX's research and development team, with assistance from their colleagues in marketing, performed a preliminary cash flow analysis. The investment cost includes $75 million spread over two years for development ($35 million this year and $40 million next year) and $8 million (in the second year) for the launch. Free cash flow (net revenues after accounting for depreciation, interest, taxes, etc.) projections for the first five years after the launch of the new product are $40, $80, $150, $100, and $60 million for years 3 through 7 (from today), respectively.

The NPV for the project is estimated to be $94 million after discounting the investment cost and revenues at 10% and 20%, respectively. The benefit cost ratio is about 2.2, the internal rate of return is 42%, and the annual return on investment is 24% with a payback in less than three years. Sensitivity analysis on the NPV was also performed by changing, one at a time, the total investment cost, the peak annual investment cost, the peak annual revenue, and the revenue discount rate by +/- 20%. The results are presented in the form of a Tornado diagram in Figure 17-1.

The project is expected to create several opportunities for GMX:

- **Valuation.** If proprietary technologies and patents are developed, the valuation of GMX will soar, helping the owners with the IPO.
- **Synergies.** If synergies evolve between the new sequencer and GMX's other products (chips and reagents), market share and long-term profitability can improve.
- **Larger revenues and margins.** If the product is successful, the revenue streams will be larger (compared to those of chips and reagents) and the margins higher (reagents are already commodities and chips will likely be commoditized soon).
- **Emerging technology.** If GMX becomes a leader in this emerging technology, its long-term competitiveness will improve.

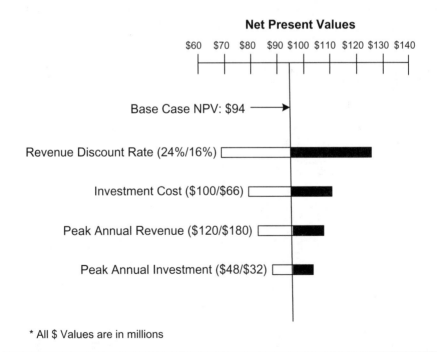

Figure 17-1 Tornado diagram

- **Control of value chain.** If the product is successful, GMX will have control over the value chain including the reagents, the gene chips, and the sequencers.

While the project sounds highly attractive, several threats also exist that must be managed effectively to make the project a success:

- **Weakening of relationships with current strategic partners.** If GMX enters into the gene sequencing instrumentation market, its existing relationship with gene sequencers may be jeopardized resulting in lower market share and a decrease in revenues of its current products.
- **Ineffective technology.** If the technology is proven to be ineffective, investment is lost and resources are wasted.
- **Not a core competence.** GMX does not have the needed technical and marketing expertise in this space, and the learning curve will likely be steep. This may result in cost overruns and schedule slippage of the project, making it less viable. Market entry can become challenging, marginalizing GMX's long-term profitability.
- **Opportunity cost.** If resources are allocated to high-risk and uncertain new technologies such as the NGS, investment in more attractive projects (e.g., incumbent products) may be compromised, ultimately weakening the long-term profitability and competitiveness.

Table 17-1 A List of new and ongoing projects

Project ID	New/ On-going	Project Name	Project Description
1	O	"All-in-one" reagent mix	Develop and launch all in one cocktail mix that can be used with GMX's flagship product AcuChip 1000 (low density array, 1000 dots) as well as the new MDA 2500 currently under development. This mix will save the users a significant amount of time and effort in preparing the test samples.
2	O	AcuTrack 100K	Develop the software application that will be used with the new HDA 100K currently under development. This software will support the high-density/low-cost array with the capability of incorporating all elements of automation as would be expected in a high end hospital lab environment that processes thousands of samples a day.
3	O	AcuTrack 2.5	Upgrade AcuTrack 2.0 software that is originally designed to work with AcuChip 1000 to support the new MDA 2500 under development.
4	O	Ambient shipping	Switch to ambient temperature shipping of the reagents, which are currently shipped using cold packs. Preliminary stability studies for most of the consumables indicated that the reagents are stable at room temperature for several days. Need to perform confirmatory studies before formally switching to ambient shipping.
5	O	Business ethics training	Train all employees in business ethics. Mandatory training needed once every two years.
6	N	cGMP certification	A growing trend in the biotechnology community is the increasing regulation and the need for quality. To lure customers in the diagnostics and pharmaceutical arenas and gain credibility, it is important that GMX's manufacturing facilities are cGMP (current Good Manufacturing Practices) certified.
7	N	CLIA lab	Open a CLIA (Clinical Laboratory Improvement Amendments) certified lab, where GMX would offer testing services for a fee using its own products. Service lab is a competitive, low-margin business but can provide more traction for GMX's products, bring additional revenues, and prevent third parties from taking its business.
8	O	Consolidating supply chain	Consolidate the existing suppliers and enter into multi-year supply agreements with top ones to reduce costs.

Continues

Table 17.1   *Continued*

Project ID	New/ On-going	Project Name	Project Description
9	O	Data storage outsourcing	Provide cloud-based data storage solutions through third-party vendors. Customers can store their data after they have completed their testing with GMX's products. The service will offer speed, reliability, ease of use, and security to retain and attract customers.
10	N	Fit for health	Help employees lead more healthy lives. This will be done by a third party that will lead employee health assessments and roll out incentives for employees to pursue better health. Employees will be given health points, which they can cash in to get discounts on their insurance. Ultimately this project is anticipated to result in fewer doctor's visits, less insurance costs, and more productivity.
11	N	Green packaging	Switch to green packaging involving biodegradables instead of the aluminum sachets and cardboard boxes currently used to package and ship the reagents and chips.
12	O	High-density array (HDA 100K)	Develop, test, and launch a high-density array that will provide 100,000 dots. With the rapid decline of gene sequencing costs, it has become a necessity in the market place to develop higher throughput chips to remain competitive.
13	N	Licensing program	Out-license GMX's IP (intellectual property) related array and software technology to other companies.
14	N	Life Mix	Develop new reagents that will help NASA with testing of materials from other planets for life. This could give high visibility to GMX and can be good for public relations.
15	O	Mid-density array (MDA 2500)	Develop, test, and launch a mid-density array that will include 2500 dots. This product will target the hospitals and diagnostic testing labs and compete with its counterpart recently introduced by GMX's major competitor.
16	N	Multi-platform AcuTrack	Convert AcuTrack 2.0 to a multi-platform application so that it will be compatible with arrays and sequencers of competitors.
17	O	Nanopore array	Develop, test, and launch novel, patent-pending gene chip technology that is based on nanometer-sized pores in a silicon chip. It holds the promise of far greater throughput, speed, and scalability compared to the state of the art. It can potentially reduce the cost of whole human genome sequencing to less than $1,000.

#			
18	N	PMP training	Offer Project Management Professional (PMP) certification training to help project managers become PMP certified and ultimately avoid or decrease project cost overruns.
19	O	Project portfolio management	Introduce project portfolio management (PPM) as a formal business process in order to streamline GMX's project investment decision process and improve the success of achieving its strategic goals.
20	N	Salesforce.com	Provide the right tools to the sales people so that they can improve their job effectiveness and close more deals faster and cheaper. This is a well-proven popular application for sales people in many industries.
21	O	Sample Prep 1-2-3	Develop and launch a new instrument that makes preparation of test samples as easy as 1-2-3. It is an instrument that will work with HDA 100K.
22	N	Six Sigma training	Provide six sigma training to the product development scientists and engineers to obtain Black Belt and Green Belt certifications.
23	N	Social media training	Provide one-day class (two sessions) for all the interested employees to train them on social media tools including LinkedIn, Twitter, and Facebook.
24	N	Supervisory training	Train all supervisors on supervisory skills in a two-day seminar offered twice during the year.
25	O	Upgrading sales systems	Upgrade the original, internally developed sales software application tool to make it more easily accessible, user friendly, and effective for the sales people.
26	N	Web interface	Upgrade GMX's website, so it can become a powerful interface for the savvy customer, who can order chips, reagents, and other GMX products via the web. The current website is not intuitive and user friendly for customer search and buying needs.
27	O	Web-based AcuTrack	Convert AcuTrack 2.0 to a web-based application. This will offer cloud services, wherein customers can not only use GMX's data analysis, visualization, and presentation tools in a software as a service (SaaS) model, but also rent server space for storage of their data.

Table 17-2 Information on the new and ongoing projects

Project ID	New/ On-going	Project Name	Benefit[1]	Initial Budget Estimate[1]	Actual Cost To-date[1]	Estimate to Complete[1]	Threat Rating[2]	Completion Date[3]	Comments
1	O	"All-in-one" reagent mix	$10.0	$5.0	$1.0	$4.5	3	1 yr	It is the juice for the arrays. Following the investment for development, the profit margins are high. Risk is low as formulations exist.
2	O	AcuTrack 100K	$12.0	$5.0	$4.0	$1.5	6	1.5 yr	This is linked to the high-density array.
3	O	AcuTrack 2.5	$6.0	$2.0	$1.0	$1.5	3	1 yr	This is required for the mid-density array.
4	O	Ambient shipping	—	$2.0	$1.0	$1.0	4	1 yr	Payback is in less than a year. Long-term savings. GMX can score points on sustainability.
5	O	Business ethics training	—	$0.2	$0.1	$0.1	2	1 yr	On-going. CEO's pet project.
6	N	cGMP certification	—	$2.0	$0.0	$2.0	3	2 yrs	This is a labor-intensive project that will require senior level QA managers from the lab. Regular operations and new product releases can be affected.
7	N	CLIA Lab	$26.0	$12.0	$0.0	$12.0	3	1 yr	A major initiative. GMX will be competing for business with its business partners.
8	O	Consolidating supply chain	—	$0.3	$0.1	$0.2	2	6 mos.	Payback is within a year. It's just a question of allocating enough resources.

264

9	O	Data storage outsourcing	$5.0	$2.0	$1.5	$0.5	7	6 mos.	Evolving cloud-based service. Security can be an issue just like with any cloud-based service.
10	N	Fit for health	—	$0.2	$0.0	$0.2	2	6 mos.	Pet project of the Human Resources VP. Saves healthcare costs in the long run.
11	N	Green packaging	—	$2.0	$0.0	$2.0	4	1 yr	Saves costs in the long run. Good for public relations.
12	O	High-density array (HDA 100K)	$40.0	$20.0	$5.0	$22.0	6	1.5 yr	Due to lack of resources, not only had a late start, but experienced several schedule slippages. Original cost estimates were low. Not sure if the demand for high-density array would be strong in view of nanopore technology.
13	N	Licensing program	$7.0	$2.0	$0.0	$2.0	6	6 mos.	Not much capital needed. Need new hires (licensing person, legal person, IP agent). Payback will be in less than a year.
14	N	Life Mix	$3.0	$3.0	$0.0	$3.0	2	1 yr	Can leverage some of the research from All-in-one mix, but some customization for NASA will be necessary.
15	O	Mid-density array (MDA 2500)	$40.0	$15.0	$10.0	$8.0	4	8 mos.	Mid-density array is the next major product for GMX. It slipped two major milestones but is on track for release in eight months.
16	N	Multi-platform AcuTrack	$5.0	$2.0	$0.0	$2.0	5	1 yr	Open platform is the buzz of the day.

Continues

Table 17.2 Continued

Project ID	New/On-going	Project Name	Benefit[1]	Initial Budget Estimate[1]	Actual Cost To-date[1]	Estimate to Complete[1]	Threat Rating[2]	Completion Date[3]	Comments
17	O	Nanopore array	$60.0	$25.0	$10.0	$20.0	8	1.5 yr	It is a novel technology. It could be a huge success, if it works. Risk is high due to uncertainty with the technology.
18	N	PMP training	—	$0.2	$0.0	$0.2	2	2 yrs	Project managers are very interested. Many managers think it is an overhead expense.
19	O	Project portfolio management	—	$1.0	$0.4	$0.6	3	6 mos.	Project is on track. Consultant is on board. License was purchased for the PPM tool.
20	N	Salesforce.com	—	$0.1	$0.0	$0.1	2	6 mos.	Commercially available software. Not much capital involved if you use software as a service in a cloud model.
21	O	Sample Prep 1-2-3	$25.0	$10.0	$2.0	$8.0	4	1 yr	Project is on track.
22	N	Six Sigma training	—	$0.3	$0.0	$0.3	2	3 yrs	Manufacturing and process teams highly interested in this. ROI is being questioned by the management.
23	N	Social media training	—	$0.08	$0.0	$0.1	2	6 mos.	Senior personnel are especially interested. There have been a lot of requests for this training.

24	N	Supervisory training	—	$0.2	$0.0	$0.2	2	1 yr	First time any GMX supervisor has received formal supervisory training.
25	O	Upgrading sales systems	—	$0.3	$0.1	$0.2	3	6 mos.	An operating necessity for the sales people; current system is antiquated and slow.
26	N	Web interface	—	$0.5	$0.0	$0.8	2	8 mos.	Low risk. Only a matter of doing it.
27	O	Web-based AcuTrack	$9.0	$3.0	$2.0	$1.0	7	1 yr	Security can be a concern. But this seems to be an industry trend.

[1] In millions
[2] On a scale of 1 to 10, from lowest to highest
[3] From today

Table 17-3   Benefit/cost information on projects that generate financial value

No.	New/ Ongoing	Project Name	Initial Cost Estimate	Benefit**	Initial BCR	Actual Cost (to date)	Estimate to Complete	Current BCR
1	O	"All-in-one" reagent mix	$5.0	$10.0	2.0	$1.0	$4.5	2.2
3	O	AcuTrack 2.5	$2.0	$6.0	3.0	$1.0	$1.5	4.0
15	O	Mid-density array (MDA 2500)	$15.0	$40.0	2.7	$10.0	$8.0	5.0
17	O	Nanopore array	$25.0	$60.0	2.4	$10.0	$20.0	3.0
27	O	Web-based AcuTrack	$3.0	$9.0	3.0	$2.0	$1.0	9.0

*Costs and benefits are in millions of dollars.
**Current and initial estimates are the same.

REFERENCES

Baney, R. and R. Chakravarti, 2012. *Enterprise Project Portfolio Management: Building Competencies for R&D and IT Investment Success.* J. Ross Publishing, Plantation, Florida.

Bonham, S. 2005. *IT Project Portfolio Management.* Artech House, Norwood, Massachusetts.

Canada, J., W. Sullivan, and J. White, 2004. *Capital Investment Analysis for Engineering and Management.* Third edition (paperback). Simon & Schuster, Upper Saddle River, New Jersey.

Cleland, D. and L. Ireland, 2002. *Project Management: Strategic Design and Implementation.* Fourth edition. McGraw-Hill, New York, New York.

Cooper, R.G. 2000. *Product Leadership: Creating and Launching Superior New Products.* Perseus Books, Cambridge, Massachusetts.

Durbin, P. and T. Doerscher, 2010. *Taming Change with Portfolio Management.* Greenleaf Book Group Press, Austin, Texas.

Dye, L. and J. Pennypacker, 1999. *Project Portfolio Management: Selecting and Prioritizing Projects for Competitive Advantage.* Editors, Center for Business Practices, A Division of PM Solutions, Inc., West Chester, Pennsylvania.

Englund, R., R. Graham, and P. Dinsmore, 2003. *Creating the Project Office: A Manager's Guide to Leading Organizational Change.* Jossey-Bass Business and Management Series, John Wiley & Sons, Hoboken, New Jersey.

Enterprise Portfolio Management Council, 2009. *Project Portfolio Management: A View from the Management Trenches.* John Wiley & Sons, Inc., Hoboken, New Jersey.

ESI International, 2013. *The Global State of the PMO: An Analysis for 2013.* An ESI International Study.

Gladwell, M. 2005. *Blink: The Power of Thinking Without Thinking.* Little, Brown and Company; New York, New York.

Goldratt, E., 1990. *The Theory of Constraints.* North River Press, Great Barrington, Massachusetts.

Harpum, P. 2010. *Portfolio, Program, and Project Management in the Pharmaceutical and Biotechnology Industries.* John Wiley & Sons, Hoboken, New Jersey.

Heerkens, G. 2006. *The Business-Savvy Project Manager: Indispensable Knowledge and Skills for Success.* McGraw-Hill, New York, New York.

Hubbard, D. 2007. *How to Measure Anything: Finding the Value of Intangibles in Business.* John Wiley & Sons, Hoboken, New Jersey.

Kahneman, D. 2013. *Thinking, Fast and Slow.* Farrar, Straus, and Giroux; New York, New York.

Kaplan, R. and D. Norton, 2006. *Alignment: Using the Balanced Scorecard to Create Corporate Synergies.* Harvard Business School Press, Boston, Massachusetts.

Kaplan, R. and D. Norton, 1996. *The Balanced Scorecard: Translating Strategy into Action.* Harvard Business School Press, Boston, Massachusetts.

Kendall, G. and S. Rollins, 2003. *Advanced Project Portfolio Management and the PMO: Multiplying ROI at Warp Speed.* J. Ross Publishing, Inc., Boca Raton, Florida.

Kim, W. Chan and R. Mauborgne, 2005. *Blue Ocean Strategy: How to Create Uncontested Market Space and Make the Competition Irrelevant.* Harvard Business School Press, Boston, Massachusetts.

Kodukula, P. 2014. *Project Portfolio Management: How to Design, Build, and Manage a Portfolio.* Workshop Manual and Notes. Kodukula & Associates, Inc., Chicago, Illinois.

Kodukula, P. and C. Papudesu, 2006. *Project Valuation Using Real Options: A Practitioner's Guide.* J. Ross Publishing, Plantation, Florida.

Levine, H. 2005. *Project Portfolio Management: A Practical Guide to Selecting Projects, Managing Portfolios, and Maximizing Benefits.* Jossey-Bass, A Wiley Company, San Francisco, California.

Maizlish, B. and R. Handler, 2005. *IT Portfolio Management Step-By-Step: Unlocking the Business Value of Technology.* John Wiley & Sons, Inc., New York, New York.

Mello, S., W. Mackey, R. Lasser, and R. Tait, 2006. *Value Innovation Portfolio Management: Achieving Double-digit Growth through Customer Value.* J. Ross Publishing, Plantation, Florida.

Meredith, J. and S. Mantel, Jr., 2008. *Project Management: A Managerial Approach.* Seventh edition. John Wiley & Sons, New York, New York.

Moore, S. 2010. *Strategic Project Portfolio Management: Enabling a Productive Organization.* Microsoft Executive Leadership Series, John Wiley & Sons, Hoboken, New Jersey.

Morris P. and J. Pinto, 2007. *The Wiley Guide to Project, Program, & Portfolio Management.* John Wiley & Sons, Inc., Hoboken, New Jersey.

Parviz, R. and G. Levin, 2007. *Project Portfolio Management Tools and Techniques.* Illinois Publishing, New York, New York.

Pennypacker, J. 2005. *Project Portfolio Management Maturity Model.* Center for Business Practices, Havertown, Pennsylvania.

Pennypacker J. and S. Retna, 2009. *Project Portfolio Management: A View from the Trenches.* John Wiley & Sons, Hoboken, New Jersey.

Perry, M. 2011. *Business Driven Project Portfolio Management: Conquering the Top 10 Risks that Threaten Success.* J. Ross Publishing, Plantation, Florida.

PM Solutions, 2012. *The State of the PMO.* PM Solutions, Glenn Mills, Pennsylvania.

PM Solutions, Inc., 2012. *The State of the PMO 2012.* PM Solutions, Inc., Glen Mills, Pennsylvania.

PMI, 2011. *Practice Standard for Earned Value Management.* Second Edition. Newton Square, Pennsylvania.

PMI, 2013a. *A Guide to Project Management Body of Knowledge.* Fifth edition. Project Management Institute, Newtown Square, Pennsylvania.

PMI, 2013b. *The Standard for Portfolio Management.* Third Edition. Project Management Institute, Newtown Square, Pennsylvania.

PMI, 2013c. *The Standard for Program Management.* Third Edition. Project Management Institute, Newtown Square, Pennsylvania.

Porter, M. 1998. *Competitive Strategy: Techniques for Analyzing Industries and Competitors.* The Free Press, New York, New York.

Rajegopal, S., P. McGuin, and J. Waller, 2007. *Project Portfolio Management: Leading the Corporate Vision.* Palgrave Macmillan, New York, New York.

Resch, M. 2011. *Strategic Project Management Transformation.* J. Ross Publishing, Fort Lauderdale, Florida.

Rothman, J. 2009. *Manage Your Project Portfolio: Increase Your Capacity and Finish More Projects.* Pragmatic Programmers, Pragmatic Bookshelf, Raleigh, North Carolina.

Saaty, T. 2001. *Decision Making for Leaders: The Analytic Hierarchy Process for Decisions in a Complex World.* RWS Publications, Pittsburgh, Pennsylvania.

Sanwal, A. and G. Crittenden, 2007. *Optimizing Corporate Portfolio Management: Aligning Investment Proposals with Organizational Strategy.* John Wiley & Sons, Inc., Hoboken, New Jersey.

Schmidt, T. 2009. *Strategic Project Management Made Simple: Practical Tools for Leaders and Teams.* John Wiley & Sons, Hoboken, New Jersey.

APPENDIX A

DISCOUNTED CASH FLOW CALCULATIONS AND SENSITIVITY ANALYSIS

A case example is presented in this appendix to illustrate discounted cash flow (DCF) calculations and sensitivity analysis. The material in this appendix is adopted from a book by Kodukula and Papudesu (2006).

EXAMPLE

Wireless in Washington (WIW) is a small telecommunications company that has a patent pending for an innovative product that increases the range of wireless hot spots by tenfold compared to competing technologies. The product has already been rolled out successfully in the Washington D.C. area, and WIW is now exploring the possibility of introducing it in three other major metropolitan markets in the U.S. The initial investment to launch the product is estimated to be $10 million. The product is expected to have a lifetime of seven years at which time newer innovations are expected to take over. A discount rate of 25% is used to reflect the uncertainty of the project cash flows. Table A-1 presents the steps involved in calculating the project net present value (NPV) using the DCF method and summarizes the results. WIW also conducted a sensitivity analysis by varying the initial investment, discount rate, annual cost, and peak annual revenue during years 3 through 5. Table A-2 presents the results of this analysis. (Figure 13-4 in Chapter 13 shows

Table A-1 DCF calculation for Wireless in Washington

1. Estimate the cost to launch the product today: $10 million

2. Estimate the annual revenues and costs and calculate the annual net revenues for the expected project life cycle. The net revenues are expected to increase and reach a peak for years 3 through 5 and decline thereafter. (Please see the chart below.)

3. Choose a discount rate for the entire project life that reflects the risk associated with the project: 25%

4. Calculate the present values (PVs) of each annual net cash flow by discounting the future values by 25%. For this, multiply the cash flow by the corresponding discount factor. (The discount factor is $[1/(1 + i)^n]$, based on Equation 11-3 in Chapter 11.) For example, the PV of the net cash flow for Year 1 is:

$$(\$1 \text{ million} \times 0.8) = \$0.8 \text{ million.}$$

5. Add the PVs of all the annual net cash flows for the entire project life cycle: $13.23 million.

6. Calculate the project NPV by subtracting the investment from the sum of the PVs of the annual net cash flows:

$$(\$13.23 \text{ million} - \$10 \text{ million}) = \$3.23 \text{ million}$$

		Year						
	0	1	2	3	4	5	6	7
Capital cost, million	−$10.00							
Annual revenue, million		$3.00	$6.00	$10.00	$10.00	$10.00	$6.00	$5.00
Annual cost, million		$2.00	$2.50	$3.00	$3.00	$3.00	$2.50	$2.50
Annual net cash flow, million		$1.00	$3.50	$7.00	$7.00	$7.00	$3.50	$2.50
Discount rate	25%	25%	25%	25%	25%	25%	25%	25%
Discount factor*	1	0.8	0.64	0.51	0.41	0.33	0.26	0.21
PV of annual cash flow, million	−$10.00	$0.80	$2.24	$3.57	$2.87	$2.31	$0.91	$0.53
PV of net annual cash flow, million	$13.23							
NPV, million	$3.23							

*$1/(1 + 0.25)^n$ where n is the year number.
Note: For the sake of simplicity, free cash flow calculations are ignored (that is, additional capital expenses, depreciation cash backs, taxes, working capital needs, etc., are not considered) and the terminal value is assumed to be zero.

the impact of input variables on the NPV in the form of a Tornado diagram.) Even with a +/− 20% change in the input variables compared to their "average" estimates, WIW's project NPV is still a large positive number showing that the project is probably a good investment. The sensitivity analysis also shows that the peak annual revenue has the highest impact on the final NPV.

Table A-2   DCF sensitivity analysis for Wireless in Washington

1. Start with the base case represented by the "average" input variables as shown in Table A-1: Project NPV = $3.23 million.

2. Increase the investment by 20% ($10 million × 1.2 = $12 million), keeping the other variables the same and recalculate the project NPV: $1.23 million

3. Calculate the % change in the NPV compared to the base NPV: −62% = ($1.23 million − $3.23 million)/$3.23 million

4. Decrease the investment by 20% ($10 million*0.8 = $8 million), keeping the other variables the same and recalculate the project NPV: $5.23 million

5. Calculate the % change in the NPV compared to the base NPV: 62% = ($5.23 million − $3.23 million)/$3.23 million

6. Similarly, change the discount rate, peak annual cost, and peak annual revenue by +/−20%, one at a time, keeping the rest of the input variables the same as in the base case, and recalculate the NPV and % NPV change for each case.

Variable			NPV	% NPV Change
Investment	Base	$10	$3.23	
	+20%	$12	$1.23	−62%
	−20%	$8	$5.23	62%
Discount Rate	Base	25%	$3.23	
	+20%	30%	$1.49	−54%
	−20%	20%	$5.37	67%
Peak Annual Cost	Base	$3	$3.23	
	+20%	$3.6	$2.48	−23%
	−20%	$2.4	$3.98	23%
Peak Annual Revenue	Base	$10	$3.23	
	+20%	$12	$5.73	−77%
	−20%	$8	$0.73	−77%

There are two aspects of the DCF evaluation that warrant further discussion:

1. Certain products, especially those in the fast changing technology and telecommunications areas, may have a limited shelf life (as in the WIW example), whereas others may have a longer life; in fact, so long that the cash flow streams may need to be estimated in perpetuity. In the latter case, it is common practice to estimate individual annual cash flows for a period of seven to 10 years and use a "terminal" value for the remainder of the project life. The three most common methods to estimate the terminal value are briefly discussed in Table A-3.

2. To keep the illustration simple, the above example did not show how the project revenues and costs were obtained over the project lifetime nor did it include "free" cash flow calculations involving interest, taxes, depreciation, etc. Two models that are commonly used to estimate project revenues from one time period to the next over the project's life are time series and constant growth rate. With the former model it is assumed that the revenue for the successive time period is based on the preceding one, whereas with the latter, as the name implies, a constant growth rate of the revenues is assumed. A detailed cash flow analysis would involve estimates of, among others, the number of product units expected to be sold during each year, the unit price of the product, fixed and variable costs, and so on. Table A-4 provides a generic example where such details are employed.

Table A-3   Terminal value calculation for DCF analysis

There are three models that can be used to estimate the terminal value of a project:

1. **Liquidation:** In this approach, you assume a certain number of years for the product's (or service's) shelf life, at the end of which the product becomes obsolete and is no longer made, marketed, sold, or supported. The sale price of the project assets at this point, if sold to the highest bidder, will represent the liquidation value of the project. Sometimes, the project may yield a negative cash flow for the terminal value, if it involves a cost burden such as environmental cleanup.

2. **Multiple Approach:** In this approach, you first select the year when you want to apply the terminal value. Then you multiply the expected cash flow for that year by a number that represents the cumulative expected cash flows for the rest of the project life following that year. For example, you may assume that a project's cash flow is calculated to be $100 million for Year 7 where you want to estimate the terminal value. Assuming a multiplier of 3.0, the terminal value for the project is $300 million. The multiplier is typically obtained by historical information related to comparable products (or services) and management judgment.

3. **Constant Growth Model:** Using this model, it is assumed that beyond the terminal year, the cash flows will grow at a constant growth rate in perpetuity.

The liquidation approach can be used when a project is known to have a finite life. If the project is supposed to generate cash flows forever, the latter methods are more appropriate. The biggest drawback of the multiple approach is that it is subjective and does not provide an estimate of the intrinsic value of the project. The constant growth model is based on fundamentals and provides more accurate valuation. While these models are commonly used in DCF valuation of companies as a whole, in the context of projects, the terminal value is more meaningful in terms of the liquidation value rather than perpetual cash flows. In today's hypercompetitive environment, the cash flow growth rate is expected to decline considerably after a few years of the product introduction. Furthermore, the rate of return in later years is lower than is expected by investors and adds very little value to the project. Therefore, it is sensible to estimate the individual annual cash flows over an expected project lifetime and add the liquidation value as part of the DCF valuation, while ignoring any "residual" cash flows over longer periods of time.

Table A-4 Generic DCF example

	0	1	2	3	4	5	6	7
					Year			
Price per unit		$1,200	$1,400	$1,400	$1,400	$1,400	$1,200	$1,000
Number of units sold		10000	15000	16000	17000	18000	16000	15000
Gross revenue (sales)		$12,000,000	$21,000,000	$22,400,000	$23,800,000	$25,200,000	$19,200,000	$15,000,000
Cost of sales		$400	$400	$400	$400	$400	$400	$400
Variable cost		$4,000,000	$6,000,000	$6,400,000	$6,800,000	$7,200,000	$6,400,000	$6,000,000
Fixed cost		$3,000,000	$3,000,000	$3,000,000	$3,000,000	$3,000,000	$3,000,000	$3,000,000
Total cost		$7,000,000	$9,000,000	$9,400,000	$9,800,000	$10,200,000	$9,400,000	$9,000,000
Gross profit		$5,000,000	$12,000,000	$13,000,000	$14,000,000	$15,000,000	$9,800,000	$6,000,000
Less depreciation		$1,000,000	$1,000,000	$1,000,000	$1,000,000	$1,000,000	$1,000,000	$1,000,000
Earnings before interest and taxes (EBIT)		$4,000,000	$11,000,000	$12,000,000	$13,000,000	$14,000,000	$8,800,000	$5,000,000
Tax rate		40%	40%	40%	40%	40%	40%	40%
Less taxes		$1,600,000	$4,400,000	$4,800,000	$5,200,000	$5,600,000	$3,520,000	$2,000,000
Earnings after taxes		$2,400,000	$6,600,000	$7,200,000	$7,800,000	$8,400,000	$5,280,000	$3,000,000
Plus depreciation		$1,000,000	$1,000,000	$1,000,000	$1,000,000	$1,000,000	$1,000,000	$1,000,000
Free cash flows		$3,400,000	$7,600,000	$8,200,000	$8,800,000	$9,400,000	$6,280,000	$4,000,000
Risk adjusted discount rate		20%	20%	20%	20%	20%	20%	20%
Discount factor		0.83	0.69	0.58	0.48	0.40	0.33	0.28
PV of cash flows		$2,833,333	$5,277,778	$4,745,370	$4,243,827	$3,777,649	$2,103,159	$1,116,327
PV of all cash flows	$24,097,444							
Project investment	$15,000,000							
Project NPV	$9,097,444							

277

APPENDIX B

SAMPLE SOLUTIONS TO CASE STUDIES/EXERCISES

This appendix provides sample solutions to the mini case studies/exercises in Chapter 17. Every exercise has several possible solutions, depending upon your interpretation and analysis of the case study information, but this appendix presents only one solution as a sample. To keep it simple, the solutions are presented in a concise format without a lot of detail.

EXERCISE 1: PORTFOLIO FOUNDATION

The strategic framework of GeneMatrix (GMX) is summarized below in terms of its mission, vision, values, and strategy. Four strategic goals (SGs) and one SMART (specific, measurable, agreed-to, realistic, and time-bound) objective for each goal are identified.

Strategic Framework

- **Mission:** To save human lives and improve quality of life through human genomics
- **Vision:** To become the most innovative company in the area of human genomics
- **Values**
  - ◆ Product innovation
  - ◆ Technology excellence
  - ◆ Customer focus

- **Strategy**
  - ◆ To focus on GMX's core competence and to develop and market product innovations in DNA microarray technology
  - ◆ To build new strategic partnerships with third-party gene sequencing manufacturers and to improve existing ones
  - ◆ To develop and market new products for seamless integration of arrays with the sequencers
- **Strategic Goals**
  1. Expand revenue streams:
     A. Introduce new product innovations
     B. Enter emerging markets
  2. Increase customer satisfaction
  3. Improve business processes
  4. Enhance skills of project and product managers

Objectives

SMART objectives are developed for each one of the above strategic goals. These objectives are presumably agreed to by the executive team and the key stakeholders.

- **SG 1A:** Introduce into the market at least three major new products to generate a revenue of at least $35 million over the next four years.
- **SG 1B:** Introduce the product portfolio into Brazil within the next 18 months and obtain at least one major client to generate revenue of $5 million or more.
- **SG 2:** Improve customer satisfaction ratings by at least 10% each year for the next three years.
- **SG 3:** Improve the efficiency of the current business processes by 15% within the next 18 months resulting in either a cost saving or revenue generation of at least $5 million.
- **SG 4:** Obtain industry-standard credentials (e.g., PMP and Six Sigma) for more than 90% of the project and product management professionals within the next two years.

EXERCISE 2: PORTFOLIO DESIGN

Table B-1 presents a sample design template for the portfolio. The template recommends project categories, investment allocations for each category, project evaluation criteria and weightage factors, discount rates, contingencies, tolerance limits for schedule and cost variances, etc.

EXERCISE 3: PORTFOLIO CONSTRUCTION

The projects in GMX's portfolio are divided into four categories along the standard balanced scorecard domains, as shown in the design template. Each project is evaluated for its alignment with GMX's strategy and strategic goals. The value generation potential, threats, and opportunities associated with each project are also assessed. For ongoing projects, their performance to date is considered in the evaluation process. Based on this analysis, go/no-go recommendations are made on each project. The results are summarized in Table B-2. It should be evident from this table that four ongoing projects in the financial value category received a "terminate" recommendation. Three of these projects (numbered 2, 12, and 21) are associated with the high-density array, HDA 100K. The strategy behind this recommendation is to focus on the mid-density array (MDA 2500) and the nanopore arrays rather than spread the resources among all three arrays. The primary reason for the "terminate" recommendation for the ongoing projects and "no-go" for the new ones is weak alignment with GMX's strategy and goals. The recommendation on project no. 13 (Licensing program) is to "hold" until clarification is provided by the executive team on the licensing of GMX's intellectual property.

EXERCISE 4: PORTFOLIO BALANCING

Assuming that the go/no-go recommendations from Exercise 3 are implemented, the total cost to complete all the surviving projects in each category and the budget needed for the next 12 months starting from today are calculated. (Project no. 13, which is on "hold," is not included in these calculations.) In the latter calculation it is assumed that the estimate to complete will be incurred at a linear rate for those projects that are expected to take longer than one year from today. These calculations are shown in Table B-3. Based on the budget needed for the next 12 months for the projects in each

Table B-1 Design template for the portfolio

	Project Categories							
	Financial		Customer		Business Process		Employee	
Category Allocation	75%		10%		10%		5%	
Level 1 Evaluation Criteria	Project cost	$100K	Project cost	$100K	Project cost	$100K	Project cost	$100K
	Alignment	Strong	Alignment	Strong	Alignment	Strong	Alignment	Strong
	ROI	15%	ROI	15%	Payback period, years	2	Learning and growth effectiveness	High
	Years	3	Payback period, years	3				
Level 2 Evaluation Criteria and Weightage Factors	Alignment	20%	Alignment	20%	Alignment	20%	Alignment	20%
	Profitability	60%	Customer satisfaction improvement	70%	Cost savings	70%	Learning and growth effectiveness	20%
	Timely completion	5%	Timely completion	5%	Timely completion	5%	Long-term impact on organizational goals	60%
	Technical risk	5%	Technical risk	5%	Technical risk	5%		
	Market risk	5%						
	Future opportunities	5%						

	Risk Level		
	Low	Moderate	High
Discount Rates	15%	20%	25%
Contingencies	5%	10%	20%
Management Reserve	10% of the total investment allocated for projects in the portfolio		

	Schedule	Cost
Variance Tolerance limits, +/–	10%	15%

Table B-2 New portfolio and recommendations

Project ID	New/ Ongoing	Project Name	Align with Strategy?	Aligned to Goal No.*	Alignment**	Recommendations and Comments
				Financial Value Projects		
1	O	"All-in-one" reagent mix	Yes	1A	Excellent	**Continue.** Customers will be very interested in saving time and effort by using just one rather than multiple reagents. The mix works with both AcuChip 1000, GMX's flagship product, as well as MDA 2500 which is currently under development. Margins are still expected to be high. Estimate to complete must be controlled.
2	O	AcuTrack 100K	Yes	1A	Good	**Terminate.** This software product is tied to project 12, HDA 100K, which is recommended for termination.
3	O	AcuTrack 2.5	Yes	1A	Good	**Continue.** This software will be required for Project 15, MDA 2500, which receives a continue recommendation. Estimate to complete must be contained.
7	N	CLIA Lab	No	1A	Poor	**No-go.** Operating a lab is not GMX's core competence. This project shows poor alignment with GMX's strategy. It will take GMX's attention away from the development efforts associated with the core products. Plus, it will create conflict with GMX's strategic partners that are selling GMX's products by competing for business with them.
9	O	Data storage outsourcing	No	1A	Poor	**Terminate.** Customers are interested in cloud storage services for the vast amount of data they generate; data storage is another key step in the value chain that looks attractive; and the project is near completion. Despite these merits, this project is not a good idea. Data storage is not GMX's core business. GMX does not need to be concerned with the security liability. This service can be effectively managed through business partnerships.

Continues

Table B-2 *Continued*

Project ID	New/ Ongoing	Project Name	Align with Strategy?	Aligned to Goal No.*	Alignment**	Recommendations and Comments
12	O	High-density array (HDA 100K)	Yes	1A	Excellent	**Terminate.** Initial schedule slippage and cost overrun are likely to continue or even get worse. High-density arrays may not have a clear niche in view of the nanopore and mid-density arrays. Since GMX is already working on the latter arrays, resources may be spread too thinly if all three arrays were to be developed simultaneously. Focusing on MDA 2500 and nanopore technology is critical.
13	N	Licensing program	Maybe	1A	Moderate	**Hold.** Deciding whether or not to out-license IP is a tough one. Out-licensing will clearly increase the market share of GMX's technology, but GMX could lose control over how it is used. Strategic direction in this regard is not clearly defined at GMX. Go/no-go on this project needs to be revisited after the direction has been articulated by the executive team.
14	N	Life Mix	Yes	1A	Good	**No-go.** This does not have a big market. NASA's funding is uncertain. Development cost is too high. Does not generate much PR (public relations) either.
15	O	Mid-density array (MDA 2500)	Yes	1A	Excellent	**Continue.** This is an important product in GMX's portfolio. It fits very well with GMX's core business and strategy. Despite initial schedule slippage, it appears to be on track at this time. Commitment towards its development by allocating the required resources can make MDA successful.
16	N	Multi-platform AcuTrack	No	1A	Poor	**No-go.** GMX's core business does not include software development. The purpose of AcuTrack software is to support GMX's products. Developing software that supports competitor's products does not make sense.

17	O	Nanopore array	Yes	1A	Excellent	**Go.** This is an important but evolving technology. It is part of GMX's core business. GMX already has patents pending in this technology. Despite the technical risks and market uncertainty, GMX should invest in mitigating the risks and minimizing the uncertainty. Development effort should be closely monitored, especially because of high investment costs, which can easily escalate.
21	O	Sample Prep 1-2-3	Yes	1A	Good	**Terminate.** No need to develop this instrument, since it works with HDA 100K that is recommended for termination.
27	O	Web-based AcuTrack	Yes	1A	Good	**Continue.** This is the web-based counterpart of AcuTrack 2.0, which works in tandem with GMX's flagship product AcuChip 1000. It will be highly attractive to current as well as future customers. It can be further enhanced in the future to work with MDA 2500 that is currently under development. The project can be scaled down, wherein the cloud storage services will not be offered by GMX. These services can be arranged through third-party providers.

Customer Value Projects

26	N	Web interface	Yes	2	Excellent	**Go.** Customers are moving in the direction of the web. This project makes the ordering process easy for them.

Business Process Value Projects

4	O	Ambient shipping	Yes	3	Good	**Continue.** A quick payback and long-term savings are expected. The project is on track with cost. GMX can earn PR points on sustainability.
6	N	cGMP certification	Yes	3	Good	**Go.** Renders credibility to GMX's products. Relatively small investment. Priority can be lowered if resources are required on other projects.
8	O	Consolidating supply chain	Yes	3	Good	**Continue.** A relatively small investment with a fast payback. Project is on track with schedule and cost.

Continues

Table B-2 *(Continued)*

Project ID	New/ Ongoing	Project Name	Align with Strategy?	Aligned to Goal No.*	Alignment**	Recommendations and Comments
11	N	Green packaging	Yes	3	Moderate	**Go.** Saves costs in the long run. Generates environmental value. Good for PR.
19	O	Project Portfolio Management	Yes	3,4	Excellent	**Go.** Expected to help GMX focus on high value-generating projects and achieve it goals. Slow decision-making process has been identified as a weakness at GMX during the last strategic planning meeting. PPM can help streamline the decision process. Project is on track and requires only a modest investment.
20	N	Salesforce.com	Yes	3	Good	**Go.** Highly regarded application in the market. Will help streamline the sales process and close leads faster. Investment cost is small because of the software as a service model.
25	O	Upgrading sales systems	Yes	3	Good	**Terminate.** This is a redundant project, considering salesforce.com.
Employee Value Projects						
5	O	Business ethics training	Yes	4	Good	**Continue.** Basically a mandatory project, because it is required by the CEO.
10	N	Fit for health	Yes	4	Good	**Go.** Will improve employee's health in the long run and reduces long-term health care costs. Plus, it is a fun project and can lead to many team building opportunities for the project teams.
18	N	PMP training	Yes	4	Excellent	**Go.** Project management was identified as a weakness in the SWOT analysis at the last strategic planning meeting. The training can help reduce cost overruns on many projects that are under way at GMX. Plus, employees are showing interest in this skill.

22	N	Six Sigma training	Yes	4	Excellent	**Go.** It is a skill/training that is catching on in the manufacturing industry. It is expected to create process and product improvements which have a fast payback. ROI has to be clearly demonstrated to convince upper management.
23	N	Social media training	Yes	4	Moderate	This project requires a budget that is less than $100,000. It should not be considered in this portfolio, but may be included in the operating budget elsewhere.
24	N	Supervisory training	Yes	4	Good	**Go.** As GMX is growing, there is a strong need to develop supervisory skills for the managers. These skills are often neglected in small companies, but are critical to developing management talent and helping employees with learning and growth opportunities at GMX.

*Please see Solution to Exercise 1.
**Excellent, good, moderate, or poor.

Table B-3   Budget estimates for the surviving projects

ID	Project Name	Time to Complete, years	Estimate to Complete*	Budget for Next Year*
		Financial Value Projects		
1	All-in-one reagent mix	1	$4.5	$4.5
3	AcuTrack 2.5	1	$1.5	$1.5
15	Mid-density array (MDA 2500)	0.75	$8.0	$8.0
17	Nanopore array	1.5	$20.0	$13.3
27	Web-based AcuTrack	1	$1.0	$1.0
	Subtotal:	—	$35.0	$28.3
		Customer Value Projects		
26	Web interface	0.75	$0.8	$0.8
	Subtotal:	—	$0.8	$0.8
		Business Process Value Projects		
4	Ambient shipping	1	$1.0	$1.0
6	cGMXP certification	2	$2.0	$1.0
8	Consolidating supply chain	0.5	$0.2	$0.2
11	Green packaging	1	$2.0	$2.0
19	Project portfolio management	0.5	$0.6	$0.6
20	Salesforce.com	0.5	$0.1	$0.1
	Subtotal:	—	$5.9	$4.9
		Employee Value Projects		
5	Business ethics training	1	$0.1	$0.1
10	Fit for health	0.5	$0.2	$0.2
18	PMP training	2	$0.2	$0.1
22	Six Sigma training	3	$0.3	$0.1
24	Supervisory training	1	$0.2	$0.1
	Subtotal:	—	$1.0	$0.6
	Total:	—	$42.7	$34.6

*in millions

category, percent category allocations are calculated and compared with the design allocations as shown below.

Category	Current Allocation	Design Allocation
Financial	82%	75%
Customer	2.3%	10%
Business Process	14%	10%
Employee	1.7%	5%

The following observations and recommendations are made:

1. The portfolio does not meet the category balance requirements specified by the design template. Financial and business process categories are over allocated, whereas the other two are under allocated. So in order to attain category balance, more projects are recommended in the latter categories. Alternatively, you may reduce the investment level in the financial and business process categories. Once the balance is gradually attained, you will need to maintain it to sustain a steady state portfolio.

2. The portfolio does not meet the triple constraint relative to goals vs. projects. A comparison of the planned organizational goals (please see the solution to Exercise 1) and goals actually addressed by the current projects (please see column 5 of Table B-2) reveals that the portfolio does not contain any projects that would help GMX achieve the goal of entering emerging markets. Furthermore, there is only one project in the "customer" category, which is not sufficient to help GMX achieve the customer satisfaction related goal. Therefore, it is recommended that the portfolio include projects that will build GMX's presence in emerging markets (e.g., Brazil), as well as those that will deliver more customer value. A shift in triple constraint balance can shift the category balance and vice versa. Close monitoring, thorough analysis, and proper control of the portfolio can help you achieve a balance that meets the design requirements.

EXERCISE 5: PROJECT RANKING BY THE EFFICIENT FRONTIER METHOD

There are five projects in the portfolio that are expected to generate direct financial value. The benefit-cost information on these projects is presented in the form of an efficient frontier in Figure B-1. Projects 27 (Web-based AcuTrack), 15 (Mid-density array MDA 2500), and 3 (AcuTrack 2.5) are on the relatively steep part of the efficient frontier. It shows that these projects have a relatively higher return potential compared to investment. The increase in return seems to be marginal for projects 17 (Nanopore array) and 1 (All-in-one reagent mix). GMX may want to continue with project 17 because of its strategic importance. Its progress must be monitored closely due to its cost overrun to-date and high threat level. Project 1 may continue for now, but if

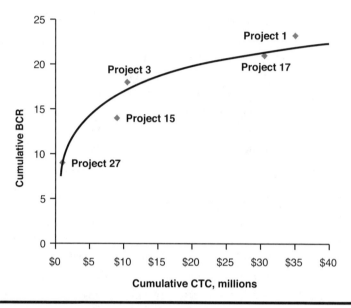

Figure B-1 Efficient frontier for financial value projects

significant cost overruns persist, it may need to be terminated or its scope revised at its next phase-gate. The benefit to cost ratio rankings in the efficient frontier analysis can be useful in deciding on resource allocation priorities, if the resources become limited.

EXERCISE 6: PROJECT RANKING BY PAIRED COMPARISON AND FORCED RANKING

Projects that are expected to generate business process value are ranked using the paired comparison method as shown in Table B-4. The results from a forced ranking of the employee value projects are presented in Table B-5. Both these rankings can be used in deciding on resource allocation priorities.

EXERCISE 7: PROJECT GO/NO-GO

Project Omega is a new project candidate in GMX's portfolio. The project schedule, cost, risk, and other information has been submitted as part of the business case. A summary of the project evaluation and a final go/no-go recommendation are given below.

Table B-4 Ranking of business value projects by paired comparison

ID	New/ Ongoing	Project Name	Project ID 4	6	8	11	19	20	Sum	Project Rank
4	O	Ambient shipping		1	0	1	0	0	2	4
6	N	cGMXP certification	0		0	0	0	0	0	6
8	O	Consolidating supply chain	1	1		1	1	0	4	2
11	N	Green packaging	0	1	0		0	0	1	5
19	O	Project portfolio management	1	1	0	1		0	3	3
20	N	Salesforce.com	1	1	1	1	1		5	1

Table B-5 Ranking of employee value projects by forced ranking

ID	New/ Ongoing	Project Name	Ranking Person (Anonymous) 1	2	3	Total Score	Project Rank
5	O	Business ethics training	1	2	1	4	1
10	N	Fit for health	5	6	5	16	5
18	N	PMP training	2	3	3	8	3
22	N	Six Sigma training	3	4	4	11	4
24	N	Supervisory training	4	1	2	7	2

Alignment

The alignment between project Omega's goal/business objectives and GMX's goal/objectives looks excellent. However, the making of sequencers does not fit with GMX's current strategy, which is to focus on its core competence involving product innovations in the DNA array technology and strategic partnerships with the current and prospective third-party sequencer makers.

Value Generation Potential

- Project Omega's financials look attractive:
  - Net present value (NPV) = $94 million
  - Return on investment (ROI) = 24%
  - Payback = Less than three years
  - Internal rate of return (IRR) = 42%
  - Benefit to cost ratio (BCR) = 2.2

- Sensitivity analysis showed that:
  - ◆ Even when the discount rate (to discount the future revenues), total investment cost, peak annual investment cost, and peak annual revenue are adjusted by +/− 20%, the NPV is still in the positive territory and relatively high.
  - ◆ The lowest NPV is $69 million corresponding to a discount rate of 24%.
  - ◆ The NPV is most sensitive to the discount rate, followed by the investment cost, peak annual revenue, and peak annual investment.

Risk Characteristics

- **Threats:** The biggest threat is the weakening of existing strategic partnerships with third-party sequence makers resulting in loss of market share for current products and associated revenues. Other threats include ineffective technology and opportunity cost.
- **Opportunities:** The biggest opportunity is that the valuation of GMX will soar because of the innovative technology. This can help with the future initial public offering. Other opportunities are the creation of synergies between the sequencer and the nanopore array (which is under development), larger revenue streams and higher margins, and control of value chain.

Recommendation

Despite highly attractive financials and future opportunities, Project Omega does not fit with GMX's strategy of focusing on arrays. In fact, Project Omega counters its strategy of building effective partnerships with third-party sequencers. Entering the sequencer market poses serious threats as well, as discussed above. Unless GMX shifts its strategy towards sequencers and realigns the entire organization accordingly, Project Omega is not a wise investment. Therefore, the recommendation is: No-Go. It must be noted that if GMX employed a two-step process for new project go/no-go decisions, where the first step is screening (Level 1 evaluation), Project Omega would have been rejected in the first step without having to go through a detailed business case analysis because of its lack of strategic fit.

INDEX